"Don and I loved all of our players and all of our teams—but the 1991 Huskies were special. Don would be honored by Mike's careful research and bringing that epic, inspirational season back in such a thrilling way."
—CAROL JAMES

"Legends, it is said, grow larger with the telling. And so it is with Mike Gastineau's joyous telling of the 1991 University of Washington football season. For some, this will be a magical trip down memory lane. For others, an explanation of what thirty years' worth of shouting has been all about. Gastineau skillfully lets those most intimately involved with that season recall and revisit it. He has created not only a loving tribute, but also a detailed portrait of a champion and the very best of times in Husky football history."
—BOB RONDEAU, THIRTY-SEVEN-YEAR VOICE OF HUSKIES FOOTBALL

"I'm so happy Mike has written *Fear No Man* because I've tried for years to put how special this team was into words. Playing on the 1991 Huskies was pure joy."
—CHICO FRALEY, LINEBACKER, '91 HUSKIES

"I woke up on January 1 and realized we had a good team—but because we were isolated in the Pacific Northwest, no one believed in us. Miami this, Desmond Howard that. Yeah, yeah. Wait 'til they see us. The Dawgs would not be stopped. Not on this day. We were there to dominate, and that's just what we did. This book tells our story."
—LINCOLN KENNEDY, OFFENSIVE TACKLE, '91 HUSKIES

"I know how much the 1991 team meant to Don James, and this book powerfully tells their incredible story. I disagree with Gastineau about who would have won if the Huskies had played my Hurricanes for the championship. But I agree with him about this: it would have been a game for the ages."

—DENNIS ERICKSON, COACH OF THE 1991 UNIVERSITY OF MIAMI HURRICANES

"Mike has proven time and again to be a diligent and gifted storyteller, especially when it comes to sports history in Seattle. He has captured some of the best, most embarrassing, and transcendent moments of our journey to a championship. The story of the 1991 UW team remains unique thirty years later. Husky fans—and fans of inspirational sports stories—will love this book."

—ED CUNNINGHAM, CENTER, '91 HUSKIES

FEAR NO MAN

DON JAMES, THE '91 HUSKIES, AND THE SEVEN-YEAR QUEST FOR A NATIONAL FOOTBALL CHAMPIONSHIP

MIKE GASTINEAU

Foreword by Nick Saban

Go Dawgs!

UNIVERSITY OF WASHINGTON PRESS

Seattle

Fear No Man was made possible in part by a grant from the University of Washington Libraries and the Libraries Excellence Fund.

Additional support was provided by a generous gift from Vicki Borland and the late Lynn Borland.

Design by Katrina Noble
Composed in Calluna, typeface designed by Jos Buivenga
25 24 23 22 21   5 4 3 2 1

UNIVERSITY OF WASHINGTON PRESS
uwapress.uw.edu

LIBRARY OF CONGRESS CATALOGING-IN-PUBLICATION DATA
Names: Gastineau, Mike, author.
Title: Fear no man : Don James, the '91 Huskies, and the seven-year quest for a national football championship / Mike Gastineau ; foreword by Nick Saban.
Description: Seattle : University of Washington Press, 2021.
Identifiers: LCCN 2021000412 (print) | LCCN 2021000413 (ebook) |
    ISBN 9780295749211 (hardcover) | ISBN 9780295749228 (ebook)
Subjects: LCSH: Washington Huskies (Football team)—History. | University of Washington—Football—History. | James, Don, 1932–2013.
Classification: LCC GV958.U5865 G37 2021 (print) | LCC GV958.U5865 (ebook) |
    DDC 796.332/6309797772—dc23
LC record available at https://lccn.loc.gov/2021000412
LC ebook record available at https://lccn.loc.gov/2021000413

The paper used in this publication is acid free and meets the minimum requirements of American National Standard for Information Sciences—Permanence of Paper for Printed Library Materials, ANSI Z39.48–1984.∞

There are no memories which cling so persistently to the mind of the alumnus, always capable of awakening a glow of enthusiasm and always recalled with pleasure, as those interwoven in the football games of his undergraduate days.

FIELDING YOST, *FOOTBALL FOR PLAYER AND SPECTATOR* (1905)

CONTENTS

.

FOREWORD

The Legacy of Don James

It wasn't long after Coach Don James walked into the team meeting room at Kent State University (KSU) in January 1971 that our football team realized things were going to be different. I was a sophomore, and from the moment Coach James uttered his first words, it was obvious that he had arrived with a plan in place for the Golden Flashes.

Coach James told us what we were going to do, how we were going to do it, and when we were going to do it, and he was abundantly clear in making known his expectations. He was on a mission to create a culture of accountability, and it was immediately apparent how this blueprint would help us be successful on and off the field.

Part of his vision was to create a family atmosphere, and to that end, his wife, Carol, was involved in many aspects of our program; as he often said, he and Carol were *already* a proven team! He wanted his players to develop and flourish post-KSU football, and as a result, he created academic support programs designed to help his players get the most out of their education and college athletics experience. Many of the countless lessons l learned from Coach James during my time as a player and coach at Kent State are the very same principles I've tried to infuse in each team I've coached.

My last two seasons playing college football at Kent State are some of the most memorable of my life. However, as my college days were coming to a close, I was ready to turn my attention to the automotive business; Coach James, it seems, had other ideas! I was always a student of the game, so I was committed to the practice of thorough preparation, watching an endless amount of film, and learning the intricacies of our game plan each week. As a result, Coach James invited me to remain on staff as a graduate assistant.

Ready to embark on Chapter Two of my life in establishing gainful employment and supporting my wife, I politely declined his kind offer. However, in usual Don James fashion, he was always a step ahead. He pointed out that my wife, Terry, was a year away from completing her graduate degree and how unfortunate it would be to uproot and interfere with her goals. He encouraged me to stay on for another season and give coaching a try, which would allow Terry to realize her dream of a master's degree in education—a win-win situation. One season turned into two, and I too was able to add a graduate degree to my resume. As the sayings go, "Hindsight is 20/20" and "The rest is history." It was the best advice I ever received, and Terry agreed.

Mike Gastineau's book is intimately familiar because so many aspects of Coach James's program mirror what we are doing today at Alabama. We have a year-round curriculum designed to maximize our players' goals. Predicated on the premise that Don James introduced at Kent State in 1971, I remain steadfast in the belief that when players develop a routine, they start buying into and believing in the culture created through the variety of organizational disciplines we have instituted for their success. It's not long before they realize that following this protocol enhances their chance to excel on and off the field.

Nearly fifty years later, I'm still using the form Coach James created to evaluate recruits. I've put it to good use at each of my head coaching stops. Moreover, several former assistant coaches who are now at the helms of their own programs across the country have followed suit. We begin with a character and intelligence assessment before delving into the measurables (size, speed, athletic ability) and other critical factors needed to play a specific position. It reinforces the importance of recruiting players who have not only the right skill set, but also the correct mindset to assimilate and thrive in our program.

My wife, affectionately called "Miss Terry" by the Bama contingent, has been a vital component to the success of our programs. She has been 1,000 percent committed every step of the way, is tuned into every facet of our operation, and, after all these years, has A to Z down pat! From hosting breakfasts for recruits and their families at our home every Sunday during official visits to tweaking halftime shows with our Million Dollar Band Director, Miss Terry ensures that every "t" is crossed and every "i" is dotted. With a fun, easygoing demeanor, she is the master when it comes to connecting with people and creating a family atmosphere for our team, staff, and fans. She too embraced the James philosophy and, like Carol, has more than made her mark on each program along the way.

When I address our team each week before the game, I don't give an emotional speech. We don't even talk about winning the game. Instead, I find stories to share that give life lessons and encourage us all to be the best we can be. That comes directly from Coach James.

Playing for Don James for three years and coaching under him for two years, I learned rather quickly to always pay attention to detail, whether prepping for a game, an off-season workout program, or a recruiting weekend. In his world and mine, nothing is too small or insignificant, and no stone should be left unturned. When I left Kent State for other coaching opportunities, I was stunned at the lack of organization and structure elsewhere; I just assumed every program functioned the same way. It was an eye opener and a very good learning curve for me.

Coach James and I spoke often. I'd ask his opinion about something, and he always had great insight. The last time we talked, he was in the hospital. I told him that since it was Monday, we'd be running progressives. That's where a player sprints 10 yards, then 20, then 30, and so on up to 100 yards. When I was a player for Don, that's what we did for conditioning every Monday. When I told him progressives was my plan for the day, he started laughing.

The 1991 Washington football team meant a great deal to Coach James. He had knocked on the door before. However, this book details the close calls and the little things the coaches and players tweaked that season that made the difference to allow them to walk through. The ultimate goal is to win the big prize. When that happens and a championship comes to fruition, it's like scaling the tallest mountain. You know you've accomplished something special.

Other than my parents, the two people who had the largest impact on my life and did the most to help me become successful were my high school coach, Earl Keener, at Monongah High School in West Virginia, and Coach Don James. Being a coach allows you to influence the lives of young people. There is no greater gift than to watch these youngsters arrive on campus wide-eyed and a bit reserved and leave the university three or four years later as strong, confident young men. I am fortunate to be in the greatest profession in the world. However, along with this profession comes tremendous responsibility. A good mentor needs to be organized and on top of their game every minute of every day in order to set the best example to help their charges be successful. No one did it better than Don James.

Coach James's 1991 Washington Huskies team was amazing. This book tells their story. I think you'll enjoy the ride!

NICK SABAN
Head football coach
University of Alabama

AUTHOR'S NOTE

Many of the quotes and details about the 1991 UW football team in this book were obtained through interviews conducted between 2018 and 2020. Thanks to the following people for taking time to talk to me:

Carol James, former Husky coaches Dick Baird, Keith Gilbertson, Jim Lambright, Randy Hart, Gary Pinkel, Larry Slade, and Chris Tormey.

1991 team members Mario Bailey, Walter Bailey, Eric Bjornson, Mark Bruener, Ed Cunningham, James Clifford, Chico Fraley, Dana Hall, Billy Joe Hobert, Dave Hoffmann, Donald Jones, Lincoln Kennedy, Orlando McKay, and Kris Rongen.

Former Huskies Tim Cowan, Hugh Millen, and Chuck Nelson. Media members Don Borst, Bob Rondeau, and Keith Shipman. Former Washington assistant sports information director Dan Lepse.

The 1991 UW football team was covered by seven Seattle area daily papers. This tale greatly benefitted from notes, quotes, and anecdotes gleaned from the pages of those papers and the prose of the pros who worked for them:

Don Borst, John McGrath, and Bart Wright of the *Tacoma News-Tribune.*

Dan Raley, Art Thiel, Bud Withers, and John Owen of the *Seattle Post-Intelligencer.*

Dick Rockne, Steve Kelley, and Blaine Newnham of the *Seattle Times.*

Gary Nelson, Larry Henry, and Todd Frederickson of the
Everett Herald.
Rick Alvord of the *Bellevue Journal-American.*
Sam Farmer of the *Valley Daily News* in Kent.
The Sun, Bremerton, Washington.

In 1990, Don James collaborated with Virgil Parker on a biography titled *James: The Pac-10 and Washington's Winningest.* That book was another valuable resource used to tell this story.

PREFACE

On October 5, 1991, I attended my first Washington football game.

I arrived in Seattle that June to begin a job at a legendary Seattle music radio station that would soon be known as Sports Radio 950 KJR, and everyone kept telling me how special the game day experience was at Husky Stadium. They were right. The game didn't kick off until 3:30 p.m., so my wife Renee and I walked through the parking lot enjoying the tailgating atmosphere on a perfect autumn afternoon next to Lake Washington. Sizzling grills filled the air with smoky goodness. Laughter was accompanied by the unmistakable sound of cans being opened.

The Huskies that day were as magnificent as any team I've witnessed as they overwhelmed Arizona. They played with joy and buoyed each other's spirits with smacks on shoulder pads, helmets, and backsides.

They were one of the first college teams to use the spread offense, which arrived in 1989 when Head Coach Don James hired Keith Gilbertson and charged him with adding zip to an offense that needed an overhaul. They ran an attacking defense willing to blitz on any down and in any situation. That made James nervous, but his defensive coaches, led by Jim Lambright, convinced him they had the unique blend of talented players capable of pulling it off.

The 1991 season ended happily, but the next season had an awkward finish. In November 1992, it was revealed that quarterback Billy Joe Hobert had taken a loan from the father-in-law of a friend, and a subsequent eight-month investigation into the University of Washington (UW) football program turned up rule violations in five other areas. The university cooperated with investigators, who concluded that no one from the football program had known of or authorized behavior that resulted in violations. Yet UW was hit with one of the harshest penalties ever issued by the Pac-10 Conference. Upset with what he felt was a punishment that in no way fit the crime, as well as a lack of support from the university administration, James abruptly resigned before the 1993 season.

That part of the story has been told in many places, most notably in Sam Farmer's 1993 book *Bitter Roses: An Inside Look at the Washington Huskies' Turbulent Year.* It's a part of Washington football history that cannot be ignored but is sometimes given so much emphasis that it can overshadow the 1991 team's accomplishments.

After he resigned, Coach James agreed to do a college football show with me, and for the next three seasons we spent an hour a week together. Thanks to Don, I got the chance to interview every major college coach in America. His wife, Carol, usually came along, and we began (only half-jokingly) to refer to her as the show's executive producer. She'd jot notes to Don to remind him to say hi to the wives and families of our weekly guests.

Carol *did* help us out on the show, but her main reason for coming each week was simple. "We spent a lot of time apart when he was coaching," she said. "I want to be with him now as much as I can." Don's resignation was controversial, and I was one of many who disagreed with his decision. But it was impossible to not see how happy he was in his post-football life. He and Carol had met when they were both fourteen, and their love for each other was warm, genuine, and inspirational.

One night, Renee and I left a Mariners game early. The season finale of the hit TV show *NYPD Blue* was airing, and Renee made it clear that under no circumstances were we missing the episode during which the main character, Detective Andy Sipowicz, was getting married. I was mildly irritated that we were going to miss the end of the ballgame, and as we pulled out of the parking lot, I saw a couple coming toward us. "Look," I said. "Look at that poor guy. His wife made him leave early too." Our car got closer, and I saw it was Don and Carol.

"Hi guys," I said.

"Hi, Gasman!" Don said as he hurried by us. "We've gotta get home for the Sipowicz wedding!"

I decided that if Don could be enthusiastic, then I could be too.

This book focuses on the 1991 team and the evolution of the entire UW football program with Don James as a coach. In 1985 Don was considered one of the top coaches in the country. Four subpar seasons later, that reputation was gone, and many fans were wondering what was wrong with UW football. But by that time, a talented group of young players had arrived at Washington. In informal meetings, they looked each other in the eye and began setting goals. First, they would get back to a bowl game; then they would get UW back to the Rose Bowl. When they accomplished that, they would aim their sights at the prize atop college football's tallest mountain and pledge to bring a national title to Seattle.

Along the way, the players and coaches learned valuable lessons. One stumble—just one day where a guy gave less than his most intense best—could lead to a slip. And in college football one slip could make a goal vanish like a wisp of smoke, never to be seen again.

But in 1991 there would be no slips. The Huskies knocked down every opponent put in front of them and authored a season so dominant that only one word is needed to sum it all up: perfection.

FEAR NO MAN

A Dark December

FOR A COLLEGE FOOTBALL COACH, A LOVELY CHRISTMAS AT HOME means only one thing: failure.

Don James wrestled the Christmas tree through a doorway, around a corner, and into the living room. He lifted it into the tree stand, and his wife, Carol, tightened the screws at the base. Then they stood back; satisfied that the tree was upright and balanced, they began to decorate it with silver and gold tinsel, beautiful shiny ornaments, and strands of lights.

Holiday music played on the stereo. Don and Carol had been married for thirty-six years, and family and the holidays were important to them. Nevertheless, when the classic song "Home for the Holidays" came on, they exchanged a knowing look. Perry Como's mellow crooning about being home at Christmas was completely lost on them because as far as the James family was concerned, there was no place like a hotel—particularly one in Southern California within a short distance of the Rose Bowl—for the holidays.

James was hired as the University of Washington's head football coach in 1975, and beginning in 1977 his teams went to bowl games ten times in eleven years. Now, for the first time since 1978, he was spending a dreary December in Seattle. In previous years, they did not decorate the house for the holidays because they were always gone; instead, Carol asked the hotels where they stayed to set up a tree in their room, and that was how they usually celebrated Christmas.

The 1988 season wasn't supposed to have ended as it did. The UW Huskies had entered the season ranked twentieth in the country and had won four of their first five games. Then they lost four of their last six games and finished sixth in the Pac-10. The final loss came to archrival Washington State by one point in the Apple Cup game after UW blew a big halftime lead. That the team's five losses that season had come by a total of 15 points was of little consolation.

James was disappointed but not surprised. In the spring of 1988, he and Carol had taken a trip to Hollywood, Florida, to visit his in-laws. While there, he had stopped by the football offices at his alma mater, the University of Miami (class of 1954). The Hurricanes were in the middle of spring football, and Head Coach Jimmy Johnson invited James to watch the team practice. As he watched, James came to a sobering conclusion.

"He told me he wasn't sure if he had any players on his team right now who could start at Miami," Carol said. Miami was in the middle of one of the greatest runs in college football history, going 44-4 between 1985 and 1988. So, to be fair to the Huskies of that era, they were being compared to the very best.

But just a few years earlier, the Huskies had been so good that teams were being compared to them. Between 1979 and 1984 Washington had gone 57-15 and regularly played in major bowl games on New Year's Day. James had been the coach for a decade, and Washington fans had come to expect greatness.

In 1985, *Sports Illustrated* had listed the top three college football coaches in America as follows: (1) Don James; (2) Don James; and (3) Don James. But in the four seasons since, UW had been 28-17-2 and had traded December destinations like Pasadena and Miami for trips to smaller bowl games in El Paso and Shreveport. It was natural for fans to wonder why the program had slipped. Some even opined that it might be time for a change at the top, and they weren't alone. After the 1988 season, James was named the Pac-10 Conference's most overrated coach in a poll of West Coast sportswriters conducted by the *Eugene Register-Guard*.

It was not in James's nature to concern himself with such things. He had arrived in the world on New Year's Eve, 1932, born in his parents' home, a double garage without indoor plumbing. He was raised in Massillon, Ohio, where he grew up among steelworkers, bridge builders, and agricultural equipment manufacturers. His father, Thomas, worked all night in a steel factory and then laid bricks for another eight hours during the day. Thomas James's workload was nothing special. It's what people did during the Great Depression to make ends meet.

Coming from that background, James took quiet satisfaction when things were going well and vowed to work harder when they weren't. "Take the blame, give the credit": legendary Alabama coach Paul "Bear" Bryant had told him that once, and James heeded that advice throughout his life and career. That career had afforded him the luxury of not having to labor as hard physically as his father had, although he could have if necessary. He wasn't tall (5'7"), but more than thirty years after college he was still within a few pounds of his playing weight. He had stayed in shape his entire life primarily by jogging. He had run the Seattle marathon in 1987, and four years earlier he had climbed Mount Rainier, a 14,400-foot peak south of Seattle that requires months of training by anyone who wants to reach its summit.

James ran his football team in a way that required maturity and discipline from his players and assistant coaches. Meetings started on time, which meant early. Players knew that when James walked into a room, they sat up and stopped talking. He had a presence about him and carried himself with the no-nonsense attitude of a CEO whose constant goal was success. After watching his team stagger to the end of the 1988 season, he knew that there was plenty of blame to take and that he and his staff had work to do if the Huskies were going to get back to where he wanted them to be. Going 6–5 on the season, with no bowl game, was not that place. He came up with an idea to make that point obvious to everyone.

A few days before Christmas, James arrived at his office with a box of presents to hand out to his coaching staff. Each gift-wrapped box contained the same thing: a new Seiko watch. Washington coaches were accustomed to getting nice watches around the holidays because most bowl games gave a new watch with their game logo on the face to coaches as a gift. James waited for everyone to open their gifts.

"These are our 'No Bowl' watches," he told the staff. "We didn't go to a bowl game this year, and this watch is to remind you that it better not happen again, or no watches will be given to anyone for any reason."

The explanation was typical of James, who possessed a keen and dry sense of humor. His inference was clear: if there is no bowl game next year, we can all use these watches to make sure we're on time for the flights taking us to new job interviews.

James enjoyed the rest of the holidays as much as he could. Since he was home, he watched other teams and coaches in bowl games. He was interested to see how the Hurricanes would do in the Orange Bowl against Nebraska. He remembered how impressive they had been when he had watched them practice the previous spring and was not surprised that they easily defeated the Cornhuskers to finish the year with an 11-1 record. Their one loss had been by just one point, to Notre Dame in October, a 31-30 setback in the infamous "Catholics vs. Convicts" game that was clinched when Miami failed on a two-point conversion attempt after scoring a touchdown in the final minute of play.

Notre Dame finished the year unbeaten and won the national championship. Miami fans were left to wonder if they might have won the national title if Jimmy Johnson had played for the tie in South Bend. Like most great college football debates, everyone had an opinion, but no one would ever know.

The discussion reminded James of another night in Miami several years earlier, when he thought his 1984 team had won the national championship. The argument in favor of that team being number one was logical. But logic often went missing in college football debates.

The Orange Bowl

ANY LIST OF THE STRANGEST, WILDEST, WEIRDEST FOOTBALL GAMES ever played would include the 1985 Orange Bowl in Miami, Florida, between Washington and Oklahoma. The last game of the 1984 season was played on the first night of 1985 and featured two teams that believed they were playing for a national championship, a penalty on a Conestoga wagon, a fireworks accident that hospitalized several fans, and a huge turnover by a running back whose name would one day be appropriated by a Grammy-nominated rapper.

UW's presence in Miami in the first place made the game unique. In the days when conference champions were tied to certain bowls, the Big 8 champ (usually Oklahoma or Nebraska) played in the Orange Bowl every year except two between 1968 and 1996, typically matched up against a southern or eastern powerhouse team.

The only time a West Coast team had played in the game was in 1950, when the Santa Clara Broncos defeated Paul "Bear" Bryant's Kentucky Wildcats. Santa Clara University celebrated the biggest win in school history by dropping football due to escalating costs. From that point on, no team west of the Great Plains appeared in the Orange Bowl until UW agreed to play OU in the 1985 game.

The Huskies were unbeaten through the first nine weeks of the 1984 season and ranked number one in the polls. As the presumptive Pac-10 champs, they were ticketed for a Rose Bowl appearance before a 16–7 loss at USC in November. That game was one of six times during a wild season that the team in the number one slot in the rankings suffered an upset.

The chaos wasn't limited to the top spot; on nine other occasions, top five teams suffered losses. Twice they played in tie games. Eighteen different schools made an appearance in the top five during the season, and by the time December rolled around, voters in both the Associated Press (AP; writers and broadcasters) and United Press International (UPI; coaches) polls turned to the Western Athletic Conference (WAC) champ and the lone unbeaten team, Brigham Young University (BYU) as their choice for number one. Each team in the final top five of the regular season was imperfect. Number five, Nebraska, had two losses. Fourth-ranked Washington had the November road loss to USC. Number three, Florida, was on probation due to an NCAA investigation that cost coach Charley Pell his job. The feeling among most fans in the country was that the Gators had no business being ranked. Their probation wouldn't allow them to play in a bowl game anyway. Oklahoma was number two with a road loss at Kansas and a tie in the Red River Shootout with Texas.

BYU's imperfection was the Cougars' membership in the WAC and the soft schedule they had played. Sure, Pittsburgh had been ranked number three when the two teams had met on Labor Day weekend, but that number proved to be wildly inflated as the Panthers went on to a 3-7-1 season. Overall, BYU was judged to have played the ninety-sixth weakest schedule out of ninety-eight Division I teams. By the time New Year's Day rolled around, BYU had upped its record to 13-0 with a Holiday Bowl win over Michigan, but even that win became a sticking point in the rising argument that BYU had no business being ranked number one.

Normally, a bowl win over Michigan would be something to crow about. But the Wolverines finished that year with a 6-6 record. It was the only season in Coach Bo Schembechler's twenty-one-year career that his team didn't win at least eight games. The resulting conclusion: yeah, BYU was unbeaten and won the Holiday Bowl, but it did that against a Michigan team depleted by injuries and befouled by inept play.

The Holiday Bowl was played ten days before the Orange Bowl, which left plenty of time for debate over who should win the national title. Second-ranked OU was the popular choice should the favored Sooners beat Washington in the Orange Bowl.

"There had been a lot of speculation that if Oklahoma won, they would win the title," Hugh Millen said. Millen, along with Paul Sicuro, was the quarterback for that UW team. "We were a little chafed that there was more chatter about them getting the title if they won than us. But nobody locked us out of it."

Millen might have been a little chafed about how his season was ending too. On October 27, after a miserable first half against Arizona, during which he fumbled the ball twice and threw three interceptions, he was benched in favor of Sicuro. "I was like Santa Claus that day," Millen said of his gift distribution skills. The Huskies came back to win, and Sicuro won the starting quarterback job. With Sicuro as the starter, the Huskies routed California, suffered their only loss of the year at USC, and defeated WSU in the Apple Cup before accepting the invitation to play Oklahoma. The game was the first time the Sooners and Dawgs had ever played each other and was the marquee matchup of the bowl season.

OU was a touchdown favorite, but UW got off to a great start. Sicuro completed four of his first six passes for sixty-three yards and a touchdown, running back Jacque Robinson scored on a run, and the Dawgs owned a two-touchdown lead in the first quarter.

"They [OU] had a great defense with Tony Casillas as the nose guard," said Chris Tormey, who was in his first year as an assistant coach for UW. "Nobody was running the ball against them, and that was our MO. We were a two-back team, and we weren't throwing the ball that much. For that game we came up with a plan to trap Casillas. We ran that trap early, and he was looking around the rest of the game, trying to make sure he didn't get blindsided."

UW's offense was largely ineffective for the remainder of the half, but the Huskies still enjoyed a 14–7 lead as halftime approached. After another drive stalled and with little time remaining until the break, James opted to let his All-American kicker, Jeff Jaeger, attempt a sixty-one-yard field goal. He missed, and the Sooners got the ball back with just eight seconds left—but that turned out to be enough time for them to do some damage.

Sooners quarterback Danny Bradley threw a short pass to receiver Derrick Shepard. He slipped between two tacklers and rolled untouched to the end zone for a sudden, shocking, tying score on the final play of the half. Oklahoma had been outplayed for most of the half but flipped the entire game's momentum with a single play.

Before entertainment spectacles became the norm at the Super Bowl, the Orange Bowl annually hosted a gaudy halftime show featuring dancers, singers, and pyrotechnics. During this night's extravaganza, a firework exploded in the stands. There were no serious injuries. However, several people suffered minor burns, and a few were transported to a hospital. The incident served as a precursor for more weirdness to come.

In the UW locker room, James approached his offensive coordinator, Gary Pinkel, to discuss his concern that after a hot start, Sicuro had cooled off. "Don was good at recognizing when a quarterback wasn't playing up to his level," Pinkel said. "We were struggling a little bit, but we decided to give Paul a chance in the third quarter to see what happened."

What happened was more of the same. Near the end of the quarter, with the game still tied at 14 and UW driving, Sicuro was intercepted for the third time. James had seen enough. "Tell Millen to get ready," he told quarterbacks coach Jeff Woodruff. "He's going in the next time we get the ball."

The third quarter ended with Millen warming up on the sideline as the Sooners lined up for a short field goal that would give them the lead. Tim Lashar banged home the kick from twenty-two yards out, and the "Sooner Schooner," a small Conestoga wagon pulled by two white ponies (delightfully named Boomer and Sooner) and used by OU cheerleaders to celebrate scores, came rolling onto the field as Oklahoma fans cheered. However, officials had thrown a flag against the Sooners for an illegal substitution on the play, so they would have to kick again. The officials then added another flag, this one for delay of game and unsportsmanlike conduct due to the apparently illegal presence on the field of the pony-powered Conestoga wagon. Suddenly, Oklahoma faced a forty-two-yard field goal attempt that the Huskies promptly blocked. The UW sideline exploded in celebration. With the score still tied, Millen took center stage.

Millen had played sparingly since his benching against Arizona. He was now being asked to create something on offense against the country's top defensive team in a game that had national title implications. He figured everyone he knew was either at the game or watching it on TV back in Seattle, and that fact dialed up the pressure. "I was pretty uptight," he admitted. His night didn't start any better than Boomer's or Sooner's. Millen's first play was a pass that was knocked down by a defensive lineman. On second down the Huskies lost four yards on a run. On third down, a screen pass fell incomplete.

Oklahoma took the ensuing punt and drove into field goal range. Lashar connected this time (with no accompanying Sooner Schooner celebration), and Oklahoma had a 17–14 lead with less than nine minutes to play. While the Sooners were driving, Millen made good use of his time. He took a walk down the sideline away from where most of the team was standing and had a conversation with himself.

"It's time to get your shit together," Millen heard his inner voice say. "These guys are from the Big 8. Nobody throws in that conference. If we were scrimmaging these guys, we would rip them. We would kill them." Millen began to imagine it was a scrimmage instead of the Orange Bowl. He envisioned a giant curtain surrounding the field and that no one could see what was going on. "When I went back out for the second series, I had this incredible peace. I convinced myself we were scrimmaging Oklahoma behind a giant curtain."

Millen may have been calm on the inside, but to anyone watching it was hard to tell. On first down his handoff to Robinson resulted in a fumble that Millen recovered. On second down he overthrew tight end Tony Wroten. But on third down, Millen threw a laser to Danny Greene for a twenty-eight-yard gain. It was only the second time all night that the Dawgs had converted on third down, and the big play seemed to rattle Oklahoma.

Two plays later Millen hit Mark Pattison for twelve yards and a TD. UW had driven seventy-four yards in seven plays and had the lead, 21–17. There was still over five minutes to play, so the Sooners had time.

But what happened next dissipated any wind they might have had left in their sails.

Oklahoma return specialist Buster Rhymes was standing at his own nine as Jaeger's kick sailed toward him. Rhymes drifted back to catch the ball. At the last second he let his eyes scan upfield to check coverage and maybe peek to see how close he was to the sideline. The ball hit his face mask and hands and bounced out of bounds at the two-yard line.

(Rhymes started 1985 with that mistake. But he ended the same year by setting an NFL record for kick return yardage with 1,345 yards as a rookie for the Minnesota Vikings. His performance got the attention of producer and rap star Chuck D, who at the time was mentoring a fourteen-year-old singer named Trevor Smith. Chuck D suggested Smith change his name to Busta Rhymes.)

After the fumble by Rhymes (Buster, not Busta), Bradley's first-down pass was deflected by defensive tackle Ron Holmes and intercepted by Joe Kelly. The Huskies scored on the next play and hung on from there for a 28–17 win. The victory capped off a remarkable day for the Pac-10 Conference. Earlier, UCLA had defeated Miami, 39–37, in the Fiesta Bowl, and USC had topped Ohio State in the Rose Bowl, 20–17.

Those results led many observers to believe that UW would be named the national champion. UW players and fans all used similar lines of logic to deduce that both the writers and coaches voting in the two polls would conclude that Washington was the best team. The Huskies had one loss, but it was on the road to the team that won the Rose Bowl. BYU had beaten Michigan in the Holiday Bowl, but that had been a below-average Michigan team. And oh, by the way, UW had beaten the Wolverines themselves, 20–11, earlier in the season in Ann Arbor.

The Pac-10 was far superior to the WAC, and three wins in three New Year's Day games made it difficult to argue that the league wasn't the best in America that season. The number one spot was on James's mind after the game. "I know we have at least two votes in the coaches' poll," James told the NBC-TV audience. "I'm voting us number one, and Barry told me he is too." "Barry" was Oklahoma coach Barry Switzer. "Washington is the best team we played, and they deserve to be ranked number one," Switzer said. "They're a better team than Brigham Young. I'll guarantee you that."

The UW players were cautiously optimistic that one if not both polls would place them at number one. "We felt we had been decisive enough," Millen said. "We weren't certain, but we felt like we had been impressive, and we allowed ourselves to dream."

"We were sure we were going to get at least one of them," Carol James said. She and Don waited in their hotel room for word the next day. "The hall outside our room was filled with reporters. Most of them seemed sure we were going to get it too. When the phone rang, we thought it was going to be good news." It wasn't.

The first call came from UPI. A few minutes later came one from AP. Both the coaches and the media had chosen BYU as the top team in the country. The twenty-point margin that separated BYU and UW in the media poll was the closest vote in that poll's history. The eighteen points that differentiated the top two teams in the coaches' poll was also one of the closest votes ever.

Fair or not, there is a point to be made that the Huskies were swimming upstream against history. For years, successful teams from the Rocky Mountain region had been overlooked in the national polls. Wyoming went 10-0 in 1950 and won ten games in 1966 (including a Sun Bowl victory over Florida State) but finished outside the top ten both times. When it was still in the WAC, Arizona State went 12-0 in 1975, including a Fiesta Bowl win over Nebraska, but finished second nationally to Oklahoma. There was some feeling that BYU's title was an overdue nod of respect to teams headquartered in the Rockies.

None of that mattered to Washington. The Huskies had played a tougher schedule, they had a more impressive win over the one shared opponent with BYU, and they had defeated the second-ranked team in the country in their bowl game.

"Washington was significantly better than BYU," said Bob Rondeau, UW's radio play-by-play man. "Fans were upset. It was the height of unfairness. There was a notion that if we could do one more game, if we could see them, look out."

James was irked by a couple of issues related to the final vote. For one thing, Florida finished third in the AP rankings and seventh in UPI's, despite the NCAA investigation, and the Southeastern Conference (SEC) had already banned the Gators from postseason play. The scandal, one of the worst in NCAA history, had already cost coach Charley Pell his job, and the fifty-nine rule violations would result in a two-year probation just days after the final polls were announced. James was in the large group that felt Florida shouldn't have been eligible for inclusion in the polls and wondered what the ramifications for his team might have been had votes not been used on the Gators. For another, two coaches (Ken Hatfield from Arkansas and Bobby Collins from Southern Methodist University) had failed to vote in the final poll. Losing a close election is bad enough. Finding out people hadn't bothered to vote made it worse.

James kept most of his thoughts to himself, at least partially because one of his best friends in coaching was BYU's coach, LaVell Edwards. "In this business, you don't have a lot of good friends," Pinkel said. "It wouldn't have mattered because [Don] couldn't have changed the outcome, but if there had been a different coach involved, Don might have been a little bit more vocal." Any complaint James had about finishing second in the polls might have taken away from what Edwards and his team had accomplished, and that would have been the last thing James would have wanted. Nevertheless . . .

"He always got over things faster than me," Carol James said. "But I saw how it hurt him. He thought that the 1984 team was his best. It was a huge disappointment for everyone."

Like a mountaineer just a few hundred yards from the summit who is turned away by an inexplicable change in the weather, James began the process of regrouping. He knew that teams capable of winning a national title didn't come along often. Even if a coach had the right team, he needed a couple of fortuitous bounces of the ball along the way. He needed players to stay healthy. But he now had evidence that under his leadership it was possible to put such a team together. Whether he knew it or not, he had already made a big decision in the days just before the Orange Bowl that would impact his program moving forward.

3

The Recruiter

ON A WARM DAY IN DECEMBER 1984, THE UW COACHING STAFF gathered outside the legendary Miami stadium that had given the Orange Bowl game its name. James made it a point to get a picture taken with each of his assistant coaches as a souvenir of the bowl game. The photographer set up next to a giant Orange Bowl logo, and one by one the assistant coaches stood next to their boss and smiled. Eventually, the full-time assistants had all cycled through the line, and it was time for the graduate assistant coaches (GAs) to come forward. Dick Baird was beaming as he took the scene in. It was his first year on the UW staff and his first-ever trip to a bowl game. The weather was perfect, practices had gone well, and now he was going to get a photograph with his boss that would serve as a permanent reminder of this high point in what he already considered a charmed life.

GAs represent the bottom rung of the coaching ladder. They are the football equivalent of interns, tasked with whatever is needed most at any given moment to help the staff and team. They work long hours, make little money, share tiny apartments or houses, subsist on cheap meals, and support each other. The ultimate payoff is an entrée into the world of college football coaching, and that's a tradeoff any young aspiring coach is ready to make.

Baird wanted to move up in the coaching ranks, so he had that in common with his fellow GAs. But young? Forget it. His peers on the UW staff were all in their midtwenties. Baird was pushing forty and had already spent several years coaching at the high school and junior college levels. NCAA rules at the time allowed for teams to have junior varsity (JV) teams that played a limited schedule of games against mostly local small colleges. That's how Baird had first met James.

"I was the coach at Olympic College in Bremerton," Baird said. "We played the Husky pups [the JV team and freshmen], which helped my program. I had gone to a couple of Don's clinics, and he was so good at teaching the 'how' part of things. He showed you how they did things and why it worked." Eventually, Baird decided he wanted to work for James, and when he ran the idea past his friends and peers in the coaching business, their feeling was unanimous. "They all laughed at me," Baird said, laughing at what still seems like a crazy notion. "They all told me, 'There is no way you fit him. Your personality and his personality? No way!'"

As only good friends can be, they were blunt and accurate. James was straitlaced and buttoned-down. Baird was laces untied and buttons missing. James was clean-cut and looked like he had stepped out of the pages of the *Gil Thorp* comic strip. Baird had a beard, long hair, and looked like an extra in a Cheech and Chong movie. But he was serious in his desire to work for James, and he had several years of experience as a coach and educator. By the time he first met with James, he had shaved his beard and gotten his hair cut. The head coach began the interview by pointing out that Baird looked different.

"Lambo [Husky assistant coach Jim Lambright] told me to clean up a little bit," Baird said. "That was probably pretty good advice," James replied. The two men talked about Baird's career and his desire to work at UW. James remained skeptical, due mainly to where Baird was in his life.

"You've got four kids, and you want to be a graduate assistant?" he asked as the meeting wound down. Baird understood why James had doubts; the idea of a GA in his midthirties was a stretch on several levels. But Baird had the support of his wife, Kim, and he had a belief in himself.

"Yes," Baird replied. "I want to prove I can do this, and I think once I do, you'll hire me." James had done his homework and already knew a lot about his prospective GA. Several of Baird's friends had contacted the coach on his behalf. Among those who had reached out was a man who James greatly admired.

"I had worked with Lenny Wilkens for five years and helped him organize and run his basketball camps," Baird said. "He and Don were friends, and he agreed to call him for me." Wilkens was the coach of the Seattle Supersonics and was fifteen years into what would be a thirty-six-year hall of fame coaching career. In 1979, he coached the Sonics to the NBA championship. He knew players and coaches and how to build a winning team; his opinion held sway with James. Wilkens watched how Baird ran his camps, how he interacted with the kids, and how he got everyone involved. He told James that Baird would be a positive addition to his staff. James got similar messages from several other people, and after the meeting with Baird he was convinced that Baird was everything people were telling him and was willing to do the work necessary. James offered him a spot as a GA.

Football is fun when you're winning, and Baird had a blast in 1984. Now, he was soaking it all in as he found himself next in line to join James for a photo. He walked up, and the two shook hands. As they turned to face the camera, James told Baird, "I don't know what position it's going to be yet, but you're hired. You've got a job next year on this staff." Briefly shocked, Baird stared at the camera for a second before responding. "So I'm being offered a job right now?" James nodded as they both smiled. The camera clicked, preserving the moment for posterity.

James eventually settled on making Baird his recruiting coordinator. A change in NCAA rules now required that a school's recruiting coordinator had to also be an assistant coach. Before 1985, the role was usually filled by people strong in administrative and organizational skills but maybe lacking in football knowledge.

One thing Wilkens had impressed upon James was that Baird had done a terrific job organizing and running his basketball camps. Running UW's football recruiting operation wouldn't be that different. And now that the NCAA mandated that the recruiting coordinator had to be a coach, Baird's experience on the field was a necessary plus. But the new coach/recruiting coordinator had no delusions of his primary strength. "Don didn't hire me for my football acumen," he said. "He hired me because I related to kids."

James and Baird approached life from different points on the spectrum and ended up complementing each other's strengths. James was the man in charge, and for young men who wanted to play college football that was an important thing. They wanted to have confidence in the leader, and that's how they related to James.

But Baird was different. He spoke their language, got their jokes, listened to their music, and knew their culture. His football background helped him identify good players. His personality helped him connect with them on a different level than most people his age. His fun-loving attitude also added a necessary ingredient to the staff.

"He was a great hire for us," Lambright said. "In meetings, he'd say anything if he thought it was going to get a laugh. I had suggested to Don that we hire Dick, and there were times when Don would look at me like, 'What were you thinking?' But Dick was a good balance on our staff for guys who were too serious."

Baird streamlined the recruiting process. The Huskies had hundreds of kids in football camps each summer, and Baird wanted to send a note to each one who might someday be a recruit. To do that, he needed more computer power than the UW football office had. So he convinced James that they needed to purchase personal computers for use by the staff. Baird also knew that most high schools and colleges were transferring from 16mm film to the emerging video technology. "We are the last ones using film," Baird told James in what was only a slight exaggeration. The times were changing, and UW had to change with them. Before long, each coach had a PC and a VCR in his office. "I wasn't the most advanced technology person in the world," Baird laughed. "But I dragged Don into what was then the modern world. He allowed me to set up a new system, and he went along with it."

During their initial interview, James had been impressed with how Baird spoke about his family. "He was a big family guy, and that was important to him." One of the reasons that was so important to James was that he constantly spoke to recruits and their parents about how the UW team was a family. During recruiting weekends, Don and Carol would host breakfasts at their home on Sunday mornings. This typically involved several dozen kids. Food was served off the dining room table, and players found seats anywhere they could around the house and ate off their laps. It gave the mornings the feel of a family gathering. In case that atmosphere was unfamiliar or unnoticed, Carol James would make a point of mentioning it. "If you become a member of the Washington football team, you'll be part of the James gang," she told them. "You'll always be a part of our family."

After breakfast, Carol would spend the afternoon writing notes to each of the recruits' mothers. "I'd talk to each kid at breakfast, and I'd try to pick up something special that I could mention in the note. That way, the mom knew I had spoken to her son. I promised [the mothers] that if they came to UW, their sons would be treated and looked after like family members. To this day, several former players call me 'Momma James' or 'Momma Carol.'"

Carol had met Don at a carnival in Ohio in the summer of 1947, and she claims that he took an interest in her at first because her parents had a rec room in the house with a pool table and a ping pong table. She was an athlete, and in addition to regularly beating James and his friends in both pool and ping pong, she boasted that she could beat them in a race too.

"She was quite a sprinter," James wrote in his biography. "She claimed nobody her age in town, boy or girl, could beat her." James proved that theory wrong by defeating her in a race. Soon after, they were an item. They attended the University of Miami together, and while Don quarterbacked the team, Carol was a cheerleader. She was so popular that she was named by varsity lettermen as the "M Club Sweetheart" in 1952. That summer, after their sophomore year, they were married.

Carol's midwestern charm was a nice counter to her husband's more businesslike attitude. Her warmth made her approachable, and as UW players got to know her and realized she was serious about them all being a family, they would confide in her.

"Some players would come to me with problems because they were afraid to talk to Don," Carol said. "I would tell them if I felt it was something where Don could help, I'd tell him. Otherwise it was between us. And either way, we would find a solution."

Talking to young football players came naturally to Carol because she'd been around them most of her life. "[Don and I] started going together when we were fourteen, and from that point on I spent a lot of time hanging out with Don and his football friends."

"You can't talk about Don James without talking about Don and Carol," Baird said. "To me, they were a team. Our family approach to running the team, and to recruiting, really worked." Baird saw how important the Sunday breakfasts were and realized that getting the parties catered would allow Carol more time to visit with prospective players. It was an example of the attitude Baird brought to his job. When he saw a need, he would come up with a solution. Baird developed a unique relationship with James. Other staff members were amazed at how often they saw him walk into James's office to discuss things. "Don always said he had an open-door policy, but several of the coaches were intimidated by him," Baird said. "I wasn't."

This is not to say that Baird didn't occasionally cross James. A gregarious and fun-loving guy, Baird lived his life with an attitude that the next good time was surely just around the corner. He admits this occasionally led to problems. "By Thursday, Don wanted everyone to put their game face on. But I can't stop laughing any day of the week. I have more fun than anyone I know. It's part of my makeup. Don gave me dirty looks all the time." Baird said he always knew when he had gone too far in the laughter department: "He would look at me and say, 'Richard!' And that was it."

But James also used Baird as a foil and a source of comic relief. His serious disposition belied a subtle sense of humor, and he liked nothing better than zeroing in on his recruiting coordinator. He constantly chided Baird about the fact that he had played football and gone to school at Washington State. Baird didn't mind being the target because he could tell that James valued his work. When he started at UW, recruiting was the last item on the daily meeting agenda. But soon, James had moved it to the first item at each meeting, and that made Baird proud. "He gets it," Baird thought to himself. "Recruiting is the most important thing."

Eventually, Baird brought this up to his boss. "I notice we've moved recruiting to the first item in every meeting. I like that. Get to the important stuff right out of the blocks." "No, that's not it," James replied. "I just have you go first to make sure you're not hung over."

Baird always laughed. James didn't usually become close friends with his assistant coaches, but Baird was a necessary exception. The two spent so much time together that they were bound to become close.

"[Baird] added some personality and spice to the systems we had in place, and he was just so gregarious and outgoing," Tormey said. "When we'd have kids on campus for recruiting visits, they could feel Dick's infectious enthusiasm. He was a big part of our success."

Baird developed a unique ranking system and used it to evaluate every potential recruit. He'd talk with the assistants who were out on the road and offer his opinion on the strengths and weaknesses of the players they were talking to. If a current player was in the football office, Baird would bring him into his office, show him tape, and encourage feedback. "Look at this guy," Baird would say. "We're looking at him. What do you think?"

James did an annual golf tour of the state in the spring and summer to stay connected to alumni and boosters. Baird was his frequent companion. After a day of golf, James would give a serious speech to the group of the day about the state of the Husky team; then Baird would speak in a considerably looser style. Attendees got the scoop from the CEO before ending their night in raucous laughter. "It was like the Don and Dick Show," Baird said.

The only downside to the golf tour was the travel. Sometimes it was in cars, but often it was in small private planes. Neither Baird nor James liked small planes, but because of scheduling concerns, these were sometimes necessary. They were flying home after a day in Yakima, Washington, when the pilot told them to brace themselves for bumps due to a storm over the Cascade mountains. "There's a bottle of whiskey between your seats if you're nervous," he informed his two passengers, who both, indeed, were nervous.

As the plane lurched through the clouds, James (who rarely imbibed) decided a shot of whiskey might help. He pulled the bottle out, unscrewed the cap, and took a nerve-calming belt before offering the bottle to his companion, who was much more seasoned in the ways of liquor consumption. Baird declined. "I don't drink whiskey," he told James. "Whiskey is risky. I never touch it."

James could not have been more surprised. "You . . . don't . . . drink . . . whiskey?" he asked. "Hell, you drink everything else." James screwed the top back on the bottle, and they shared a laugh as they continued their bumpy journey back to Seattle.

We Need to Get Gilby

THE SEASONS IMMEDIATELY FOLLOWING THE OKLAHOMA WIN HAD been, by the standards set in James's early years, lean. The 1985 team followed up the dramatic Orange Bowl season with a comparatively pedestrian 7–5 year that included a humiliating 21–20 loss to Oregon State at Husky Stadium (the only time in James's career he lost to the Beavers).

Washington was a 38-point favorite, and at the time the Beavers' win was the largest overcome point spread in college football history. Before the game, *Seattle Post-Intelligencer* columnist Steve Rudman referred to the Beavers in print as the "Barney Fife of college football." After the game, an OSU player found Art Thiel (who also wrote for the *Post-Intelligencer*) and jabbed his finger into Thiel's chest while bellowing, "Barney Fife, huh? Barney Fife?"

The '85 Huskies dropped two of their last three games before ending the year on a positive note with a win in the Freedom Bowl over Colorado. The 1986 Huskies were better in the regular season with eight wins but were clobbered in the Sun Bowl, 28–6, by Alabama. Running back Bobby Humphrey shredded UW's defense for 159 yards, quarterback Mike Shula threw two touchdown passes, and linebacker Cornelius Bennett was named game MVP after stacking up eleven tackles. "Alabama was beating us off the edge all day that day," Baird said. "Bennett was just unstoppable."

Larry Slade was in his first year as Washington's secondary coach. "You could see the difference. We had big guys, but the speed difference was so huge, and you could see the impact of that."

The 22-point loss was the largest bowl game defeat in the James era and caused him to reassess his program. "The Alabama game planted the notion that maybe we've gotten too big and fat," Rondeau said. "Bigger is not necessarily always better. That commitment took a while to manifest itself, but it started after the Sun Bowl." James typically looked for size first in a recruit. The only thing better than size was more size. But that afternoon in El Paso made him realize that the Huskies had to get faster.

"If you can't get a verifiable time on a guy, don't bring him up for a visit," James told his coaches. James was mindful of the fact that some high school coaches would fudge a player's time if they thought it meant a better chance at a scholarship offer. "There's not a high school coach in America who doesn't know the number to say when a coach asks how fast a player is, but if we can't document a kid's speed, then we are not going to recruit him," James said. That hard line meant UW would occasionally miss out on a good player. But James felt that they had become victims too often of misinformation. "We got caught up in too many speed mistakes, and we became too slow as a team."

A 6–4–1 season in 1987 was followed up by a win over Tulane in the Independence Bowl. For a program that had started the 1980s with back-to-back Rose Bowl trips and then a trip to the Orange Bowl, Shreveport, Louisiana, felt like a step backward. "It was awful," Rondeau recalled. "It had zero buzz to it, a small crowd; it was cold, [and] they're playing Tulane. To their credit they won the game."

In the run-up to that game, James was also looking for a new assistant coach. His defensive line coach, Jim Heacock, was leaving to take the head coaching post at Illinois State. The man he now wanted to hire, Randy Hart, had been on his radar for a while due to a long list of coincidences. For starters, they shared northeast Ohio roots since Hart was born and raised in Cleveland. It's possible James first heard Hart's name when he was the defensive coordinator for Michigan in 1967 and Hart was a guard for Woody Hayes at Ohio State. They first met at the 1972 Tangerine Bowl, when Hart was an assistant for Earle Bruce at the

University of Tampa. Hart recalls, "I remember Don, and I chatted [with him] briefly, and that was it. But you never know."

Hart was an assistant at Purdue in the spring of 1978, when he visited Seattle to study what the Dawgs were doing on defense. After Purdue he worked for Bruce again, this time at Ohio State. While recruiting the Canton area for the Buckeyes, he occasionally ran into James's brother Tommy, who had played at Ohio State and professionally for the Cleveland Browns. Bruce and his entire staff were fired by Ohio State after the 1987 season, and Hart was at home mulling over his limited options when his phone rang. James was on the line and asked Hart if he was interested in coming to Seattle. "Don, it's a week until Christmas," Hart said. "I've got a wife, two kids, and no job. Are you kidding me? Yes. I'm lacing up my shoes right now, and I'm on my way."

In Seattle for his interview, Hart quickly realized he had to do more than impress James. "Carol was as much the person who was going to hire you as Don. Carol had to put the stamp of approval on you, and with me, I was lucky enough that she did."

The Independence Bowl win was nice, but James always said that his team's goal every year was to win the Pac-10 and go to the Rose Bowl. It had been six years since that had happened, and UW supporters were anxious for a holiday season in 1988 that would include a return to Pasadena. But those hopes were dashed by the series of close losses in the second half of the season that concluded with the staff receiving their 'No Bowl' watches, and James was hearing about it. "According to my 'fan' mail, the alums didn't like it," James said. "You would have thought the world had come to an end around here. But we weren't any more pleased with the won-loss record than the fans."

Unlike the fans, James was in a position to do more than just complain. Two years of emphasizing speed in recruiting meant the Huskies were getting faster. Now, they had to get better at how they did things. For the first time in nine years James had no bowl game to prepare for, but the future was very much on his mind as he picked up his phone the day after the '88 Apple Cup loss and placed a call to Moscow, Idaho.

Keith Gilbertson, who had just concluded his third season as the head coach at Idaho, was approximately 180 degrees apart from James in terms of how he was feeling. The Vandals 9–1 record was the best in school history, and Gilbertson's 28–9 record in three years made him the winningest coach percentage-wise in school history. Gilbertson had known James since 1976, when he had served as a GA for him at UW. He was happy to hear James's voice, and they discussed their games from the previous day before James got down to business.

"I want to run something by you. I'm getting ready to make some staff changes and I'm interested to know if you'd be willing to come back to Washington," James began.

Gilbertson hadn't been expecting an offer like that from James. "I don't know," he finally responded. "I'm a head coach now, and things are going pretty good." James knew Gilbertson would be focused on the Vandals' upcoming playoff game and hadn't expected an answer right away.

"Okay. Just think about it, and let's talk in a few weeks," he said. "Good luck against Montana." Gilbertson hung up and allowed his mind to race. He was, indeed, a successful head coach. He was proud of what he had accomplished at Idaho. But this was a chance to work with Don James. "He was the guy who got me going," Gilbertson said. "He helped me get my first big-time job [as the offensive coordinator at Utah State in 1977], and I had always wanted to be on his staff because I thought so much of his program."

The next day, James did something he had never done at Washington. He fired an assistant coach. Offensive line coach Dan Dorazio was dismissed. "I was just not pleased with the way the offensive line has played the last couple of years," James said. "This was one way I could make some changes in the offensive line so we could get going again." The decision was not easy. Dorazio had played for him and then coached with him at Kent State. They had known each other for close to twenty years. He had every right to feel as if he were being made a scapegoat for UW's subpar season. But in what might be the best example ever of the loyalty James had from the men who worked with him, Dorazio was philosophical about his ouster. "Coach James is consistent, fair, and honest," Dorazio told *Sports Illustrated*. "He's a great human being. He told me he was disappointed in the offensive line play and that it was my responsibility."

Meantime, Gilbertson's team defeated Montana and the Northwestern State Demons to move into the semifinals of the Division I-AA playoff tournament. The morning after the win over the Demons, James again called the victorious head coach. "How'd you guys do yesterday?" James asked.

"We did really good," Gilbertson replied. "We had 35 points and 375 yards of offense . . . in the first half." There was a pause on the other end of the line. Finally, James spoke. "Thirty-five points and 375 yards in the first half?"

The two men laughed at the absurdly good numbers Gilbertson's team had put up. James then brought the conversation back to the idea of Gilbertson's coming to UW. They discussed some hypothetical details of how that kind of move might work before James concluded the conversation by inviting Gilbertson to interview for the job once his season was over. That happened the next week, when Idaho lost to Furman.

Early December can be a confusing time for football coaches. Some are preparing their teams for bowl games or the playoffs. All of them are diving into recruiting and spending many of their days and nights trying to woo seventeen-year-old kids who they hope will be the next big thing. At the same time, some of them are being wooed by other schools in search of an upgrade to their current coaching situations.

In Gilbertson's case, his success at Idaho had not gone unnoticed, and James wasn't the only one inquiring about his future plans. The University of Texas at El Paso (UTEP) Miners wanted to hire him to replace Bob Stull, who was leaving the school to take the head coaching job at Missouri. Coincidentally, prior to his stint at UTEP, Stull had worked for James for several years as an assistant coach at Kent State and UW. Gilbertson and his wife, Barbara, spent the weekend of December 17 in El Paso, and it was believed that he was the Miners' top choice. But early the next week, he pulled his name from consideration. "It was a great opportunity," he said. "I liked the area and the people there, but I'm not a Texas guy, and I think you need to know how to recruit that state to be good at that school."

Gilbertson's discussions with the Miners led to a situation not of his making that drew some verbal fire from James. When UTEP athletic director Bruce Hovius announced that Gilbertson had withdrawn from consideration for the job, he also told reporters, "Keith is going to the University of Washington to be their new offensive coordinator."

That put James in an awkward spot because he planned on keeping Pinkel as his offensive coordinator. He wanted Gilbertson to coach the offensive line while working with Pinkel to come up with new ideas that they could try on offense. He had been up front with both men about this division of labor and was ticked off that Hovius was making assumptions. "It's strange to see guys making statements about other jobs at other schools," he said. "I don't want to play games with other people's lives." So if Gilbertson took the job, would his arrival and the infusion of new ideas in any way rankle Pinkel? Probably not, given that it was Pinkel who had made the suggestion in the first place.

"We were pretty conservative on offense, and we were struggling," Pinkel said. UW's offense had averaged over 30 points per game in 1984. The offense that season had been simple, basic, and effective with two running backs behind the quarterback, a tight end (sometimes two) on the line for extra bulk, and one or two receivers. "We didn't run one play that season with three receivers on the field," Hugh Millen said.

But by 1988 the Huskies' average was a touchdown less per game as defensive coordinators had caught up to what they were doing. James knew they needed a change, and Pinkel had an idea. He and Gilbertson had worked together for James in 1976 and remained good friends. Pinkel recruited eastern Washington and on trips there often made a short detour to Moscow, to visit with the Vandals' coaching staff. What he saw on those visits was not only different from what Washington was doing, but it was also the future of football.

The Huskies had a limited number of looks they could throw at a defense. Idaho was limitless by comparison. The Vandals might use one running back, and he might go in motion before the snap, leaving the quarterback by himself behind the line but with up to five receivers as targets. Sometimes they would line up four receivers on one side of the ball and one on the other, using the so-called "no-back" look. Millen's team didn't run one play with three receivers all year. Gilbertson's offense didn't run one play with less than three receivers.

"It was fun to watch and it was fun to play in," Gilbertson said. "It was basically, 'Go out, get open, and we'll throw it to you.'"

Pinkel thought the offense would work at Washington, and his suggestion to James was direct. "The things that they're doing over at Idaho with one back and no back—we need to get Gilby in here if we can get him." Pinkel knew that offensive football was moving away from what UW had been doing and toward what teams like Idaho were doing.

"It says a lot about Coach James that he saw the big picture," Pinkel said. "He was working with our defense, trying to defend some of the offenses we were seeing, and he saw that the game was changing, and he was sharp enough not to stay set in his ways." Still, the type of offense Gilbertson favored would be a radical departure from what UW had done for fourteen years under James.

"Don's philosophy was 'Don't screw it up; don't turn it over; we'll be good at punting; we'll play great defense; and we'll do the right things on offense,'" Gilbertson said. "That worked for a long time, but the game was expanding." From his series of conversations with James, Gilbertson could tell he was ready for something different. And he knew Pinkel was ready to play a different way too.

But Pinkel was staying at UW, which meant that if Gilbertson left Idaho, he would be leaving a head coaching job to take an offensive line coaching position. A lot of people would question such a move, and James worried that might be an impediment to Gilbertson's taking the job. Eventually, when James brought up the issue of titles and exactly what they would call Gilbertson at UW, he was cut off. "I don't care about my title," Gilbertson told James. "But I want the chalk. I want the chance to put in what we do with you guys, and it will be fun." Gilbertson was ready to join Washington as long as he knew he had a say-so in the offense.

That comment put a smile on James's face. He had a sign on his desk that had become one of the bedrock cornerstones of his philosophy. It was an idea he had first heard from the man some consider the greatest Michigan Wolverine ever, Bennie Oosterbaan.

Oosterbaan was an All-American football player for legendary Michigan coach Fielding Yost in the 1920s. (He was an all-conference basketball and baseball player too.) He then coached and worked in the school's athletic department from 1928 until 1972. James met him in 1966, when he was hired as Michigan's defensive coordinator. The two men had remarkably similar personalities, and James took several ideas from Oosterbaan and incorporated them into his philosophy. One was a simple piece of wisdom Oosterbaan often said: "Isn't it wonderful what can be accomplished when no one cares who gets the credit?"

Now, sitting across from him in his office, Gilbertson was the living embodiment of that idea. "Gary and I have been friends for a long time, and you guys can call me whatever you want." On December 23, Gilbertson confirmed he was leaving Idaho to take the offensive line coach job at UW.

"Hiring Gilby was really important for Husky football," Pinkel said. "We got a guy who was really knowledgeable about the one back offense. We were able to work really well together. Maybe it's because we were good friends, but that part of it was simple. There was no ego. We both wanted to have the best offense, and with his input we immediately started to get better and better."

"I'd like to give 12 and 0 a try."

By 1991 Don James had won 129 games at Washington, including eight bowl game wins. He had won the Rose Bowl three times and the Orange Bowl once, but a national championship had eluded him. "I'd like to give 12 and 0 a try." (PHOTO BY DOUG GLANT)

JIM LAMBRIGHT
Washington Defensive Halfback

Defensive coordinator Jim Lambright. "Lambo's intensity was beyond the limit," Chris Tormey said. "And the new defense fit his personality." (PHOTO BY CORKY TREWIN, COURTESY UW ATHLETICS)

Lambright was the only member of the staff who played at UW (on the 1964 Rose Bowl team). "Where did you go to school?" he would ask good-naturedly when he had disagreements with others on the staff. "I went to school right here." (PHOTO BY UW ATHLETICS, COURTESY OF THE LAMBRIGHT FAMILY)

"Everything changed when he walked in . . ."

Offensive coordinator Keith Gilbertson. "Everything changed when he walked in," said Kris Rongen. "He had a flair and a swagger, and he instantly transformed our program." (PHOTO BY JOANIE KOMURA, COURTESY UW ATHLETICS)

Recruiting coordinator Dick Baird during pregame warm-ups before the Huskies' win at USC. When he found a need, he always helped out. (PHOTO BY JOANIE KOMURA, COURTESY UW ATHLETICS)

Miami, 1984, the day before the Orange Bowl—an important moment in Huskies football history. As this photo was being taken, Don James (*right*) was offering his graduate assistant Dick Baird a full-time job. (PHOTO BY UW ATHLETICS, COURTESY DICK BAIRD)

Defensive backs coach Larry Slade. "The best place I coached as far as having guys who were students of the game was at Washington. It was as good a situation like that as anywhere I've ever been." (PHOTO BY BRUCE TERAMI, COURTESY UW ATHLETICS)

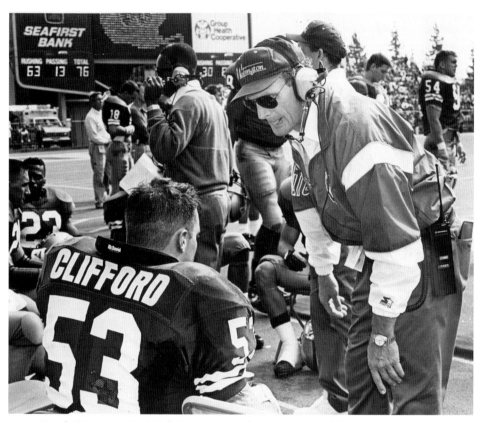

Randy Hart in typical high-intensity mode, with James Clifford. (PHOTO BY
BRUCE TERAMI, COURTESY UW ATHLETICS)

Chris Tormey coached the linebackers, but his most important accomplishment related to the 1991 Huskies happened in 1987, when he convinced Virginians Donald Jones and Ed Cunningham to travel across the country to play football at Washington. (PHOTO BY JOANIE KOMURA, COURTESY UW ATHLETICS)

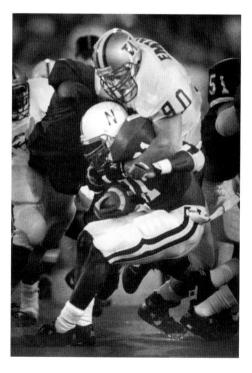

Quarterback Billy Joe Hobert (12). "He changed after Brunell got hurt," said Ed Cunningham. "He emerged in a way no one foresaw. He went from this happy-go-lucky country kid to a real competitor." (PHOTO BY JOANIE KOMURA, COURTESY UW ATHLETICS)

Steve Emtman (90) brings Nebraska running back Derek Brown to a complete stop. "He made himself the number-one pick in the NFL draft that night," said Randy Hart. (PHOTO BY MARK HARRISON, COURTESY *SEATTLE TIMES*)

Center Ed Cunningham (79) hoists Mario Bailey (5) into the air to celebrate another touchdown. Bailey ended his career as the leader at Washington in several receiving categories. (PHOTO BY BRUCE TERAMI, COURTESY UW ATHLETICS)

Ed Cunningham (79) sets a wall of protection for Mark Brunell during the 1990 USC game. Cunningham called it "the most fun game I ever played at Husky Stadium." (PHOTO COURTESY UW ATHLETICS)

Guard Kris Rongen (72) sets up in pass protection. His "block" of a Cal player is something Golden Bears fans bitterly remember. (PHOTO BY JOANIE KOMURA, COURTESY UW ATHLETICS)

Wide receiver Orlando McKay. "We knew we were good, but I don't think any of us realized we were going to be the only national championship team for Washington for thirty years, or maybe forty or fifty. Who knows? We didn't understand that part." (PHOTO BY JOANIE KOMURA, COURTESY UW ATHLETICS)

Running back Jay Barry (42) had 718 yards rushing on the year and teamed with Beno Bryant to give UW a one-two running back combo that was devastating to opponents. (PHOTO BY JOANIE KOMURA, COURTESY UW ATHLETICS)

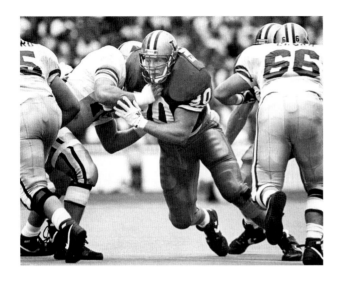

Voice of the Huskies Bob Rondeau observed, "Steve Emtman leading by example was like, 'either you play as I do, or I'll kill you.'" (PHOTO BY JOANIE KOMURA, COURTESY UW ATHLETICS)

Safety Shane Pahukoa. Fast, rangy, and tough. "The MVP of that defense," according to Larry Slade. (PHOTO BY JOANIE KOMURA, COURTESY UW ATHLETICS)

Linebacker Donald Jones (48). He was so good, according to James, that "it was unfair to offensive linemen." Like the one he left on the ground here en route to WSU quarterback Drew Bledsoe. (PHOTO COURTESY UW ATHLETICS)

Linebacker Chico Fraley (39) eyes an opposing quarterback. He gave his father his 1990 Rose Bowl ring. "I'm getting another one next year." (PHOTO BY JOANIE KOMURA, COURTESY UW ATHLETICS)

Linebackers Dave Hoffmann (54) and Donald Jones (48). Hoffmann said he could look into the eyes of offensive linemen and tell what they were thinking. "Which one of us is coming after the quarterback? You don't know, do you?" (PHOTO BY JOANIE KOMURA, COURTESY UW ATHLETICS)

Dana Hall (5), James Clifford (53), and Brett Collins (46) head for the sidelines after another stop. (PHOTO BY BRUCE TERAMI, COURTESY UW ATHLETICS)

Linebacker Jaime Fields (3) on the new attacking defense: "Let's go! 100 miles per hour. We're going to attack from every position!" (PHOTO BY COLIN MEAGHER, COURTESY UW ATHLETICS)

Cornerback Walter Bailey en route to the end zone with an interception versus Arizona. "When we went onto the field it was a straight party out there. We were going to hit someone in the mouth and have a great time." (PHOTO BY BRUCE TERAMI, COURTESY UW ATHLETICS)

The defense that wouldn't rest. Washington's opponents ran 791 plays; 417 of those plays (52%) resulted in a tackle for loss, no gain, a turnover, or an incomplete pass. (PHOTO BY JOANIE KOMURA, COURTESY UW ATHLETICS)

Basketball on Grass

WHILE JAMES WAS RETHINKING HIS OFFENSE AND ADJUSTING HIS coaching staff, his players were also engaged in a series of informal meetings that addressed the 1988 season and what they had to do to get Washington back to its proper standing in the football universe. Many of the people in those discussions had been freshmen in 1987. A few had played, but most had redshirted, spending the season practicing with the team and getting acclimated to college academics while sitting out games. They all saw how much fun it was to win enough games to be invited to a bowl, even if it was in Shreveport, Louisiana.

"We loved the Independence Bowl," linebacker Chico Fraley said. "We all had fun there, but in 1988 we had too much internal bickering and we didn't get it done." Randy Hart agreed with Fraley's assessment. When the Huskies started the year with three straight wins, anything seemed possible. But their slide to a 6–5 finish exacerbated divisions within the team.

"The losing was what caused it," Hart said. "We had a few guys who thought they were better than they were. Then, the articles started appearing in the papers about how Don had lost his luster. He didn't know how to coach. They were thinking, 'We've got the wrong guy here.'"

"When I got there, I felt a negative vibe," said wide receiver Orlando McKay. "It was easy to think, 'We suck. We're terrible,' based on how we were playing. Every game was a struggle, and we weren't doing things right." But rather than wallowing in despair, McKay chose defiance. "This can't be us," he said after 1988. "This isn't the squad I watched on TV last year. I remember we all kept saying to each other 'This is ridiculous. We came to UW because they win; they win bowl games; they have high national rankings. This is unacceptable. We've got to be better than this, and we will not let this continue.'"

"We all knew Coach James was making changes, and we knew we had to change too," tackle Lincoln Kennedy said. "We were staying home for Christmas, and we were embarrassed because that's not what we had signed up for. We wanted to have the type of success that Washington had always had, and we realized that it was going to be up to us to get that success back."

While the young players on the team vowed to themselves and each other that 1988 was a one-time-only thing, the upperclassmen stepped up an effort to get the program back on track. "I remember Dennis Brown [a defensive end entering his senior season] was a driving force," Fraley said. "He kept telling us we all had to pull our weight if we wanted to make sure this didn't happen again."

The discussions led to immediate results. Fraley noticed that competition in the weight room heated up, film rooms became more crowded, and players used spare time to discuss how they could all get better. "The expectation was that we had to do everything we could to make sure we were in a bowl game in 1989."

The players felt a bond forming that allowed for frankness without emotion. They challenged each other, feeding off each other's perceived strengths and weaknesses in an effort to improve at everything. The resiliency of youth moved to the fore, and each day the memory of 1988 grew smaller in the rearview mirror. "Our group had an incredible optimism about the future," said McKay. "We all developed a new attitude, and it was almost like a pact."

McKay was a speedster from Arizona who was the type of player the Huskies were now making a priority in recruiting. "A track guy who plays football" is how recruiting services described him. He was the Arizona state champion in the 100-, 200-, and 400-yard dashes and he had only played football for two years in high school, so that description wasn't too far off. But it bugged him to be called "a track guy," so he made getting better at football a priority. Time was a priority too. McKay and fellow receiver Mario Bailey had both played so much in 1988 that they each had just three years of eligibility left in an offense that didn't necessarily throw the ball all over the yard. But the status of wide receivers at UW was about to take a new direction.

"Everything is changing," assistant coach Jeff Woodruff told his receivers. "Keith Gilbertson is coming here, and everything we do on offense is going to be different." McKay had never heard of Gilbertson. When Woodruff told him that he had coached at Idaho, he was not impressed. "Idaho?" McKay scoffed. "IDAHO? Do they even have a team? What is that? NAIA football?" Woodruff popped a tape into a VCR and smiled. "Wait until you see what he's bringing with him."

The tape flickered on the screen, and they saw an offense that had first come to life at Granada Hills High School in Los Angeles in 1970. "Cactus Jack" Neumeier coached the Highlanders football team at the time, and he conceived an offense that he first called "basketball on grass." Neumeier used multiple receivers and one-back or even no-back looks, which added more receivers and spread the defense out across the field to create holes. The scheme eventually became known as simply "the spread offense."

"Basically, my offense spreads the defense across the field," Neumeier told the *Los Angeles Times*. "A lot of teams spread the defense the depth of the field, but my idea is to spread them sideline to sideline, so you never get two defensive backs to cover one receiver."

Neumeier's offense flourished in 1976, when a sophomore named John Elway became his quarterback. Elway passed for 5,701 yards and 49 touchdowns in his high school career, and the offense and the otherworldly numbers it put up caught the attention of his dad, Jack, who was coaching Division II football in the Los Angeles area. After the 1978 season, Jack Elway took a new job as head coach at Division I San Jose State University (SJSU).

Elway hired Dennis Erickson to be his offensive coordinator and then had Neumeier come up to San Jose to show them both how to install his offense, which immediately had two new devotees. Elway had success with it at SJSU, and when Erickson left after three years to become the head coach at Idaho, he took it with him to the Big Sky Conference. His offensive coordinator (and eventual successor) at Idaho was Gilbertson, and it was Gilby's version of the spread that McKay and Bailey were watching.

"My eyes just lit up," McKay said. He watched Idaho zoom up and down the field, carving up defenses with plays that featured as many as five players in a dizzying array of pass patterns that zigzagged across the field. The quarterback often released the ball after just a two- or three-step drop, which accelerated the pace even more. Finally, McKay asked a question: "Does this mean more throwing?"

"Does it mean more throwing?" Woodruff practically shouted. "Let me tell you what's going to happen: you guys are going to catch hundreds of passes!"

Meanwhile, Gilbertson was evaluating the players on the offensive line and was mystified as to why they were struggling. They were an experienced group of players who looked good, were big and strong, and were all competitive in the weight room and mat drills. (Mat drills are an off-season drill used by coaches to test players' agility, strength, stamina, and ability to work as a team. Players are divided into small groups, and each group is then brought onto a wrestling mat and given quick commands.)

"Mat drills are a great indicator of what a guy can do," Gilbertson said. "These guys could all change direction, run, jump, move, and bear crawl, and they're all big guys. I'm watching these guys, and again I kept thinking, 'How in the hell are we not doing better?'"

"We weren't very good, and the team was splintered," said Ed Cunningham. Cunningham was a center who had come to play football in Seattle after growing up in northern Virginia. But the bickering left him so unhappy and "worn down" after the 1988 season that he considered transferring. He stayed because he would have had to sit out a year if he left due to NCAA transfer rules. And despite the issues within the team and within the offensive line he said he felt the core of something potentially good coming together. Gilbertson could see that too, but he also felt that negative vibe upon his arrival. When he walked into his first meeting, he noticed players spreading out across the entire room. Some sat together, but others sat by themselves, and he immediately realized the group had some divisions.

"What the hell is wrong with you guys?" Gilbertson asked. "I don't know what's holding you back, but we're going to figure it out because you look too good doing mat drills and in the weight room to not be doing better out there on the field. Gentlemen, we are going to be a good offensive line."

For his second meeting, Gilbertson presented the linemen with a seating chart. Instead of sitting all over the room, they would sit next to each other. "With the offensive line there's a group dynamic," he told them. "And it has to work."

Gilbertson preached to them daily about the importance of becoming closer as teammates. "You don't have to be best friends," he told them, "but you have to like each other. You have to be accountable to each other, and we have to function as a family. We can fight in our meeting room, but when we go out on the field, we're fighting the other team."

"He called us out on the way we had been doing business," Kris Rongen said. Rongen was a guard who had arrived at UW in 1987. "At his suggestion we had pizza dinners together every Thursday night, and as we started hanging out, it all changed from a daily grind to believing in something much greater than just being there. We all quickly realized he was legit. Everything changed when he walked in."

About that time, Gilbertson's position group had grown by one. Lincoln Kennedy had come to UW as a highly recruited defensive lineman out of San Diego. He was a big, strong, affable kid who made a dramatic impression in his first Husky Stadium appearance when Lambright timed the players in forty-yard dashes.

"It was the first time I ever walked on turf," Kennedy said. "I was a California kid, and we played on grass and dirt. I took off, I finished, but when I tried to slow down, my foot caught on a seam, and I took a big fall. I was on the ground thinking, 'How embarrassing is this?'"

Kennedy looked up and saw Lambright standing over him, stopwatch dangling around his neck. His coach gave a long exhale and began shaking his head. "That was my introduction to Husky Stadium and Astroturf," Kennedy said. "I was like, 'Yeah, I'm an athlete all right.'" Kennedy *was* an athlete, but after one season the coaches thought he was an athlete playing the wrong position. James set up a meeting with Kennedy.

"We're going to change what we're doing on defense," James said. "I'll give you a choice. You can stay on defense, but you're not going to play much. Or you can move over to offense. We've got a new guy coaching over there, and he would love to have you. But it's your choice."

Kennedy called his high school coach, John Shacklett, and asked him what he should do. "If you switch to offense, you'll be an All-Pro in the NFL one day," Shacklett told him. "You're that good. You're a better offensive player than you are defensive, and you should make the move." The next day Kennedy told James he was all in.

"I appreciated that Coach James gave me an option and didn't force it on me," Kennedy recalls. "In college, they don't have to do that. From that day forward I had respect for his integrity and more important, I had respect for the program. I wanted our program to have success." But he still didn't know where the overall program was going. "We didn't know where the defense was going. We didn't know where the offense was going. We didn't know anything."

By the time the Huskies began three weeks of spring football practices, there was an uptick in energy and enthusiasm. But as practices began, there was one more hurdle for Gilbertson to clear: he had to show a group of skeptical receivers that he knew what he was doing.

"Gilby had this very specific trot when he came onto the field," McKay said. "It's like his 'cool guy' run; he swayed his head from side to side. Here comes this guy with this weird trot and his polyester pants and his purple shirt. We all thought it was hilarious."

In addition to being amused by Gilbertson's running style, McKay found it hard to believe an offensive line coach could tell him anything about how to be a successful wide receiver. "Wide receivers are divas by nature," said McKay. "We think we know everything about the position, and no one can tell us anything." But he quickly realized he was wrong: "As soon as he opened his mouth, you knew. When Gilby talked about route running, he knew all the terminology, and we figured out quickly that he knew what he was talking about. He was a mad scientist cooking up offensive potions. He was always figuring things out that nobody had thought of yet."

Gilbertson cemented his connection with his linemen on the first day of spring football practice. It was scheduled to begin at 8:30 a.m. He told his players he wanted them to meet ninety minutes earlier, which would leave them enough time to get taped and dressed for practice. The entire offensive line was in their seats ready to talk at 7:00 a.m. But there was one problem: no Gilby. The players looked at the clock and each other with ever-widening eyes. No one involved in Husky football was ever late. After ten minutes Gilbertson finally walked in. "Okay, guys. I had some friends in town, and we were up late so . . . change of plans. Go get taped and dressed, and then we'll meet on the field and go over what we have to go over out there."

Gilbertson exited the room, and the players sat in their seats stunned. "Then, we all just started laughing," Cunningham said. "We *knew* at that moment that this was going to work. It felt like he was one of us. He had boundaries, and he made those clear, but he related to us."

As they both had assured James, Pinkel and Gilbertson worked together with no friction. Like everyone else, Pinkel was excited to install a new offense. "We mixed some of the things that we were doing with the I formation with some of Gilby's one-back schemes, and it was really fun," Pinkel said. "We started looking like other teams that were running that type of offense, and the fact that we were good at it immediately was a confidence boost."

That boosted confidence was on display one afternoon late in the spring when the UW's athletic director, Mike Lude, visited the football offices. He was curious about how spring football was going and especially interested to find out how the players were adapting to the new offense. Eventually, he walked into Gilbertson's office.

"Mike, we're going to win a national championship," Gilbertson said. Lude stared at Gilbertson without saying a word as the statement hung in the air. "This is a group of special guys here. They're all fast, athletic, and strong. This could be something."

An Attacking Defense

JAMES STOOD IN FRONT OF THE MEDIA, HIS EYES SCANNING A STAT sheet and his mood souring by the second. His team had given up 34 points and nearly 500 yards in a home loss to a decidedly average Arizona State team. Finally, he spoke.

"As a coach, you'd rather be standing on the sidelines knowing you had a great defense." That James was not, in fact, a coach with a great defense was being rammed home game after game. The Sun Devils were just the latest opponent to prove the point.

UW's 1989 season had started promisingly enough with a powerful 19–6 win in Seattle over Texas A&M. While pregame conversation centered on the Dawgs' new "big play" offense, postgame analysts couldn't stop talking about a UW defense that dominated the Aggies, at one point shutting them down on ten consecutive third-down plays.

"That was fun," said Lambright. "It would be naïve for me to think that we would be able to dominate the way we did out there, but that's what you hope for."

The defense was stout the next week in a rout of Purdue, but cracks began to form during a subsequent three-game losing streak to Arizona, Colorado, and USC. The Huskies were outgained in all three games and gave up an astonishing 420 yards rushing to Colorado. USC manhandled them while piling up nearly twice as many yards. They rebounded to beat Cal and UCLA, but in both games, the defense continued to give up total yardage that was unacceptable.

"I remember the week of the Arizona State game," defensive back Dana Hall said. "Lambo kept saying to us that there was no way Justin was coming into Seattle and throwing for 500 yards." ASU quarterback Paul Justin had posted numbers that defied logic in the Sun Devils' game the week before versus WSU, completing 33 passes in 47 attempts for 534 yards in a wild 44–39 ASU win. "No way he does that against us in Husky Stadium," Lambo had told his players all week.

Lambright was right. Justin threw for "only" 339 yards but was in command all afternoon as the Sun Devils defeated UW, 34–32, in a game in which UW never led. "They came in and absolutely killed us," Hall said. "They threw the ball up and down the field all day."

A postgame headline in the *Seattle Times* took an overt shot at a program that was now 8–9 in its last seventeen: "Huskies Look Good—For a Big Sky team." "Until Washington improves the defense," columnist Blaine Newnham wrote, "it will be involved in a bunch of scintillating but not very satisfying games. Like just any other good Big Sky team." The Big Sky is a lower-level league that regularly featured high-scoring games. Newnham's inference was clear. The defense was not Division I caliber.

The players and coaches knew that the team's offense might be a work in progress as players implemented a new system. But no one expected the defense to be this porous, especially after the strong start. For a few weeks now the defensive coaches had been lobbying for something different, and by the time the staff gathered on the morning after the ASU loss, James had made up his mind that the Huskies were going to make a big change. "We were using a lot of fronts and a lot of different looks, and we weren't doing anything to the standard any of us wanted," Lambright said. "We needed to simplify things."

"We had a good-looking playbook," Randy Hart said. "We had good players, and we had all this speed on the field. But we were making them think too much. My thought was, 'Let's quit trying to be geniuses and just attack.'"

The Huskies had been running an "up-scheme" on certain second-down situations all season. They would place all eleven players at or near the line of scrimmage. Sometimes they would blitz; sometimes they would drop players back. The team had gotten pretty good at disguising the look, so opponents couldn't tell. In the meeting, Hart asked, "Why don't we just leave them up there all the time? Let's cut 'em loose. What do we have to lose?"

James announced that was exactly what he wanted to do. Instead of burdening players with strategy, reads, decisions, and various defensive options, James wanted the coaches to preach four things: Get off the block. Strike a blow. Pursue the ball. Tackle. "This was a big change for Don," said Lambright. "It's when we truly became an attacking defense." "It wasn't a free for all," Hart said. "You had to be where you were supposed to be, and you had to be disciplined."

It was a defense made by and for Lambright. One of his philosophies as defensive coordinator was to encourage his players to hit each other harder in congratulations than when they brought down an opponent. "After a tackle, you make sure to put your face mask in your teammate's face mask." UW defensive players heard that all the time in practice. Lambright was among the first defensive coaches to give players credit for half tackles. Players who arrived second, third, or even fourth to the party were credited with a half tackle as long as they had a hand on the ball carrier. This encouraged groups of players running toward the ball. An attacking defense felt like an extension of that philosophy. "It fit Lambo," Hart said. "Jim's an aggressive, confrontational, competitive guy. He'll challenge anybody."

Before Lambright met with his players to tell them about the planned changes, one of those players wanted to talk to him. Linebacker James Clifford lettered for UW as a true freshman in 1988 and was having a sensational 1989 season. He wound up leading the Pac-10 in tackles with 164 and emerged as a defensive leader.

"I'll never forget going into Lambright's office the day after the ASU game," Clifford said. "I was scared." Lambright was a no-nonsense coach who worked his players hard. As Hart said, "He had those eyes that turn into laser beams, and when that happened, chances are you had pissed him off."

Dana Hall told a great story about Lambright's intimidation. One night during training camp, Lambright was doing bed check and saw a player sneaking off into the shadows. He didn't see who it was for sure, but he thought it was Hall. He confronted the cornerback the next day. Hall denied it. He told the truth, and Lambright believed him. But Hall said it was still difficult. "I'm 6'3" and I tower over Jim Lambright. But he's got those blue eyes, and sometimes they looked white. The fear he put into me was unbelievable."

It was the same fear that Clifford felt now. But something needed to be said. He told his coach that he and his teammates were no longer trying to get better. They were too focused on thinking about how the coaches wanted them to play, and all that thinking caused them to be hesitant and tentative on the field. Clifford said it felt like players were just trying to survive practices and games, just trying to get by.

"I thought Coach was going to air me out," Clifford said. Instead, the man on the staff with the deepest Washington roots looked across his desk at another man with deep Washington roots (Clifford was from Seattle) and responded: "James, I appreciate you coming in here. If I thought you were full of shit, I'd tell you. But I want to tell you this instead: It has already been addressed." Lambright paused while Clifford soaked up what he had just heard. "It has already been addressed," he repeated. Clifford left the office, excited to see what that meant.

When James arrived at UW in 1975, he brought most of his staff from Kent State with him but he also kept Lambright from previous coach Jim Owens's staff. James knew he needed a local connection for credibility and recruiting, and Lambright was as grounded in the Pacific Northwest as Sasquatch.

Born and raised in Everett, Washington, Lambright was the son of a commercial fisherman. The first time he saw Husky Stadium was when he and a couple of buddies slipped through a hole in a fence and snuck into a game in October 1957. UW beat Oregon State that day, and Lambright was hooked on being a Husky. After high school, he earned a scholarship to play football there. He was on the 1963 UW team that lost in the Rose Bowl to Dick Butkus and Illinois. His senior season he was named to the 1964 All-Coast team, an honor voted on by sportswriters and broadcasters to honor the best players on the West Coast.

After graduation, Lambright coached at Fife High School in Fife, Washington, for one year and at Shoreline Community College (north of Seattle) for three. Coaching salaries being meager in those days, Lambright supplemented his income by joining in the family business; he spent most of his summers on commercial fishing boats in the Gulf of Alaska. If coaching had not worked out, that's likely how he would have spent his life. During the winter he taught and coached ice skating and curling. The possibility exists that somewhere, at this very moment, a skip and a lead are having a beer and reminiscing about their days under Coach Lambright at the Granite Curling Club in Seattle. Curling's loss was football's gain when Owens hired him in 1969. James promoted him to defensive coordinator in 1978 and assistant head coach in 1987. He liked to remind the others, particularly WSU alumni Baird, of his long-time Husky heritage.

"Where did you go to school anyway?" Lambright would jokingly ask Baird when they had a difference of opinion. "You know, I went to school right here. I played here."

Lambright first came to national prominence as a coach during the 1984 season, when his defense, nicknamed "Purple Reign," crushed opponents. That defense used as many as five linebackers in certain schemes. He was considered the guru of the eight-man defensive front that the Huskies were now using regularly. Defensive coaches from around the country made pilgrimages to Seattle to get tips from Lambo.

The team greeted news of a defensive switch with unanimous enthusiasm. Lambright told them reading and reacting was being moved down the depth chart with a new aggressive philosophy taking its place.

"It was heated and exciting because they were changing things up," said Fraley. "The read-and-react style put us at a little bit of a disadvantage. The new defense was designed to let us move and run, and we were all excited about that."

Orlando McKay remembered linebacker Jaime Fields being amped up afterward. "Let's go! Let's go!" McKay recalled Fields saying. "A hundred miles an hour! We're going to be bringing it on every play. We're going to blitz and attack from every position!"

Coaches told players the plan was simple. Know your gap, know your assignment, do your job, and do your job aggressively. Thinking was replaced by barely contained chaos. "It was pretty easy for our guys to figure it out," Hart said. "Our new strategy became, 'Go North!'"

"They talk about how you have to play downhill," linebacker Dave Hoffmann said. "This defense allowed us to start playing steep downhill. To do that, you've got to read quickly and be aggressive and nasty, or some big offensive lineman is going to pancake you. But if you were fast and nasty, you could have a really good time."

One of the fast, nasty players who was looking to have a really good time was a defensive newcomer. Donald Jones was from Gladys, Virginia, a crossroads twenty miles south of Lynchburg. He appeared on UW's radar when linebacker coach Chris Tormey was recruiting another Virginian, Ed Cunningham. "We figured that with all these trips to Virginia to get Ed, we should try to pick up another guy," Tormey said.

Jones found his way to defense thanks to Lambright's interest in offensive players whose skills might be better used on his side of the ball. "I always looked at backup speed people on offense and wondered where else they could play," Lambright said. Jones was a fullback who redshirted in 1987 and had just three carries in 1988. He started 1989 still struggling to find playing time until Lambo began envisioning him as a linebacker. "We didn't want to limit a guy with that kind of strength and quickness," he said.

At the same time James was explaining to Lincoln Kennedy that the coaches saw a brighter future for him on offense, he was also telling Jones that the key to more playing time would involve switching to defense. "A guy with your ability . . . we have got to find a way to get you on the field," James told him. "We'd like to move you to defense. You'll play linebacker, and you're going to play right away. Now, we still think you can be a great running back, and I'm not going to force you to play defense. It's your decision." Jones took a day to think and pray about the decision before telling James yes.

Jones had been on the defensive side of the ball for several weeks now, and the coaches liked what they saw. But Lambright liked what he imagined Jones to be. As he began his preparations for the Oregon State game, he watched tape of the Beavers from the previous week against USC and was blown away at the lethal combination of speed and size displayed by linebacker Junior Seau, who was having an All-American year for the Trojans. As Lambright watched Seau wreak havoc on the Corvallis dam builders, he envisioned Jones doing the same thing.

"They came to me and said this was the week we were going to start rushing the passer, and I was the guy to get the job done," said Jones. "The coaches kept telling me, 'You're just as fast [as Seau]. You're just as strong. You can do this.'"

Putting eight men on the line of scrimmage would increase the stress on the secondary, but coaches explained that the burden would be short. If defensive backs could cover their man for three or maybe four seconds, the opposing quarterback would either be knocked on his rear end or running for his life. Hall was among the players who immediately benefitted. "You're starting at cornerback this week," Lambright said to Hall. "We want you to be physical, and when the receiver comes off the line, beat the crap out of him."

After two days of meetings, it came time to debut the new style on the practice field. The defensive players loved the idea as soon as they heard it. The offensive players became believers as soon as they saw it.

"We scrimmaged on Tuesdays," Gilbertson said, "and we lined up for the first play. I looked at them, and they were all at the line of scrimmage. I thought, 'Damn. What's this?'"

"You could immediately see the excitement on the defensive side of the ball," McKay said. "Guys were flying around, running to the ball, and pursuing. It was something I had never seen before. And the fact that they were so fired up got us fired up on offense."

"We were having fun," Hall said, "and the offensive guys—the players and the coaches—they hated us."

By Saturday, UW's defenders were like kids at Christmas, anxious to show off their new toys. After OSU's first two drives ended in missed field goals, it was time for the Dawgs to unwrap the big box from Santa. Jones was inserted into the game, and the defense looked like bulls storming the streets of Pamplona.

On Jones's first play, he sacked quarterback Matt Booher. On second down, he forced an illegal procedure call against an OSU lineman. On the next play, Booher dropped back to pass, sidestepped the onrushing Jones, was crushed from the other side by defensive tackle Dennis Brown, and fumbled the football.

For Oregon State, the rest of the first half resembled a long, skidding car crash that wouldn't end. In just eighteen minutes, the Huskies had outgained the Beavers 163–11 and outscored them 37–0. They sacked Booher three more times and blocked two punts. Jones abused the Beavers' line so thoroughly that at one point when he again forced tackle Brad D'Ancona to move before the snap, the officials became confused and called off-setting penalties, announcing that both D'Ancona and Jones had been moving before the snap. "Who said defensive players can't move?" Lambright loudly protested.

Gilbertson took a minute from planning his offensive attack to appreciate what he was watching on defense: "It was crazy. Poor Oregon State. Everyone was up by the line of scrimmage, and they had to try to guess who was coming." The final score was 51–14, the most points and largest margin of victory in a conference game for UW since a 50–7 rout of Cal in 1982.

"We were just kind of flying around," said Clifford. "We were like bees, swarming all over the place." The players weren't the only ones buzzed up after the game.

"Donald Jones is unfair for tackles," enthused James. "And once he gets an idea of what he's doing out there, he can be our Junior Seau."

The Huskies closed the regular season with a 20–9 win over WSU in the Apple Cup as the defense unleashed a second consecutive destructive performance. Eric Briscoe intercepted Cougar quarterback Brad Gossen's first pass of the day and returned it for a touchdown. Gossen was sacked eight times, and the Dawgs now had 16 sacks in two games after getting just 12 in their first nine.

"We blitzed and put a lot more pressure on the quarterback," Clifford said. "We proved we don't have a Big Sky defense." With seven wins they also proved they were good enough to be back in a bowl game. While they wanted the Rose Bowl, their midseason sputter made that not possible. Instead, they would be matched up against Florida at the Freedom Bowl in Anaheim.

Gary Darnell was Florida's interim head coach. He had replaced Galen Hall midseason after Hall had resigned in the wake of an NCAA investigation. Florida was set to hire Gator legend and 1966 Heisman Trophy winner Steve Spurrier to head the program after the Freedom Bowl. Having an interim coach can sometimes bond a team together in an "us against the world" fashion but more often leads to a loss of focus. Maybe that explained what Hart saw when he arrived at the stadium a few hours before kickoff and took a walk to burn off some nervous energy. As he thought about the game plan, loud laughter disrupted his focus. "Their entire defensive line was up in the stands laughing and eating nachos," Hart said. "They didn't appear to be taking the game seriously. I thought if their guys were kicked back eating nachos two hours before kickoff, the game could be a good one for us."

Nachos or not, at least one Florida player had UW's attention. "We knew all about Emmitt Smith," Kennedy said. "It seemed like every time you turned on ESPN, they were talking about him."

Smith came into the game as the most decorated Florida player since Spurrier, whom he had just joined as the second player in school history to be a unanimous All-American. Smith held fifty-eight Florida records and was Florida's all-time leading rusher with 3,928 yards. But UW wasn't cowed by anything Florida had, including a great running back. The defense couldn't wait to show off their new strategy in a nationally televised game, and the offense was gaining confidence in the new system each week. That confidence was evident when UW scored on the opening possession of the game. Then, Florida counterpunched by taking advantage of Washington's new aggressiveness.

"Our whole focus was Emmitt Smith, Emmitt Smith, Emmitt Smith," Hall said. "Lambo told us, 'Anyone else on the team can beat us, but Emmitt Smith will not beat us.'"

"Everybody was looking at Emmitt because he had the name and the credentials," said Fraley. "If you were on defense, you wanted to hit him. He had a bull's-eye on his chest." That plan didn't look so hot at first.

"On the first play, they faked a handoff to Smith," Clifford said, "and all eleven guys ran right at him. If we had had an extra guy on the field, he would have gone to him too. Meanwhile, their quarterback has the ball and is running down the sideline untouched." The Gators tied the game with Donald Douglas's sixty-seven-yard run, and Hart began to wonder if pregame nachos might be a new innovation in college football.

If Douglas had known what was coming next, he might have run through the end zone, out the stadium ramp, and up the street to Disneyland. He would have had more fun there. For the rest of the game, UW held the Gators to 164 total yards, leading to a 34–7 rout. They held Smith to seventeen yards, by far his lowest output as a starter. "I just couldn't believe everything was falling apart," Smith said after the game.

UW's defense not only ruined Smith's day, but the players were verbal about it too. "You better have them take you out," Clifford said after one play. "You're going to get hurt." When Smith came out for the opening series of the second half, Clifford told him he couldn't believe he was still in the game. By the next series, he wasn't. Smith's college career ended with him on the sidelines, pads off, helmet off, a spectator in Florida's loss. In Smith's defense, he was heading to the pros, ready to take advantage of a new rule that allowed juniors to enter the league draft. "The lure of the NFL will shut a running back down fast," said Hart. It made no sense for Smith to stay in a lopsided second-tier bowl game that was already decided.

"They had no idea what we were doing on defense," Baird said. "We just smoked 'em, and Emmitt didn't want any part of it. He wasn't going to stay out there and get hurt." Gilbertson was thrilled with the offense. The Huskies had the advantage in total yards, 433 to 231, they had zero turnovers, and they had held the ball for nearly forty-two minutes.

But as dominant as the offense was, even Gilby was blown away by the defense. "Florida had seen two weeks of it on tape," he said. "It wasn't like they didn't see it coming. But we were rolling, and they couldn't do anything. Athletically they were great, and we just took them apart."

"We were starting to become good enough to know how good we could be," Cunningham said. "Our defense could pressure or not pressure, whether we were in man or in zone. They could switch from one to the other, and by doing that, they were able to dictate what was going to happen."

"We showed everyone that Washington was someone to be reckoned with," said McKay, who had five catches for 83 yards. "We're back. Don't forget about us. You saw us in '84. Well, get ready because 1990 is going to be a big year for us."

"I can't wait until next year. I wish it started tomorrow," Clifford told reporters before firing an ominous warning shot: "You have no idea what's going to happen next year. We have a kid named Steve Emtman, and if we can do what we did today and just totally dominate a team, you can't imagine what we're going to do with this guy added to our defensive line. Just wait and see. He's going to be unstoppable."

1990

"HUSKIES NOT READY FOR PRIME TIME USC"

So screamed the headline above a story by *Seattle Post-Intelligencer* columnist John Owen before UW faced USC at Husky Stadium. Owen wrote that the "game could be a blowout, a devastating disappointment for what appeared to be one of Don James's better Husky teams." He based his thoughts on both current events and history.

History, as it usually did, favored the Trojans. Since the formation of the Pac-8 in 1964 USC had been king of the castle more often than not, winning the conference title seventeen times in twenty-six years, including the last three in a row. During its recent run of success USC was 21-1-1 in conference play, and UW was among those feeling the Trojans' wrath. USC had won the last four meetings and five of the past six against the Dawgs. Overall, James was 6–8 as a head coach against the Men of Troy.

Current events also seemed to tip things in USC's favor. Both teams came into the game unbeaten, but the Trojans' wins over eastern powerhouses Syracuse and Penn State looked more impressive than UW's close calls over San Jose State and Purdue.

The Trojans had the gaudier history, but Washington's past would be on display for the game since it had chosen the weekend of the USC game to celebrate the hundredth anniversary of Husky football.

A Centennial Team, saluting the best players in Husky history, was announced the night before the game. In a nod to the success enjoyed during James's tenure in Seattle, half of the twenty-four players honored had played for him.

Aware that the game would be high profile due to the anniversary celebration and USC's recent dominance, James asked his team to do something special. Part of game week routine at UW was something called the "twenty-four-hour rule." In the twenty-four hours before kickoff, he wanted no nonsense, no goofing around, nothing but 100 percent focus. The week of the USC game, James told players he was invoking the twenty-four-hour rule on Monday. It's an ask that demands an incredible amount of mental discipline, and it was a move James had made only one other time at Washington.

"We were getting ready to play the Cougars in 1976, when Jackie Sherrill coached them," Keith Gilbertson recalled. "On Monday that week, Don set the tone. 'There is no joke telling, there is no screwing around, and there is no levity this week. There is no laughing in the meeting rooms, the locker rooms, or the practice field. There is not going to be one happy moment until we kick their ass.' He was seething. He was hot."

James was angry at how Sherrill had reacted to the news that running back Joe Steele, one of the top recruits in the state, had committed to Washington. When Sherrill found out, he called the James household. Carol answered the phone and said her husband had left for his office. Sherrill then allowed his anger at losing out on Steele to get out of hand. "Just because your husband beat USC and UCLA, he thinks he's a knight on a white horse. And I want to tell you he's cheating really bad in recruiting." On and on the tirade went before Carol finally got a word in. "If you have something to say about Don, you should say it to him," she coolly said before ending the conversation. James was furious when his wife told him the story. That led to the first-ever week-long implementation of the twenty-four-hour rule. The Huskies won the Apple Cup that year, 51–32.

USC was favored by five points, and given the conditions, it should have felt right at home. The game kicked off at 3:30 p.m. on the last day of summer, and the sunny skies and a game-time temperature of 92 degrees made it feel more like a day at a Southern California beach than Seattle. But instead of towels, beach umbrellas, and sunscreen, the Trojans spent the afternoon looking for a fallout shelter.

UW led 24–0 at halftime, and the scoreboard alone didn't do justice to the level of ass-kicking witnessed by the 72,617 fans at Husky Stadium. The Trojans netted just forty-three total yards in the first half, and forty-four of those came on two pass plays. That meant that on twenty other plays USC gained a total of minus one yard. The Trojans were penalized ten times and faced seven third downs of long distances ranging from five to thirty-eight yards in the first half.

That first half explosion was partially the result of James's taking advantage of the former players who were in Seattle for the centennial celebration. Before the game, several of the players spoke to the Huskies. The current team's emotional barometer rose rapidly as past Dawg legends spoke about what it meant to be a Husky.

"You have to go out there and represent what Husky football is all about," former linebacker Michael Jackson roared at the team. Jackson had been one of James's first recruits in 1975 and played on the team that defeated Michigan in the 1978 Rose Bowl. "When another team comes into our house, you've got to make them feel that."

Donald Jones said several other legends gave similar speeches. "It got me so fired up that I couldn't wait to get out there and play and show those guys respect. That's the culture we had. We wanted to represent for those guys; we knew they would be watching us, and we knew it was a big game."

The game ended with Washington winning, 31–0, and the Centennial Team presumably happy with what they saw. The final score stayed reasonable because James, as always, played his backups and refused to run it up. But there's little doubt UW could have done much more damage. They outgained USC, 410–163, and handed the Trojans their worst loss in the conference since 1960, when UW crushed them, 34–0. The size of the win and the way his team did it left James shaking his head. He admitted that if someone had told him before the game that the final score would be 31–0, he would have assumed USC had the 31. "Considering all the things the Trojans had going for them—they'd beaten us four times in a row, they hadn't lost a league game since 1987, they've won three league championships in a row. . . . You keep adding things up that they've done, and it's hard to believe."

USC quarterback Todd Marinovich came into the game as a Heisman Trophy contender, and he spent the early part of the day trying to rally his overmatched teammates. "It seemed every time he made a first down, he'd say, 'It's time now. We're moving,'" Jones said. "And then, we'd stuff him. We expected a dogfight, but it was total domination."

Husky Stadium is built with roofs atop both upper decks. Their primary function is to keep fans dry on rainy days. But they also serve as acoustic deflectors and funnel noise from over 70,000 fans directly down onto the field. That became a daylong unsolvable problem for the USC offense. On one drive, Marinovich stepped away from the center three times to plead with officials to ask the raucous crowd to quiet down. On that drive, USC was penalized for illegal procedure and delay of game. Marinovich dropped a snap on one play and was sacked on another. USC was also called for a personal foul. By then, it was third down and 38. Marinovich took exactly one snap all day in Husky territory, a first down at the forty-five-yard line. He was immediately sacked.

Emtman was primary among those responsible for the destruction of the USC backfield. He had Marinovich's recent *Sports Illustrated* cover taped to his locker the week of the game. "That was a good story on him," he said. "But today was a different story."

Marinovich gave the postgame quote of the day. "It's never over 'til it's over, but this one was over really early," he said. "I've never been shut out in my life. It's pathetic. It's embarrassing. We never did anything to shut the crowd up." He paused before delivering a thirteen-word coda that true Husky fans can recite by heart:

"I saw purple. That's all I saw. No numbers. No faces. Just purple."

Marinovich saw purple. What he heard that day was an afternoon-long roar that still echoes in the ears of everyone there to witness it. For Lincoln Kennedy, the game marked his first start on the offensive line. "It was obscenely loud," Kennedy said. "I remember yelling at people on the sidelines and in the huddle, and they couldn't hear me."

"The energy was incredible, and I still get goose bumps thinking about it," Jones said. "It had never been that loud. I couldn't hear anything."

"I had never felt the kind of energy in the stadium that I felt that day," said Rondeau. "It was palpable, visceral, and absolutely electric. The whole thing just fed off itself. This was the days before replay screens or hype music. It was all very internal and intimate."

"That game is why I came to go to school and play football at Washington," Cunningham said. "Of all the games I played in that building, that was the coolest."

"That's when it started to flourish," Chris Tormey said. "That's when it really took off. We had no idea that we were going to explode like that."

The Huskies rose from number twenty-one to number twelve in the rankings, but the schedule makers did them no favors. Next up was a road game against Colorado. The Buffaloes were coming off an 11–1 season in 1989; their only loss had been in the Orange Bowl to Notre Dame. They had defeated UW in Seattle the previous season, 45–28, in an emotional game played just one week after their 1988 starting quarterback, Sal Aunese, had died. Aunese had been diagnosed with inoperable stomach cancer just six months earlier.

Now, a year later in Boulder, the Buffaloes were again the victors, this time 20–14. In the weeks before, the Buffs had given up a game-tying touchdown against Tennessee and a game-losing touchdown against Illinois, both in the fourth quarter. Motivated by those collapses, their defense stiffened against UW and intercepted quarterback Mark Brunell twice in the end zone in the final ten minutes of the game to preserve the win. "Two heavyweight football teams," Rondeau said. "That was as physical a game as I ever saw, and it was as great a game as I ever saw."

"Both of those Colorado losses helped us," cornerback Walter Bailey said. "[The players] were similar to us. Great athletes and a great defense. We knew we had to match their intensity."

The Huskies followed that game up with routs over Arizona State, Oregon, Stanford, Cal, and Arizona. The average margin of victory in the five games was 33 points, and considering that Oregon, Cal, and Arizona were all destined to go to bowl games, the wins weren't coming over a bunch of tomato cans. The buildup to the Cal game is comical in retrospect. The Bears came into the game on a four-game winning streak (the school's longest in twelve years), and the players were vocal about their confidence.

On the day before the game, UW had finished a walkthrough and was meeting in their team room when the Bears arrived at the stadium for their Friday practice. As they came by the closed door to the Huskies team room, several Cal players banged on the door and barked various predictions of doom. An incredulous James abandoned his planned remarks and asked his players, "Do I even have to say anything?"

The Bears kept up the verbal assault on game day. "Don't be surprised if we're up at halftime," fullback Darius Turner remembered one player yelling during warm-ups. "We're due for a blowout!" Finally, having heard quite enough, tackle Siupele Malamala approached Gilbertson.

"Can I get thrown out of the game before the game?" he asked his coach.

"What do you mean?" Gilbertson replied.

"If I kick someone's ass in the tunnel before the game, can I get thrown out of the game?"

"I'll tell you what, Siupele. Let's not chance it."

UW belted Cal, 46–7 ("They were due for a blowout, all right," Turner said), and by now had risen to seventh in the national rankings. Arizona was next up, and if the Huskies won and UCLA lost to Oregon UW would clinch the conference title and return to the Rose Bowl for the first time since 1981. The Huskies held up their end of the deal. They crushed the Wildcats, 54–10, at Husky Stadium. After the game, players waited in the team room for the result of the Bruins and Ducks game. The game wasn't televised and had kicked off thirty minutes after the Dawgs and Wildcats. In the days before the Internet and cell phones, word of mouth was the coin of the realm. Players spread the news that UCLA was ahead by 11 points with seven minutes to play. But then word arrived that Oregon had scored and now trailed by only three points. A few minutes after that, the Ducks got the ball back and scored again to take the lead with two minutes left.

When the final score was relayed to the room—Oregon, 28; UCLA, 24— James bellowed, "It's over!" His team cheered and surrounded the coach with hugs and backslaps. Within a minute or so, Rose Bowl president Roy Cohts stood in front of the Huskies with an announcement: "The Rose Bowl committee would like to formally invite the Washing. . . ."

That's as far as he got. Players, coaches, and staff in the room exploded with a roar, a release of emotion that took a long time to dissipate.

"There is nothing more exciting than driving to that stadium and going out and standing on that rose in the middle of the field before the game," said Lambright, who was heading to Pasadena for the fifth time, once as a player and now four times as a coach.

"As a player, you don't get many opportunities like this," said Hart. "And as a coach, you never know if it's going to be your last one." Hart played in the game in 1968 as Ohio State finished an unbeaten national championship season with a 27–16 win over USC. He had also coached in the game for Woody Hayes in 1970 and for Earle Bruce in 1984. His long and successful career had taken him to the Peach, Liberty, Bluebonnet, Holiday, Fiesta, Citrus, and Cotton Bowls. He was more qualified than anyone to assess postseason games. "The Rose Bowl is IT!" he declared.

Pinkel was happy with the bowl news because it would make things less tense between him and his family. "Around my home, no one was allowed to say the "R" word until we were there," he said. "My kids would call it the flower bowl."

"I felt like this team had a chance to be champions," Gilbertson said. "But I wasn't sure because I'd never won a championship in the Pac-10. I keep pinching myself. Maybe we are special."

"It's a thrill to see the kids enjoy it," James said. "That's what I'm getting out of this, enjoying it with these kids."

Eventually, word reached the locker room that the number-one-ranked team in America had lost. Georgia Tech roared from two touchdowns behind to defeat top-ranked Virginia, 41–38. The fifth-ranked team also lost, as Iowa's Nick Bell ran for 130 yards in the first quarter of what would end up a 54–28 rout of Illinois. Then, the Huskies found out that Colorado had staged a dramatic comeback against number three, Nebraska. The Cornhuskers led, 12–0, after three quarters. Colorado All-American running back Eric Bieniemy lost four fumbles on the day but atoned for his miscues by scoring four touchdowns in the fourth quarter as Colorado shocked the Huskers, 27–12. Fourth-ranked Auburn played at Florida that night. Most of the players watched this one on

TV as the Gators blew open a close game with 27 unanswered second-quarter points en route to a 48–7 win.

When the dust finally settled on one of the wildest days in college football history, four of the top five teams in the country had lost. Second-ranked Notre Dame and sixth-ranked Houston both won, as did number seven, UW. Players, fans, and observers all waited anxiously to see how the polls would look. When they were released, the media and the coaches agreed:

1. Notre Dame
2. Washington

As excited as everyone was that UW had not only clinched a Rose Bowl berth, but had also played its way into the national championship picture, the talk soon turned to why Notre Dame was ranked first. "No. 2 Injustice?" was the headline above a story written by Gary Nelson in the *Everett Herald*. Nelson pointed out Notre Dame's only loss of the season had come at home against Stanford. UW had beaten Stanford on the road, 52–16. *Chicago Tribune* college football writer and AP poll voter Ed Sherman wondered why so many voters had chosen Notre Dame ahead of UW: "I'm perplexed by the way Washington's been treated," he said. "Washington is getting ripped off."

"AHEM!" came a loud clearing of the throat from Boulder. Colorado fans wondered how the Buffaloes could be ranked behind UW in both polls when they had defeated the Huskies earlier in the season. The entire discussion was a yearly event on the college football calendar in the days before any kind of playoffs. Every four years in November Americans would debate who should be president. But every single year in November Americans (maybe in greater numbers than for presidential elections) would debate who should be number one in college football.

James didn't care that his team wasn't ranked at the top. He was just happy to be in the mix: "It's good to have the national championship still on the table. We talked to our players about that. We're in a really good position."

The Huskies were ranked number two in the country, and they were 21-point favorites at home over a fading UCLA team. Meanwhile, Notre

Dame had a brutal road game at Tennessee. An Irish loss and a UW win would leave the Huskies ranked number one. Optimism ran so high that the university made a request of UW students.

In 1989, after the Apple Cup win over WSU, students stormed the field and tore down one of the goalposts. Police attempted to stop them, and an hour-long melee ensued on the field. Mace was used to disperse the crowd, and the entire imbroglio left everyone angry. The students had been inspired to some degree by a column in the UW student newspaper, *The Daily,* that was titled "Tear 'em Down." Sportswriter Todd San Jule opined that the Huskies would win the Apple Cup and wrote that fans should take the celebration to the field. "Once you reach the playing field," San Jule wrote, "you'll see a pair of goalposts on either side of the stadium. You've seen it done many times on television before. . . . You've always wondered what it's like to tear down the goal posts. The time is now to find out."

Police and university officials were upset with the behavior of the students, some students were upset at what they saw as an overreaction by the police, and no one wanted to see a repeat of that scene. But after *The Daily* again ran a playful editorial encouraging the students to celebrate by removing the goalposts, the university assured them that police again would be dispersing the crowd with mace. James even wrote a letter to the editor asking the students to be respectful.

Game day arrived with an unseasonably warm temperature of 56 degrees. But it was raining, and the wind that came with it was the real problem. "It was a classic pineapple express," said Rondeau, invoking the nickname that had been used for years on the West Coast to describe storms that began near Hawaii and brought warm temperatures, wind, and lots of moisture. The bad weather didn't dampen the enthusiasm. Arriving fans were given roses to take into the game to celebrate the previous win, and in the final hour before kickoff, the public address announcer gave a few updates on the Notre Dame-Tennessee game. As expected, the Irish were struggling in Knoxville, and each announcement was greeted by a roar and a waving of roses from the Husky faithful.

On the field during warm-ups, Gilbertson had an uneasy feeling. "I wish they'd stop announcing that score," he thought to himself, mindful that the UCLA players could use it for motivation. On the Bruins' side of the field, that's exactly what happened. The players heard the cheers when it was announced that Notre Dame was trailing. They had seen the newspaper stories where university officials begged fans to not tear down the goalposts.

The game began, and the Huskies couldn't stay out of their own way. Maybe it was the conditions, maybe it was because they were coming off an emotional win the week before, but the Dawgs could not achieve consistency. "It was the *Twilight Zone*," Gilbertson said. "It was one of those days where we'd call stuff and guys would look the wrong way or go the wrong way. It felt like every series ended with me saying, 'What are we doing? This is week ten.' And UCLA had a nice plan. [Offensive Coordinator] Homer Smith was a smart guy."

"It was a weird, perplexing feeling from the start," said Rondeau. "UW had been dictatorial defensively that year, and all of a sudden here was this game plan that was dictating to them what was going to happen. Smith figured the only way he could keep them at bay was to do things fast, and that's what UCLA did."

UCLA was playing with freshman quarterback Tommy Maddox. To contain UW's aggressive defense Smith set Maddox up in a shotgun formation most of the day. He ended up with twenty-three completions in forty-one attempts for 239 yards and two touchdowns.

"The game plan they had was perfect, especially against our defense," said Cunningham. "They put Maddox in the shotgun and let him throw quick slants and outs. They were very patient. And I was awful. It was my worst performance as a Husky."

UCLA's best play of the day was a simple handoff from Maddox to running back Brian Bowen on third down and one at their own twelve. The Huskies lined up in an aggressive, blitzing defensive alignment called a strong safety crash. Shortly after the snap, Fraley moved to the outside of fullback Shawn Wills, who was blocking on the play.

"One of my biggest mistakes ever," Fraley lamented. "If I had hit the fullback, it would have slowed the play down, but I tried to slip by him to get to the QB faster."

"They hit us with a lead draw, and that was the downside to playing that style of defense," said Tormey. "You live by the sword, and you die by the sword. We had eleven up, they creased us on a draw play, and one guy was out of his gap. When you're in zero coverage, no one has eyes on the ball."

If Fraley had gone inside, Brown would have run right into him. Instead, he was easily blocked out of the way, and Brown rolled unimpeded on the Husky Stadium turf like a golf ball on a downhill fairway, so alone on the play that for most of the run he was the only player visible in the picture on TV.

"He could have run all the way to Spokane if he had wanted to," James said. "That was a bad call on our part. A strong safety crash should only be called against a tight end formation. Then the weak safety can get back and help in the middle. At least we should have had a checkoff to get us out of a bad call."

"That took the pop out of them for a while and put them back on their heels," Brown said after the game. Orlando McKay agreed. "All of a sudden, our confidence was shaken."

Fraley is right about his role in the miscue, and Brown and McKay were right that the play took some of the starch out of UW, but there was still 49:25 left in the game, and UCLA only led 7–0. Later in the first half, the Huskies suffered another setback. Running back Greg Lewis was working on a streak of nine consecutive 100-yard games. On a lousy weather day, he figured prominently in the Huskies' attack. But he suffered a hyperextended knee in the second quarter and was largely ineffective after that. "Once we lost Greg, we just kind of drifted through the game," said Mario Bailey.

Still, the Huskies had plenty of opportunities to regain control, and they grabbed the lead, 14–13, late in the third quarter. UCLA responded with a touchdown pass to Scott Miller and a field goal by Brad Daluiso for a 22–14 lead midway through the fourth quarter.

"The Huskies are trying to hitch up their britches and gut it out here," ABC-TV announcer Keith Jackson told his audience as UW got the ball after the field goal. But the drive after the supposed tightening of the britches stalled, and they punted. The wind and rain had subsided a bit in the middle of the game, but now, as the afternoon grew dark, both had picked back up. The wind off Lake Washington was blowing at twenty miles per hour, with gusts to thirty-five. Miller was the UCLA return man. "The wind was just shifting all over the place," he said later. "I never should have tried to catch the ball." Miller fumbled the punt, and UW's Jay Barry recovered. Four plays later, on fourth down, Brunell hit Bailey for a touchdown. After a successful two-point conversion, the Huskies had somehow managed to tie the game at 22.

The wild afternoon of wind, rain, punts, fumbles, miscues, and other twists and turns wasn't over yet. UCLA tried to move the ball but was stymied and had to punt. There were still over two minutes left in the game, and the Huskies had all three of their timeouts left. The fans regained their belief that UW would win, and the noise level escalated. But on their second play, Brunell overthrew McKay near the Husky sideline. The errant toss was picked off by safety Eric Turner. It was Brunell's first interception in 129 passing attempts. UCLA quickly advanced the ball into Husky territory and with ten seconds remaining brought on Daluiso to attempt a forty-three-yard field goal. "The wind was swirling, and I couldn't get any indication which direction it was going," Daluiso said.

As rain pelted the field, Daluiso's kick left the ground and looked good. Then, buffeted by the gusting wind, it fluttered toward the left goalpost. For a brief second, it looked like the Huskies might escape with a tie. But the ball scooted past the upright (with a little room to spare), and UCLA had their amazing, improbable upset win, 25–22.

"They came out flat and figured they could roll over us," Miller crowed after the game. "I don't know what their problem was, but it was their mistake."

"For a number-two-ranked team they were lacking a little intensity," safety Matt Darby said. "They probably looked at our record and thought they could roll over us, but we laid it to them."

"I haven't gotten over that game," McKay said almost thirty years later. He had led the Huskies with four catches for sixty-seven yards, but in defeat he focused on the four balls that had come his way that he didn't catch. "I'll never get over it. I watched it a few years ago, and I wanted to throw up. I blame myself a ton. I had multiple opportunities to come up with plays. I did not live up to the standards I set for myself that day."

In retrospect, it's easy to see how the Huskies were in a position to get tripped up. They had clinched a Rose Bowl bid. They had steamrolled everyone else in the conference to that point. The fan and media focus all week had been on the sudden opportunity to win a national championship. Some of that naturally seeped through to the players.

"All we could talk about all week was how we were going to win the national championship and meet the president," said Cunningham.

"I don't remember feeling that way," said Kennedy, "but in the back of our minds, I'm sure there was some, 'Hey, look at this. We can win the national title.'"

"In everyone's mind, there was a little bit of, 'We're there. We're going to win the national title,'" said Bailey. "It was there that week. We had just reached the top of the mountain, and we hadn't expected that. We were rolling past everyone, but we didn't have a clue that we were that good, so we were overconfident."

Terry Donahue had been the head coach at UCLA since 1976 and now had a 7-5-1 record in thirteen games against James, but this one left him barely able to process what all he had seen and in need of a new word, which he invented for reporters to sum the day up. "It was the doggonedest thing I've ever been involved in," Donahue said with a laugh.

James wasn't laughing about anything. "You know, we read a lot of nice things about us last week," he said. "All that talk about the national championship. We tried to use it as motivation, but maybe the more good things you hear, the softer you get, and the more people are going to come after you. The national championship dream is dead."

8

Winter, Spring, Disaster

THE STING FROM THE UCLA LOSS CARRIED THROUGH THE WEEKEND. In the immediate aftermath, Kris Rongen was forced to pull the plug on a huge postgame party at his house (a decision no college student makes lightly). "It was a funky bad day and a funky bad night," he said. "It was supposed to be a great celebration and a lot of fun. Instead, it was, 'How did we just lose?'"

"I couldn't get out of bed for a couple of days," Cunningham wrote in an ABC sports retrospective piece years after the game. "I was depressed. It was the worst loss I was ever involved in. It's my most bitter defeat playing competitive football."

Unfortunately for Washington State, they were next up on the schedule. Hoffmann said any lingering depression about the UCLA game or canceled parties dissipated. "Guys were pissed, but we didn't spend a lot of time worrying about woulda, coulda, shoulda. Our attitude was, 'Let's go finish the job. Let's crush anyone in front of us.'"

Dana Hall recalled that after losing the 1988 Apple Cup in Pullman, the Huskies were irritated to discover that there was no hot water for postgame showers in the locker room. Several players remembered that, and it further fueled their anger. "We wanted to leave no doubt, we wanted to demolish them," Hall said.

Like the week before, Gilbertson found himself uneasy on the field during warm-ups. But it had nothing to do with scores being announced or a feeling that his team might not be ready. As he walked out onto the field, he was startled to see his boss running toward him.

"What's wrong?" Gilbertson asked. James pointed at the stands while delivering a one-word response without breaking stride as he passed by: "Bomb!" James replied.

Security officials at WSU had found a homemade explosive device in the student section of the stadium, the discovery of which led to one of the oddest announcements in sports stadium history. "If you see anything strange under your seat," boomed the announcer, "please stand up and raise your arms so police can investigate. Please take this as a serious announcement."

Up in the radio booth, Bob Rondeau laughed about one detail of the story. "The WSU students who pulled off the prank put a bomb in the WSU student section. Talk about Couging it." "Couging it" is a derisive term Husky fans (and sometimes even Cougar fans) use to describe any mistake made by the WSU football team.

James, Gilby, and the rest of the Huskies quickly evacuated. The stadium was searched, and nothing else suspicious was found. The original homemade bomb was ultimately labeled as harmless, but the game was delayed for thirty minutes. When the game finally started, the only thing that exploded was UW. The Dawgs drubbed the Cougs, 55–10, piling up the most points ever scored in an Apple Cup game and matching the 1914 game for the largest winning margin in Apple Cup history.

A month and a half later the Huskies began 1991 with a 46–34 win over Iowa in what was at the time the highest-scoring Rose Bowl in history. Washington's defense asserted its dominance early as the Dawgs first two scores came courtesy of a blocked punt return by Hall and an interception return by Charles Mincy. Brunell ran for two touchdowns and passed to Bailey for two more and was named the game's MVP. Greg Lewis, who had had arthroscopic knee surgery after the UCLA game, ran for 128 yards in his final game as a Husky.

The game looked close because Iowa scored 20 points in the fourth quarter after James had taken most of his first-team players out. Iowa was aided in their comeback by the recovery of two onside kicks. "I guess some of you guys know now why you are backups," James infamously told his team after the game. He was irritated and embarrassed that Iowa had made the game competitive enough that he had to put his first-team offense back in the game in the fourth quarter. That's high on the list of things that embarrass a coach because, among other things, it shows that the second team did not maintain the intensity necessary to successfully finish the game.

"He did not like how that game ended," said McKay. "He wanted to finish every game. He didn't care about blowing the other team out; he just wanted to make sure we finished and looked good until the end of the game."

But James was excited about his third Rose Bowl win (and his first since New Year's Day, 1982). He was now 9–3 in bowl games as a head coach at Washington. "Considering a bowl game matches you against a team that has had a highly successful season, it's a record of which I'm proud," he said.

The players were happy too. But in the back of their minds, they realized they had unfinished business. After the game, Fraley gave his Rose Bowl ring and watch to his father, who immediately declined the gift. "Chico, I can't take this," Charles Fraley said. "This is too important, and you should keep it."

"No," Fraley told his father. "You take it. I'm getting another one next year."

Next year began with the off-season workout program the week after the Rose Bowl. It was voluntary, but most players knew better. For every person who loves being in the gym, there's usually at least one who is there but not excited about it. But in the case of UW football in the winter of 1991 participation and enthusiasm were unanimous. "We didn't have to kick anyone's ass or ask, 'Where were you?'" Hoffmann said. "Guys were chomping at the bit."

"It started the first day in the weight room after the Rose Bowl," said Fraley. "I remember Emtman had come up with a drill we called 'suicide squats.'" The idea was to start with 90 percent of your maximum weight on a bar. You did eight or ten squats. Then you took off a plate and repeated the squats. You kept going until there was nothing left on the bar." The drill required three spotters, and Fraley said players couldn't walk afterward.

Hoffmann also came up with something new for players who might be bored with the weight room. He and a group of teammates would push his Chevy Blazer along a side road behind the athletic complex. "I started doing it in high school in San Jose. My little brother and I would trade off. He didn't really have a choice. I'd push for about eighty yards while he steered. Then we'd trade. In high school, other guys joined us, but nobody ever came twice. But everyone at UW was jacked about it because it was something different."

Get stronger. Get tougher. Get faster. That's what the winter months are for, and now, with one of the most talented group of players UW had ever had, players who were already strong, tough, and fast were improving. "It was intense," Gilbertson said. "No one missed a weight session. No one missed a mat drill. No one missed speed school." Speed school?

Using techniques taught by Kevin McNair, the Huskies worked on improving their speed every Tuesday and Thursday. McNair was a former track star at Stanford and former coach at the University of California at Irvine. He was curious about why some people could run fast and how fast runners could become even faster. Eventually, he began working with professional and college football teams interested in increasing their team speed. James began to incorporate some of McNair's methods, which included kinesiology, and showed that the entire body (not just the legs or feet) affected how fast one was.

Gilbertson said the emphasis on improving team speed came from the top. "Coach was adamant that we were going to recruit bigger, stronger, faster, quicker guys, and when they got here, we were going to make them even bigger, stronger, faster, and quicker, or they wouldn't be here."

"Don's forte was developing the kids we recruited," said Hart. "Our off-season program was phenomenal. The kids started believing in themselves because they were seeing the results. Don was great at developing talent. That was his ace. He was unlike anyone I ever worked with in that regard."

"There was an emphasis on plyometrics," Cunningham said. "We started learning how to run with form and efficiency, and our fitness level went way up. Our defensive guys had to be in soccer-like fitness because they went fast, and we scored a lot, so they were often back out on the field without much time to rest."

Most of UW's top players had now been in Seattle for at least three years. In the winter of 1989, their discussions had revolved around getting the program back on track. In the winter of 1990, it was all about getting back to the Rose Bowl. Now, it was about maintaining focus for the entire upcoming season. "That UCLA game hung over us all winter," Gilbertson said. "It was like having a big knob on your forehead."

When spring practice began, the intensity on the field matched that of the winter workouts. By then, Gilbertson was officially running the offense. After the Rose Bowl, Gary Pinkel had been hired as the new head coach of the University of Toledo. Assuming the Rockets' top job meant a chance to be the boss and a return to his Ohio roots. Both he and Gilbertson could take satisfaction in what they had achieved. The offense had gotten better, neither man had made a big deal about who should get the credit, and everything had worked out. Now, with Pinkel departing, Gilbertson moved up to become the offensive coordinator.

"From a young age, this is what I've wanted to do," Gilbertson told Gary Nelson of the *Everett Herald*. Accompanying the story was a photo that showed Gilbertson, at two years of age, sitting in his father's lap. His dad was reading a book about bears to his toddler. The book? *Playing the Line*. It was written by Chicago Bears lineman Bulldog Turner and was subtitled "A sensational player tells how to do it." Goldilocks and the Three Bears? That was a story for *other* kids.

Coaches like spring football because they can work with players daily without the pressure of getting ready for a game each week. There's more time for teaching and installing new plays or schemes. The downside is that with no game to look forward to, players are left to take out any aggression or accrued frustration on teammates. "We were a collective team, but the offense and the defense were two different entities," James Clifford said. "In spring practice, we were trying to disrupt everything [the offense] did. And vice versa."

After missing the 1990 season with a knee injury, Clifford was now back in the fold. He was a team leader who made getting together outside of football a priority. Teammates regularly convened at the house of his grandfather, Garland Morrison, in Seattle to eat grilled salmon. Morrison was a pretty good fisherman, and the players were usually eating fish that had been recently pulled out of nearby waters. Morrison built a boat called the *Uff Da* and allowed his grandson and his teammates to use it to fish on Offutt Lake near Tenino, Washington, south of Seattle. They fished with varying degrees of success (Clifford said Emtman "couldn't catch a fish to save his life"), and their lack of success was duly noted when they returned to shore. "The old guys who were friends of my grandpa were talking so much shit to all the guys it was unbelievable."

With spring practice under way fishing was put on hold. The coaches were generally pleased by the effort and intensity. It's one thing for players to say they'd learned their lesson against UCLA. The daily effort, execution, and intensity on the practice field backed those words up and gave them meaning. One afternoon, the intensity was dialed up after a drill in which the second-string offense was having an easy time moving the football against the first-team defense in a scrimmage. When they scored, Emtman stormed off the field with his helmet in hand.

When he got to the sideline, Emtman encountered one of the yellow benches that could hold a dozen or more players. The huge wooden structure was empty now and blocked Emtman's way. With one hand he flipped it over and out of his path, sending towels, water bottles, and other football accoutrements flying. He then swung his helmet in an arc and slammed it against an equipment trunk.

"ONES!" he screamed for the first-string team. "RIGHT HERE! NOW!" In the past, he might have let a more experienced lineman talk to the team because he was not a player given to making speeches, preferring instead to lead by example.

"Emtman leading by example was like, 'Either you play as I do, or I'll kill you,'" laughed Rondeau. "He commanded that kind of respect and that fear among everyone else. This was not a guy you wanted to piss off."

On this occasion his teammates *had* pissed him off, and it was time for a brief discussion of who was who and what was what. Emtman pointedly told them that their quality of play was unacceptable, and he would not tolerate it. Not in a game. Not in practice. Not ever. The speech was an extension of what coaches had already noticed in meetings, where he was less likely to remain quiet when he saw something he didn't like.

"You did not want to put a tape on in front of Emtman where you were not playing hard," Larry Slade said of Emtman's demeanor during film sessions. "You did not want that experience." Emtman was growing as a leader, and his emergence was not lost on Slade's fellow coaches.

"We were excited about it," Lambright said. "We believed this wasn't going to be just a good team. We were dominant. And we knew they had the potential to be even better. We knew we could crank this thing up."

Thursday afternoon, April 18, the Dawgs had things cranked up, and once again, the offense was making plays against the defense. As great as UW's defense was, the offense was also loaded with talent and by now was growing in confidence.

"The defense always had a bit of swagger under Lambright, but the offense didn't really develop it until Gilbertson arrived," Keith Shipman said. Shipman covered UW for KCPQ-TV and was the host of James's weekly TV show. "Gilby brought that attitude with him. They had started showing it in 1989 and 1990, particularly on the offensive line." By the spring of 1991, the offense had as much self-confidence as the defense.

A lot of that confidence came from Gilby, but it also came from the on-field leader. Mark Brunell was using a good spring to build on the momentum he had at the end of the 1990 season. His MVP day at the Rose Bowl had landed him on some early preseason All-American lists. He was surrounded by a veteran bunch who had enough experience with their new offense that they were impressing the sometimes difficult-to-please Gilbertson. "It was a wild day of practice," he said. "We had as good an offensive scrimmage as I had ever imagined. We're throwing and catching and running and going back and forth. Boom! Boom! Boom!"

Every "Boom" that Gilby's offense was delivering was met with words of disapproval from Lambright. "The defense was getting their tails handed to them by the offense," said Hart. "We were playing terrible, and Lambo started in on them."

"I am sick and tired of this bullshit," Lambright yelled at his team. "We are going to pick it up starting right now and play like we're going to play, or we'll run you guys until your tongues fall out." By now, everyone on defense was angry, and the only good news was that practice was almost over. The Dawgs moved into the final segment of the day, which involved work on their two-minute offense.

"It was one of those days where we were all tired of hitting each other," Fraley said. "Practice was always competitive, but this day it was wild. It was heated." Chris Tormey agreed. "The more success the offense had, the more our guys kept upping their intensity."

On one play, Jones and Emtman both were able to get past their blockers and arrived simultaneously at the point where Brunell was standing. The quarterback was wearing a gold bib over his jersey indicating to defenders that he was not to be tackled.

"It was an 11-on-11 drill, and we got too aggressive," Jones said. "I made an inside move on Lincoln, and I had a direct line on Brunell. Emtman had a line on him too, and we just couldn't slow up." The duo were at full speed when they crashed into Brunell, who crumpled to the turf and grabbed his knee.

"You could hear the breath go out of everyone when that happened," said Walter Bailey. "It was like it was in slow motion. You could tell Don [Jones] was trying to pull up, but he hit him on the knee right when he released the ball."

"To see him in that much pain, I knew it was bad," said Fraley. "I felt sick. He was in great shape and had worked so hard, and he was set up to have the greatest year ever."

"That was the saddest day of my career," said Jones, who stood above his supine quarterback as tears welled up in his eyes. "I thought our season was over. I thought we had just lost the national championship, and I was the reason why."

No one yet knew for sure what the injury was, but everyone knew it was bad. Ultimately, it was determined that Brunell had suffered severe damage to both the medial collateral and anterior cruciate ligaments in his right knee. He needed surgery and would miss at least six months. The best-case scenario was that he might be able to return for a bowl game—if the Huskies could get to a bowl game without him. Brunell's backup was Billy Joe Hobert, and in the immediate aftermath of Brunell's injury, the anticipation of what he might do as the Huskies' starter was mixed.

"Billy Joe didn't look like a great player in practice, and Mark was the Rose Bowl MVP and a superstar player," said Jones. "He was so dynamic, and he was one of the best players in the country. We felt we needed him."

"Mark was tremendous; he knew the offense, and he was the captain," Kennedy said. "I thought we were heading in the right direction, and now I didn't know where we were going to go."

"We knew we had the best team," Cunningham said. "There was no doubt we were better than everybody, and it was like, 'Oh, man, there goes our Ferrari.'"

"We didn't feel good," said McKay. "We're talking about a Rose Bowl MVP who is now hurt. And we did not think we had multiple quarterbacks on the roster who could be Rose Bowl MVPs. We didn't think, 'Oh, no problem. Billy Joe will probably be the Rose Bowl MVP and lead us to a 12–0 record. It's all good.'"

But Fraley had confidence in Hobert. "I didn't have a concern. We thought our defense was pretty good, and our mantra was that if the offense scores more than ten points, we'll win every game. The defense had respect for Billy."

"Here's the deal guys," Hall told his teammates. "We don't know what Billy Joe's going to be and we don't know what the offense is going to do, but we don't care. The question is how many points can we score and how many turnovers can we create? If we give the offense short fields, they can't help but be successful."

Walter Bailey agreed with his fellow defensive back. "Billy Joe came from a pedigree of winning, so we felt like if we all did our jobs, it just wouldn't matter. We had great leadership, and we had an expectation: we are going out to win a national championship. Whoever we were playing first was going to get hell. They were going to get thunder and lightning and any other havoc we could give them. We felt if the offense couldn't get it done, the defense would win the game."

McKay remembers taking solace in the confidence of Mario Bailey. "We don't have Mark; now we've got this young gunslinger from Puyallup," Bailey told McKay. "We're going to be fine. We've got an experienced group, and as long as I'm here, we're going to win." "And he was right," McKay laughed. "If the quarterback could just get it in his general direction, he'd make a play. Mario's unbelievable confidence helped us through that situation."

Eric Bjornson had confidence in Hobert; his problem was he didn't have confidence in himself yet. And he was now the team's backup quarterback. "I was upset about the injury and nervous about what it meant to me because I wasn't ready experience-wise to be in a game. It was a massive blow and we had concerns, but we all had a lot of confidence in Billy. He was smart and talented; he could make all the throws and make all the checks. I sat with him in the quarterback room every day, and he knew everything. I knew he was ready."

Gilbertson, Hart, and Tormey came away from the day with different feelings. Gilbertson's reaction might be termed extreme: "I was so upset, I couldn't sleep. So I came into the office at about 5:00 a.m. to watch video. I wanted to kill someone. I just couldn't decide who."

Hart maintains to this day that Brunell's gold bib was part of the reason the injury happened. "He's a good athlete. If he hadn't been wearing a gold jersey that day, he would have felt the pressure and gotten out of there. But in his mind, he's thinking, 'No one's going to hit me. They're my guys.' Everyone was angry. We felt guys weren't giving their best effort so we're yelling at them to correct that, and all of a sudden, we created a disaster. That incident woke us all up to the importance of knowing the team and knowing how to practice."

Tormey, who had the unenviable task of calling Brunell's parents to inform them of the injury, remembers an overwhelming feeling of frustration: "There was no good explanation or reason for [the accident]. It never should have happened. It was stupid. It's one of the darkest days I ever had in coaching."

A few days later, after his surgery, Brunell was sitting in his hospital bed and looked up to see the smiling face of Carol James. She hugged him and was happy to see he was in good spirits. He told her he had already begun to think about how his rehab schedule would look (he was the son of a coach, after all). They talked for a few minutes, and Carol told him how sorry she was and how hopeful she was that he'd make a full recovery. Then Brunell told her something that put her at ease. "It's in good hands with Billy Joe. We're going to be okay." Carol allowed herself to think for the first time since the injury that maybe, just maybe, things were going to be all right.

Cunningham's uncertainty about what would happen without the team's "Ferrari" turned to confidence as he watched the new quarterback assume his role: "Billy changed. That's when he emerged in a way no one foresaw. He was gifted; he could run; he was big; he was funny; but he was a horrible practice player. But after Brunell got hurt, he went from this happy-go-lucky country kid to a real competitor. He had an edge; he'd get mad, at us and himself. Those final practices of spring with him at quarterback were really important to us."

9

Not Bad for a
60-Point Underdog

BY THE TIME PRESEASON PRACTICE STARTED IN AUGUST, THE SHOCK of Brunell's injury had worn off. Despite Hobert's lack of experience, few doubted that he had enough ability and more than enough moxie to assume control of the team's offense. Never lacking in confidence, Hobert's demeanor was one of a guy who knew he could do the job. "From the first time I met Billy Joe, he had this confidence about him," said Clifford. "He had a sense of control; you could tell that he thought he belonged. He had confidence and swagger. And that plays."

"He was such an arrogant prick," Rongen laughed. "He was so cocky. How can you not get behind that? He was the general in the huddle, and he immediately commanded our attention."

"We had moments of doubt," Lambright said of the quarterback situation. "You would have paid good money to listen to all the talk about it. He was crazy, and there was a chance he might not have gone to sleep early the night before. But he had so much confidence in himself that I ended up feeling confident in him."

Lambright's confidence was fueled in part by the belief he shared with everyone else connected with the team that the Huskies defense was the best such unit in the country and would be so dominant and so good that no one injury to any player would bring the team down. "We just won't let anyone score," Clifford said with a laugh. "We felt like we could do that."

"Nothing against Billy Joe," said Hoffmann, "but we needed someone [at quarterback] to come in and not screw up. We were concerned, but it wasn't fear. We felt like if he could stay within himself, we'd be fine."

If Hoffmann and Clifford sound like they're damning Hobert with faint praise, they were only echoing the thoughts of Hobert himself, who was everything everyone thought. Brash. Cocky. But also aware of what was happening around him. "I had a just-wing-it personality, but I didn't have to be spectacular," he said. "When you're surrounded by that much talent, you could screw it up if you try to do too much. Don't try for 21 when you have 17 in your face. Just go."

Hobert's personality and willingness to say anything made him a favorite among the reporters. Whenever he spoke, notebooks were flipped open, recorders and cameras were turned on, and great quotes would almost immediately start falling out of his mouth. After he reacted to a hit on his knee that needed nothing more than ice by holding his leg and screaming in pain, he later told reporters, "I'm a drama major, and I was just getting extra credit."

When *Seattle Post-Intelligencer* reporter Dan Raley informed him that his teammates considered him a "blue-collar guy," Hobert responded, "I like that type of image. I don't want to be a pretty boy. I don't like being pampered. I just want to go out and kick ass. I don't mind looking ugly. I wouldn't mind if I had a scar on my face."

Told that players made fun of him for growing up in cow country, Hobert said, "I've never milked a cow in my life. I've rolled around in the hay, but that's a different story." Once, he cut an interview session short because he had to get to class. "It's a class in women's studies, but why don't you say it's Chemistry 5000 or something."

Hobert's name fit him perfectly. A guy with his personality couldn't have a bland name. It had to be something like Billy Joe. And of course, there was a story behind it. William Joseph Hobert, known as Bill, was a star pitcher on his high school team in the 1960s. He later volunteered for the army, became a squad leader, and was killed in action in Vietnam.

His brother, Terry, wanted to name his son after him, but his wife, who hated the war, didn't like the idea. So instead of William Joseph Hobert, Washington's new quarterback was given the name Billy Joe.

Like Hobert, Emtman had grown up in rural America. Unlike Hobert, he wasn't a quote machine for the media, but that didn't mean he didn't regularly impress people with the things he was able to do. Emtman was running a cat and mouse drill once with fellow defensive linemen. What he did, they did. Emtman jumped; they jumped. Emtman dropped and rolled; they dropped and rolled. Emtman took three quick steps to the right; they took three quick steps to the left. Emtman did a backflip from a standing position and landed on his feet. They stood with their mouths hanging wide open after watching their 6'4", 280-pound teammate spin in midair like a gymnast. "He looked like a big Cadillac doing a somersault," said defensive tackle D'Marco Farr.

On another occasion, during a pickup basketball game with members of the football and basketball teams, Emtman again left everyone watching speechless. He first dunked a basketball and then a few plays later rocketed a teammate's missed shot home with a thunderous tip-jam. Dan Lepse, UW's assistant sports information director, saw both plays. "There's no way," Lepse thought, "a guy that size should be able to do things like that."

Lambright was impressed with Emtman's superlative feats of athletic skill. Impressed, not surprised. "Just look at where he's from," he said. "The middle of a cornfield. The middle of nowhere. He was a farmer, and he was a simple man. His heart was corn and a plow, and his work ethic was unmatched. From the moment he came here, he was always a step better; everything that he did was a little more than you expected. You looked at him and thought, 'My God, there is no way we can lose with this guy.'"

Carol James had been impressed with Emtman from the first time she had met him at one of the recruiting breakfasts. "Some guys just impress you when you look at them," she said. "The first time he walked into our house, I thought, 'Hmmm. What have we got here?'"

A near-perfect physical specimen, Emtman spent the summer before 1991 finding ways to get even better. He lost fifteen pounds and trimmed his body fat from an acceptable 8 percent to a minuscule 4 percent for what everyone assumed would be his final season at UW. Just a junior in terms of eligibility, it was a foregone conclusion that Emtman would opt to enter the NFL draft in April 1992. Further evidence of that probable plan came when word got out that he had purchased a million-dollar insurance policy against injury.

Emtman's dominance in the middle of the defense led to teams double-teaming him as a method to try to reduce the carnage he caused. When they did that, gaps opened up in the line that could be exploited by UW's fast and talented corps of linebackers. Perhaps mindful of that, one anonymous Pac-10 coach was asked by *Sporting News* to name the top linebacker in America. "Pick any guy at Washington," came the reply.

The defense was bigger, stronger, faster, and more experienced than they had been at the start of the 1990 season. And lest anyone doubt that Lambright would allow the players to collectively rest on their laurels, he had a special video made of all the mistakes they had made in the 1990 season. He used the video to remind his players that they could always be better and also to learn from past missteps. "What we wanted to do was see what went wrong on those plays and look at different ways to correct it," he said. "Maybe by putting more pressure on the offense and or changing the direction of the pressure or relieving the pressure."

Lambright's defense was loaded with talent and experience, and he had every intention of pushing the players to the limit. "In the past, we might have said, 'We need to be more cautious.' But with the players we have and our style, I don't think we're going to be very cautious defensively anymore."

As August slid toward September, hype around the team built. UW was ranked fourth in the country in both the preseason AP and the *USA Today*/CNN polls. (The coaches' poll changed media affiliations in the late 1980s from UPI to *USA Today* and CNN.) Both polls picked Florida State as the top team in America. The writers (AP) had Michigan and Miami as numbers two and three, with the coaches reversing that order. Both agreed UW was number four. The *New York Times* and *Newsday* were the first newspapers to use computers to create rankings. After entering the data they had collected from teams across the country, both sets of computers spat out Washington as number one. The head coach was unimpressed. "The computers," James said, "have not seen us practice."

James didn't want all the attention, but he also knew there wasn't much he could do about it. The fans were hoping for an unbeaten season and a national title. So were the players. It would have been disingenuous for the coaches to pretend otherwise. "We did not play that down," Lambright said. "Our attitude as coaches was, 'This is something we expect. We want this.' Don probably wasn't thrilled with all the talk, but he also wanted it to be the best UW team ever." Lambright said the whole thing reminded him a bit of 1982, when the Huskies returned several players from a team that had won the Rose Bowl. Preseason confidence and positive feelings filled the air around the team that year too. But it paled in comparison to what was happening in 1991. "The expectations and grandiose talk and the sense of dominance surrounding us this time are amazing," Lambright told reporters during training camp in August. "When people are saying all these good things about you, you'd better start working harder because the risk is greater that you could become complacent. Because the second you believe it, you're going to wind up like we did last year in the UCLA game."

Washington had never opened up a season with a conference road game, but that was how the schedule fell in 1991. James had expressed concern about the Stanford game throughout training camp because, like most coaches, he would prefer an opening game at home against a lesser opponent. Instead, it was off to "the Farm," the nickname given to the Stanford campus since it had once been a horse farm owned by university founders Leland and Jane Stanford.

The night before the game, Rondeau; his analyst, Sam Adkins; sideline reporter Bill Swartz; and engineer Lloyd Jones were in a car driving up to San Francisco for dinner. Due to Rondeau's love of horse racing, they would forego the five-star culinary options available in one of the world's great dining cities to instead eat and watch a few races at Bay Meadows Racetrack. As they crawled through traffic, Rondeau asked everyone how many games UW would win. Everyone agreed the Huskies would lose at least one, maybe two. Rondeau, not a man given to hyperbole, waited for everyone to finish. "I think they're going to win every one of them," he said.

If that prediction were to become true, it would start with a road win against one of the best teams in the league. Stanford featured two players who would end up being drafted in the first nine picks of the following year's NFL draft: running back Tommy Vardell and tackle Bob Whitfield, who pulled exactly zero punches in his prediction of what UW was facing. "Any team we play is just another team for us," Whitfield said. "Washington is a great team, and I think they have the best defense I've ever played against, but we don't fear any team anymore. Things are changing around here, and our biggest concern right now is how many points we're going to beat Washington by."

Whitfield said he thought his team might win by 60 points. They might. On a different day. Against a different team. UW shattered Stanford, 42–7. Hobert calmed any lingering fears teammates had about his lack of experience with twenty-one pass completions in thirty-one attempts for 244 yards and two touchdowns. Statistically, it was the best debut performance by a quarterback in the James era. Hobert immediately got everyone's attention by completing his first six passes. "He's making his first start, and he hits six bullets in a row," Cunningham marveled after the game. "[In] my first start, I whiffed a guy."

"It wasn't just that he was playing well," Clifford said. "It was his countenance. His presence: 'I'm the guy. This is what I'm doing, this is my play, this is how I'm calling it, and I'm not going to doubt it. I've got this, and I know what I'm doing.'"

"He entered the Stanford game with unbelievable confidence," said McKay. "If he had bombed out in that game, we might have had some concerns. But he looked sharp from the start, and it was done after that. We believed in him, and he was rolling."

Hobert's personality shone through in his first start too. Cunningham was using a wet towel jammed down the backside of his pants to stay cool. The towel soaked through his pants, and some moisture got on Hobert's hand and was at least partly to blame for an interception he threw when the ball slipped out of his hand. "I'm not blaming you," Hobert said to Cunningham. "But please wipe off your butt."

Hobert had played a little bit in 1990, so while the game was his debut as a starter, he at least had gotten his feet wet. Tight end Mark Bruener had played plenty in the 1990 season—as a tight end for Aberdeen High School. His first college game experience came as a true freshman, and he made an impression on Stanford linebacker Dave Garnett. Twice Bruener pancaked Garnett, leaving the senior embarrassed, frustrated, and angry. "He was yelling and screaming at me," Bruener laughed. "He was trying to kick me off of him. He yelled, 'How can you be doing this to me?'"

Garnett would have been even more upset if he'd known how close Bruener had come to being his teammate. UW had jumped in to recruit him late in the process after a tip from legendary Tumwater High School coach Sid Otton, who told Randy Hart, "Take a good look at the tight end over in Aberdeen because he'd really help you." Hart returned to Seattle and began to put together a contact package to send to Bruener. When James learned about the new target, he instructed Hart to offer a scholarship immediately. "I don't have any information on him," Hart protested.

Since the 1986 Sun Bowl loss, James had developed a recruiting system he expected everyone to follow. From the initial contact, through the process, to the decision, there was a way things were done, and Hart was following those guidelines. James loved and trusted the system, but he also still trusted his gut. "If Sid Otton says he can play for us, then he can play for us," he told Hart. "Offer him [a scholarship] immediately."

Stanford had already made an offer to Bruener. His mother, Arlene, wanted him to take it, but his father had other ideas. During recruiting visits to Stanford, Cardinal coaches had each player introduce his parents, and each said a few words. When Bruener introduced his parents, his mom spoke first. "We're so happy to be here, and we're very excited about Stanford's interest in our son." Then his dad stood up in a room full of red-clad Stanford coaches, recruits, and their parents. "My name is Fred Bruener. All I've got to say is, 'Go Dawgs!'"

After the first game of Bruener's career, Stanford coaches could only wonder what might have been. And UW's coach was uncharacteristically effusive in his praise of a freshman. "That was incredible," James said about the pancakes. "He's done more things as a freshman than any tight end we've ever had."

The Huskies scored on seven of their seventeen possessions, and while the offense was strong, the defense was simply oppressive. They had nine tackles for loss, forced seven turnovers, and held Stanford to twenty-eight yards rushing. Stanford had ten possessions in the second half. Four resulted in three and outs, three ended with fumbles, and one ended in an interception.

"We had full control," Clifford said, "and we could impose our will. [You could tell from] looking across the line they didn't have a chance, and they knew they didn't have a chance. They had no answers for what we were going to do to them defensively. It was just easy. That's a crazy way to put it. We did what we wanted." "Not bad for a 60-point underdog," Emtman deadpanned after the game.

The Huskies' first touchdown of the game came on a short run by Jay Barry on a play that added yet another wrinkle to UW's evolving offense. Barry lined up in a slot receiver position, leaving no running backs behind Hobert. Seeing this, Stanford's defense rightfully assumed the Huskies were going to pass, and several players edged closer in anticipation.

Hobert then signaled for Barry to come back to the backfield, presumably to help block. At the snap, Stanford attacked, looking to get to Hobert before he could pass the ball. But Hobert quickly slipped the ball into Barry's hands, and the junior running back pinballed off a couple players and into the end zone. In the TV booth, Keith Jackson and Bob Griese both agreed that UW scored on what looked like a broken play. James laughed when he heard that.

"It was a run all the way," he said. "It's called '25 dive.' And now, teams have to wonder if the back is back in the backfield to protect the quarterback or to run." James had a crafty side that was on full display in this conversation. He was using the media to take a statement made by the media to sow confusion into the game plans of future teams on the schedule. "It's all part of our strategy," he said with a sly smile.

UW was now 26–7 under James when it had more than one week to prepare for a game. The good news was the Huskies had two weeks before the next game. The bad news was it was another road game. The worse news was that Nebraska was the opponent, and historically, the Cornhuskers rarely lost games played in Lincoln. James knew all about how difficult it was to play there. He knew that his players, who fancied themselves national title contenders, were about to get a tough test in a very difficult arena, and he was just hoping they could get a good night's sleep before the game. He knew from personal experience that wasn't always a guarantee in Lincoln.

91 Y F Z Delay

ANDY GUSTAFSON WAS TICKED OFF THE WAY ONE IS WHEN ONE receives surprising bad news. And make no mistake; the news Gustafson had just received was both surprising and bad. His University of Miami football team was on their first road trip of the 1953 season, and in terms of length, it was a doozy: from the southern tip of Florida to the middle of the country to play the University of Nebraska. The journey required a long charter flight aboard a Pan American World Airways Clipper.

On their arrival in the heartland, the players first worked out. Next, they checked into the legendary Cornhusker Hotel, which featured three hundred air-conditioned rooms from $3.80 to $8.00 per night. "Mid-America's Most Popular Hotel—Host to the Most!" blared a newspaper ad. The hotel featured "five-channel radio and recorded music systems in all rooms," and TVs were available by request. The Cornhusker was *the* spot to stay in Lincoln in 1953. It was also a popular destination for conventions.

"Andy Gustafson's face turned a dark hue when he checked his warriors into the Cornhusker Hotel only to discover that it was headquarters for the Nebraska state Shriners convention," *Miami News* reporter Ralph Warner wrote. "The Shriners were boisterously happy during long periods of the night as only Shriners can be." Gustafson worried that the sounds of a hotel full of Shriners on the loose on a Friday night would undercut his team's ability to get a solid night of sleep.

Over 39,000 fans filled Memorial Stadium the next day, with scalpers getting as much as six bucks per ticket. Hurricanes quarterback Don James (described by Warner as "diminutive Don" and "the little quarterback") completed four passes in eight attempts for sixty-two yards but Nebraska prevailed, 20–16. Coach Gustafson was left to wonder if a quieter environment the night before the game might have benefitted his team.

James may have had the revelry of the Shriners still ringing in his ears when he made his travel plans in 1991. His team would not stay at the remodeled Cornhusker Hotel but instead would bunk at a Holiday Inn outside of town. It was clean, quiet, and surrounded by cornfields. It was the type of place no self-respecting Shriner would ever choose for a convention, which made it perfect for James's needs. But he would still face one Friday night distraction. "We got off the plane, went right to the stadium, and got dressed for the run-through," Clifford said. "We went out to practice, and they couldn't get the lights on, so we were all standing around in the dark."

Nebraska employees tried to figure out how to turn on the lights at *their* stadium, and UW players began milling around. Clifford and Hoffmann were looking for Nebraska's legendary weight room when they found themselves in front of a huge case that housed the Big Red's numerous football trophies. There were forty conference championship awards dating back to 1894, when the Nebraska team was known as the Bugeaters; fourteen trophies from bowl game wins; and, at the center of the case, the 1970 and 1971 national championship trophies. The duo was startled by a voice that came from behind them. "Hello guys; how are you doing?"

They turned around and were face to face with Nebraska coach Tom Osborne. Clifford and Hoffmann introduced themselves. "Great to meet you," Osborne told them. "Look around and have a great time." Osborne disappeared back into the shadows, and Clifford and Hoffmann continued their self-guided tour. Back on the field, James's anger was noticed by some of the players.

"At first, it wasn't a big deal," said Mario Bailey. "We thought it was funny. But when it pissed Coach James off, it really started going downhill fast. That made us madder. You're Nebraska, and you can't get the lights to work? Okay. Whatever. That just means we're gonna kick your ass." Finally, as twilight faded into black and it became obvious that UW wasn't going to get any actual work done, an agitated James ordered his players onto their buses. The bus engines roared to life, and the drivers began the trip back to the hotel. Gilbertson was looking out the window and laughed at what he saw. "As soon as we pulled out of the parking lot, click, click, click. All the lights came on." James, speaking to no one in particular, said, "They found the light switch when it was time for Osborne to practice, didn't they?"

By the time UW got back to the hotel, there was a message for James from Nebraska informing him that the lights were on and his team was welcome to come back to practice. Not practicing on the day before the game was breaking with James's routine, but if there was one thing he valued more than routine, it was the itinerary. A return to the stadium would mess up the evening schedule, and James politely declined the offer. That evening schedule included meetings during which the players took written tests about Saturday's game. That was part of the routine the night before every game, home or away. Another part was an odd refreshment choice.

"Hot chocolate was our big night-before-the-game treat," said Bjornson, "which is kind of a stupid thing to have for a football team. It's got caffeine and sugar. But wherever we were, you'd get to the hotel, and guys were asking, 'How's the hot chocolate?' And I remember Nebraska had good hot chocolate."

"Guys were filling up on hot chocolate and pouring on the whipped cream," said Hoffmann. Some players would loudly slurp their hot chocolate during the meeting, which drove Hoffmann crazy. "I was ready to put them behind bars."

"It was the dumbest thing ever," Bjornson laughed. "We'd get dehydrated; it messed up your sleep. It was a weird tradition. Someone told me once that our yearly hot chocolate bill was over a hundred grand." (If that's true, the markup on hot chocolate makes it a business worth exploring.)

Randy Hart wasn't worried about hot chocolate. But he did worry about Nebraska's offensive line, which, in the Cornhusker tradition, was huge, with four of the five starters tipping the scales at over 300 pounds. Option football, where the quarterback could keep the ball, give it to his big fullback, or pitch it to a speedy halfback was Nebraska's bread and butter. The Cornhuskers' early numbers behind their mammoth offensive line were scary particularly if you were a defensive line coach. In two games Nebraska had piled up 130 points and 1,146 yards rushing. "That's more yards than we gave up all last year," Emtman pointed out. Against Utah State, the Huskers set an all-time NCAA record with 44 first downs. Nebraska backs were *averaging* 8.6 yards per carry, and after talking with coaching friends from other schools, Hart was even more nervous than usual.

"That defense you're playing won't work on option football," they said. "They'll be around your guys too quick." Hart was thinking about those conversations as the team bus made its way through game day traffic. Eventually, he tapped Lambright on the shoulder. "Jim, is this defense going to work against Nebraska? Is this physical attack stuff going to work against the option?"

"Well," Lambright replied, "it should."

"Yeah. I know. In theory. But theory and reality are sometimes different. What if it doesn't work? What's plan B?"

"If it works, we'll be fine. If it doesn't work, we're in trouble."

Hart sank back into his seat. He appreciated Lambo's honesty, but that wasn't the answer he wanted to hear. Meanwhile, Orlando McKay was soaking up all Nebraska had to offer in wide-eyed amazement. "I had never seen anything like it. There was a sea of people in red. Businesses were closed. The town looked like a ghost town. Every human in Lincoln was going to this game."

At the time, visiting teams at Memorial Stadium got from the locker room to the field through the stadium concourse. Security guards partitioned off a tiny corridor for the players with yellow rope. Those small ropes were the only thing separating players from boisterous fans, who informed them in blunt terms that they were in trouble. McKay made his way through the gauntlet and arrived onto the field. "It was nerve-wracking," he said. "It felt like a de facto playoff game. If we wanted to be in the conversation for the national title, we had better win. Then, I got on the field, and there they were. The mighty Cornhuskers. What we were about to embark on felt epic."

As Nebraska came onto the field, 76,304 mostly red-clad football fans stood and roared. The game was the 180th consecutive sellout at Memorial Stadium, dating back to November 1962. Nebraska had been victorious in 155 of those games.

Keith Jackson welcomed fans to the national broadcast of "a college football game with national dimension. The Washington Huskies, number four; the Nebraska Cornhuskers, number nine. The winner will have a chance at a national championship. The loser—probably not."

The wise guys were all over Washington. Nebraska began the week as a two-point favorite in Las Vegas. By game time, the line had switched, and UW was listed as a one-point favorite.

Early on, Hart's worst fears were realized as Nebraska was able to move the ball. The first play of the game was a sixteen-yard run by Derek Brown through the heart of the Huskies defense. Then, on Nebraska's second possession, the Cornhuskers smartly moved seventy-six yards in six plays for the game's first touchdown: a twenty-seven-yard run by Brown. "Right now," Jackson told viewers, "the Nebraska offensive front is blowing Washington off the ball." He was right, but the Huskies settled down, and the next four Nebraska possessions ended in punts. The trouble was that the UW offense kept stifling itself. One promising drive was derailed by a pair of holding calls. Another ended in an interception.

Early in the second quarter, Nebraska punter Mike Stigge unloaded a sixty-eight yard beauty that put the Huskies inside their own two-yard line. By now the game was being played under a nearly full moon that had risen over the stadium, and like triggered wolves, the Nebraska fans were howling, raining down noise and mayhem on the visitors.

"They were gnarly, hardcore, and in your face," Hobert said.

"It was the most intimidating stadium I'd ever been in," said Kennedy. "We had seen some places, but there was no place like Nebraska. And we knew early on that we were in a fight and we weren't in a comfortable setting."

"The fans were crazy and nasty," said Rongen. "It was jaw-dropping, but I wasn't nervous. I knew this was something I would remember."

"We were a little bit in awe just being in Nebraska," Mario Bailey admitted. "The crowd was right on you, and it was the loudest place I'd ever been. I couldn't hear Billy call signals." For the moment, Bailey's being unable to hear signals didn't matter.

With his players backed up against the end zone, Gilbertson called five consecutive running plays. Fullback Matt Jones ran for seven yards, Jay Barry gained fourteen more on three consecutive carries, and then Beno Bryant rolled sixteen yards. The crowd quieted down, and the Huskies started feeling better. "That sequence gave us a lot of momentum," Kennedy said. "We started believing we could do things."

The Huskies then took four big bites out of the Nebraska defense. Hobert hit Bailey for twenty-five yards; Bryant again gained sixteen on a run; Hobert hit receiver Curtis Gaspard for fourteen more and then ran the final nine yards himself as Washington completed a stunning ten-play drive. For the first time, UW players could hear their fans cheering, the noise coming from a tiny sliver of purple tucked into a corner of the stadium. The score remained 7–6 because of a bad snap on the extra point.

Nebraska then struck a blow that had personal overtones for UW fans. Receiver Jon Bostick was named the Washington state high school player of the year in 1987, when he was a star at Interlake High School in Bellevue, Washington. Fans were surprised when Bostick chose to play football at Nebraska. His choice illustrates the status of UW's football reputation at the time. While he was in high school, the Huskies went 22–12–2. They played in the Freedom Bowl, the Sun Bowl, and the Independence Bowl. They were good but not great. Nebraska was 29–7 during those three years, played each year in a marquee New Year's Day bowl game, and finished in the top ten all three years. While it might seem counterproductive for a receiver to choose run-crazy Nebraska, Bostick loved it there. "You wouldn't necessarily know there was a game at Washington if you drove into Seattle on a Saturday morning," he told Blaine Newnham of the *Seattle Times*. In Lincoln "all the restaurants will have signs up predicting the score. The town will be red from one end to the other. Radios will be on everywhere."

Those radios now spread the news that Bostick had just been on the receiving end of a scoring strike from quarterback Keithen McCant that put Nebraska back on top. The scoring play came at the expense of cornerback Walter Bailey. "When a team is running successfully you can overreact as a cornerback," Bailey said. "He lost me, I got beat, and I felt horrible."

But it was only for a moment. Emtman grabbed Bailey by his jersey and Hoffmann slapped him on the helmet. "Don't worry," they yelled. "We're going to make up for this. You're going to make up for this."

"I felt relief," Bailey said. "I felt like they still believed in me."

On Washington's next drive, Hobert threw his second interception of the game. But Dana Hall thwarted Nebraska with an interception of his own at the eight-yard line. "On the sideline, we kept saying, 'Keep fighting; keep fighting,'" Hall said. "We will find a way to make a play and get through this. Somehow, we're going to find a way to win this game.'"

The Dawgs moved into field goal position after Hall's pick, but Travis Hanson's forty-nine-yard attempt was no good, and the half ended with Nebraska leading, 14–6. "They're not stopping us," Gilbertson emphasized. "They can't even slow us down. Don't commit penalties. Don't drop the ball, stop making dumb mistakes, and you'll be way ahead in this game."

UW had outgained Nebraska both on the ground and in the air, and the Huskies had more first downs. But they had committed five penalties for fifty-five yards (Nebraska had just one for five yards), and they turned the ball over twice. They had a bad snap on an extra point and a missed field goal. But they trailed by only a touchdown. Ed Cunningham stood up to speak. "I had become a leader at that point, and I was vocal and demanding," he said. "I was speaking to our offense, but I was keen to the idea that the defense was in the room next to us and they could hear me."

Cunningham began his speech by acknowledging that his poor snap to Hobert had caused a fumble and stalled a drive. He then began a teamwide critique in which each word was louder than the last. He got so worked up at one point that he broke a chair before concluding his tirade. "Those guys," he said as he jerked his thumb over his shoulder at the defense, "are doing their job. We need to do our job!" Barry and Bryant spoke up in agreement.

Bruener, with all of one college game under his belt, watched Cunningham and had a realization. "I'm still a kid," he thought to himself. "But I'm playing with men now." The freshman tight end was struck by what happened next. "I remember the coaches just kind of stood back and watched. Coach James didn't say much of anything before we went back out. It was like they all realized there was nothing they could say to better motivate us."

UW got a field goal on its first drive of the second half to make it 14–9. After Washington stopped Nebraska's next drive, the Big Red got a huge break when Bryant fumbled a punt inside the five. Nebraska recovered and scored on the next play to grab a twelve-point lead. The crowd roared as it sensed a familiar feeling in Lincoln: the visiting team was in trouble.

"That was a time we could have closed it up, hung it up, and quit," James said.

"We knew they were a great team; we knew it would be a struggle. And when we were down 21–9, we knew we were in a little trouble," said Chris Tormey. Bryant figured the fumble was probably his last play of the night. Donald Jones put his arm around his teammate and said a few words. Others tried to pick him up. And Hobert tried to pick them all up.

"We're going to win this game," he said. "We're not dead! There's plenty of time, fellas, plenty of time!"

Bryant looked at the cocky young signal caller making his second career start in one of the toughest places imaginable. "I wanted to say, 'Billy! Don't you know what the score is?'" More Huskies probably felt closer to Bryant's opinion of their current situation than Hobert's. But at least one guy was right with the quarterback.

"It's 21–9. So what?" Mario Bailey yelled. "We're going to win this game."

UW began its next series with Bryant not only still in the lineup, but also carrying the rock on first down for five yards. "You can be upset with a guy," Gilbertson said, "but if he has talent, you're not going to stay upset with him." Hobert then hit his partner in confidence, Bailey, for sixteen yards, and suddenly UW was rolling. The Huskies got to the

Nebraska thirty-three, and on third down Hobert threw a perfect strike to McKay, who rolled into the end zone. The UW sideline erupted.

The celebration was short-lived. Washington was called for holding. James exploded like a man whose team had been called for six penalties for seventy-one yards while his opponent had been called for three for just fourteen. The coach waved his arms and screamed at the referee. The linesman, who had to stand near James, was the recipient of some well-placed verbal bombs as well. "That play broke my heart," James said.

UW now was looking at third down and twenty-seven. Hobert scrambled for nineteen yards, setting up a fourth and eight. In the UW coaches' booth high above the field, Gilbertson began to slip his headphones off. "I was nervous, and I'd been drinking water and Coke and coffee. I had to pee so bad."

Then he heard James's voice: "We're going for it."

It was still the third quarter, and Washington trailed by only twelve points. The prudent move, the one you'd expect from Don James, was to punt and hope the defense could get the ball back quickly. Not only was James eschewing caution, but he also decided against calling a timeout.

"The game was getting away from them, and they had to do something," Rondeau said. "It was a great testimony to their faith in Billy. Chances are Nebraska was a little taken aback by that because it was very un-Don-like. Nebraska might not have been in the defense they wanted to be in, and that's the beauty of not calling a timeout."

The decision from James briefly surprised everyone in the booth, but as Dick Baird put it, "None of us was going to say, 'Hey, Don, are you *sure* you wanna do that?'" The decision had been made, and now James needed a play. Fast.

Gilbertson scanned his play chart. "91 y f z delay," he said to James. The call was relayed to the huddle. Cunningham remembers that despite the precarious position the Huskies were in, there was a sense of calm. "Billy didn't make a big deal about it being fourth down. He just called the play. We all felt like we were going to get it."

McKay felt a surge of adrenaline when he heard Hobert call the play. "91 y f z delay," he thought to himself. "I'm Z. They're calling my number, and the ball is coming to me unless I'm covered."

The Huskies broke the huddle, and McKay saw Nebraska cornerback Tyrone Legette on the line of scrimmage. "That's good," he thought. "All I've got to do is press up the field and hit the brakes, and he'll fly right by me like in the movie *Top Gun*."

At the snap, McKay came off the line fast, then hesitated briefly before again accelerating. "I'm not even sure why I did that," McKay said, "but I think Legette thought it was a stutter go, so he started running." Legette also had his feet positioned as if he thought McKay would cut toward the sideline. The play was designed so he could cut either direction. He quickly cut inside and was wide open when Hobert delivered the ball. McKay gained fifteen yards on the play and thinks he should have gotten more but admitted his overriding thought when he caught the pass and knew he had the first down was to not fumble. "I put both my arms on the ball, and I was just thinking, 'Someone please tackle me.'"

Bryant sliced through the middle of the Nebraska defense for fifteen yards and a touchdown on the next play, and presto! UW was back in the game. About the only guy in the stadium moving faster than Bryant was Gilbertson, who was making a beeline to the men's room.

As the fourth quarter began, Nebraska still had the lead and the ball. This is where the Huskers were usually devastating. Historically, they ran the option, they ran it to perfection, and by the fourth quarter they had worn teams out. But Lambright had prepared his defense on how to best stop the option. "It's just disciplined football," he told his players. "If you've got the lead blocker, take the lead blocker. If you've got the quarterback, take the quarterback. And if you've got the pitch guy, don't worry about what the lead blocker or the quarterback are doing; go get the pitch guy."

After the Bryant TD, Nebraska faced a third and two and ran the classic option play to the right. Easy. McCant pitched the ball to Brown, who was following fullback Lance Lewis. Fraley fought off a block by Lewis and wrapped his arms around Brown's legs. As Brown struggled to gain the one more yard necessary to get the first down, Shane Pahukoa arrived and leveled him with a hit that elicited a gasp from the crowd. "I got there first," Fraley said, "and Shane finished him off."

The Huskies got the ball and quickly and confidently moved sixty-nine yards in six plays. The final play was an eight-yard pass to McKay, and UW had its first lead of the night, 22–21. Cunningham grabbed the sideline phone after the touchdown to talk to Gilbertson. "Let's not make the mistake of getting conservative," he excitedly said. Gilbertson laughed out loud. "Ed, I don't think I've ever called a conservative play in my history."

Two plays later, McCant fumbled after a hit by Jaime Fields. Paxton Tailele recovered for UW, and here, finally, was a chance to take control of the game. The Huskies gained six courtesy of Bryant on first down, but a second-down pass fell incomplete; to make matters worse, the Huskies were called for a personal foul, so they faced a third and long. Hobert targeted McKay on a deep pass down the sidelines. Nebraska cornerback Kenny Wilhite arrived about the same time as the ball did and knocked the pass away. The Huskies were too far away to try a field goal, and now that they had the lead, they would punt the ball and put the game in the hands of their capable defense.

But wait! Flag on the play. Officials ruled that Wilhite had interfered with McKay, and the subsequent penalty gave the Huskies a first down. Like any pass interference call, there was an element of subjectivity. But multiple replays from different angles seemed to indicate the road team had finally gotten a huge break. Washington took quick advantage and five plays later had a first and goal at the three. Nebraska called a timeout, and Hobert jogged over to James to figure out what the Huskies were going to do. Word came down from Gilbertson: "43 iso option." The play was a fake to the fullback, with Hobert having the option to pitch to the halfback or run it himself. UW was going to give Nebraska a little bit of its own medicine. James knew Hobert liked to keep the ball on this play, and he knew they were looking at a chance to get some necessary breathing room in what he felt was a game that was far from over, so he had one more message for his quarterback: "Billy," he said sharply to make sure he had Hobert's attention in the noise and chaos. "This is a big play coming up."

Hobert looked his 5'7" head coach in the eye from his perch eight inches higher: "No shit, Don."

In three words at a critical moment, Hobert had managed to swear at his coach without even calling him "coach." "I couldn't believe it when I heard it come out of my mouth," Hobert said.

"There were times when you just wanted to strangle him," Gilbertson laughed, and that thought may have briefly crossed James's mind.

"He looked at me out of the corner of his eye," Hobert said. "I think it shocked him to hear it as much it shocked me that I said it. I think he was going to say something, but then he realized it was just a heat of the moment thing."

Most of Hobert's teammates did not hear the exchange. But Mario Bailey did. "At the moment, we were worried, and we were trying to get the play in. But afterward, in the locker room, we were cracking the hell up. Only Billy could get away with that."

Hobert ran the ball into the end zone, and the Huskies now had an eight-point lead. The defense forced another three and out, swarming around McCant on three incomplete passes. Stigge hadn't punted in either of Nebraska's first two games. Now, he lined up to punt for the ninth time against UW. Three plays later, Barry took a handoff, started toward the line, popped to his right, and scooted around defensive end Travis Hill, weaved through a little traffic, and put the game in the ice-box with a beautiful eighty-one-yard run. It was the longest touchdown run for a Husky since Joe Steele rumbled eighty-three yards for a score versus Stanford in 1977.

The final score showed Washington as a 36–21 winner. Nebraska hadn't given up that many points to a visiting team in Lincoln since the 1955 Big Seven championship game, when Oklahoma blasted the Huskers, 41–0. In the history of Nebraska football, no team had ever picked up more first downs than the thirty-one Washington got. The fans had been on the Huskies all night, screaming at them, mocking them, and doing their best to intimidate them. But as the Washington players exited the field, they were stunned at what happened next: the Nebraska fans gave them an ovation. They knew good football, and they knew good football teams. They were disappointed by the result, but they appreciated what they had just seen.

"The most surprising thing that ever happened to me was that ovation," Hobert said. "That was when we realized we were really good." Walter Bailey agreed. "That ovation . . . that's when I knew we were special."

"It was the most gracious thing I ever saw an opponent's fans do," Rongen said. "They didn't get teams coming into their house and putting a physical beatdown on them. That ovation was thrilling."

"It was fun to play them," Hoffmann said. "It was like a great UFC fight. There was an appreciation between the players which you could see and feel."

The Huskies rolled up 618 yards, more than twice what they'd allowed (304). For the season, Nebraska would end up leading the country in rushing, but after they got seventy-four yards on the ground during their first drive, Washington's defense held them to just sixty-one yards the remainder of the game.

Emtman led the charge with eight tackles and a sack. "He made himself the number one pick in the NFL draft that night," Hart said.

"They could have put five guys on him," Rondeau said. "It was such a mismatch, it was laughable. There was a play where he chased a guy the width of the field and ran him down. He showed them he was going to be able to do anything he wanted to do. He dictated how that game was played."

Meanwhile, the offense used every idea in Gilbertson's toolbox. When it got things going, Nebraska was utterly helpless. "Gilby was always thinking several plays ahead, moving the team down the field and into the end zone," Keith Shipman said. "That's what helped them beat Nebraska." It was during the Huskies' comeback that their domination bordered on the unbelievable. In 14:54 they outscored Nebraska 27–0, piling up 257 yards on offense while holding the home team to two yards. Hobert completed eight passes in eleven attempts during the run for 98 yards.

"He started throwing dimes, and he was just killing them," Donald Jones said. "That's when I knew he was a baller. We had never played against a crowd that hostile. The energy against us was aggressive. We needed someone to step up and make plays, and he did it. He was *the* guy. Make no mistake about it; the way he played, he won that game for us."

"That night," Bruener said, "you could feel his competitiveness permeate through the team." The young, inexperienced quarterback had delivered the goods. One reporter asked James what he had done to help

Hobert with his confidence. James laughed, perhaps thinking back to how Hobert had addressed him during the rally. "I'm not sure he's the kind of guy who needs a lot of help with his confidence," he replied.

Nebraska defensive coordinator Charlie McBride offered an accurate assessment of his team's play. "I think in the first half they [the Cornhuskers] felt pretty good about themselves. The second half they [the Huskies] just wore our asses out. Simple as that."

Dick Baird spent the game in the press box in his usual position, standing behind Lambright and Gilbertson and assisting them in any way he could. He'd yell out personnel groups that were entering the game and point out things he saw that others might have missed. He watched Lambright adjust his defense after Nebraska's fast start and watched Gilbertson stay patient with his players until they finally got it going. "To watch those two go back and forth during that game was incredible," Baird said. "The stadium was rocking, and then we started coming back and kicking their ass. It was one of the greatest games I ever got to be a part of. It was the experience of a lifetime."

11

Crush Their Souls

WHEN THE WEATHER IS GOOD, HUSKY STADIUM IS A PLACE OF unequaled beauty from which to watch college football; it is a huge, double-decked structure located on the shores of Lake Washington. On game day, the lake becomes another stadium parking lot as thousands of fans leave their cars at home and instead navigate various waterways in boats of all sizes to come to the game. It's easy to hear the revelry of seafaring Huskies fans enjoying a pregame ritual that's come to be known as sail-gating. Mount Rainier is easily viewed from the stadium as it looms over Seattle, some seventy miles to the south. A look east reveals the Cascade Mountains, while the Olympic Mountains are viewable to the west. As autumn begins, leaves on trees in nearby neighborhoods begin to change and add beautiful bright hues of red and yellow to the palette. The entire scene is a delightful feast for the eyes.

The first Saturday in October was a sparkler in Seattle, a warm day with clear skies and a light breeze that made for perfect conditions to watch UW play Arizona. The game kicked off at 3:30 p.m., which allowed fans (be they on water or land) extra time to reminisce about the previous weekend's home-opening 56–3 win over Kansas State. That game featured the return of Mark Brunell. Just over five months after his devastating knee injury, expected at first to sideline him for at least six and maybe nine months, Brunell came jogging onto the field in the final seconds of the third quarter to a huge ovation.

"That was a great moment," Brunell's roommate Orlando McKay said. "I had watched the rehab process, the dark days that he had to go through. He was determined, but I also saw his frustration. I kept telling him, 'It's going to be all right. You're going to be good.' But people don't always recover from those kinds of injuries. Sometimes, a blown-out knee means you're done."

In his return, Brunell completed one pass and threw an interception. He would have better days stat-wise at UW. But the fact that he was there qualified as a miracle to his teammates and fans. "Mark worked his ass off to get back," said Rongen. "If the doctor said, 'You need three treatments,' he got six treatments. If they said go run a mile, he ran two miles. It was mind-blowing that he was back so fast."

The Dawgs defense recorded fifteen tackles for loss, including eight quarterback sacks. KSU ran only two plays in the first half in Washington territory, and one of those was a punt. An exasperated Wildcats head coach, Bill Snyder, told reporters, "I thought we'd do everything better. But Washington is probably as good as any team in the country right now."

What Snyder didn't yet know was that the Big 8 team the Huskies had run through a wheat thresher was going to end up winning seven games that season, which would become the start of his own remarkable twenty-seven-year run of success at Kansas State. What Washington fans didn't yet know was that they were about to see a performance against Arizona that would eclipse the previous week's win.

During the week, defensive coaches at UW heard through the rumor mill that the Arizona offensive line thought it was ready for the challenge of facing the Huskies. That line was anchored by tackle John Fina, who would go on to play eleven years in the NFL. Hart kept stoking his players' inner fire with what he perceived as slights, be they real or imagined. "I hear they are really getting ready for you guys," he yelled that week at practice. He focused much of his attention on Emtman. "They've got a plan for you, and they are going to shut you down."

Fraley came in for some verbal motivation from Hart too. "It's tough for me to remember a time when Randy wasn't yelling at me," Fraley said.

"Fina's going be a big star in the NFL," Hart bellowed at Fraley. "He'll crush you. You won't be able to get off his block, and once he grabs you, you're done. He's gonna kick your ass!" Fraley and his teammates were also getting a big, regular dose of chatter from the man in charge of the UW offense.

"Coach Gilbertson had a big mouth, and he liked to talk trash," Fraley said. "If one of his linemen beat you, you'd hear Keith start riding you. The dynamic between Gilby and Lambright was interesting because Lambo did not want to hear Gilby criticizing the defense. But his mindset was, 'If you want someone to stop talking, shut 'em up.'"

The coaches were concerned about a letdown after the easy win over KSU, so they spent the week verbally blasting the players in practice, and by Saturday the team was wound up tight and ready to go. Then, the coaches got a cherry to put on the sundae.

Tormey and Hart were walking through the athletic complex before the game when they ran into Arizona's offensive line coach, Pat Hill. "Nick Fineanganofo is looking forward to playing Emtman," Hill said. Fineanganofo was Arizona's starting guard, and Hill's comment was innocent enough; players always want to play against the best possible competition, and successful athletes are wired in such a way that they always believe they will win, both as an individual and as part of a team.

Tormey and Hart quickly made their way to the locker room, where Hart dialed up Emtman's intensity even higher. "I hear Fineanganofo can't wait to play against you," Hart said. "You better be ready, because he is."

As Cunningham walked out for the coin toss, he sized up Fineanganofo and the rest of the Arizona captains. "He was a huge guy; a big, massive man," Cunningham said. "But he looked scared to death. He couldn't stand still. Maybe Emtman had shot him a look during warmups, but whatever had happened, he looked like he was heading into the coliseum and knew it wasn't going to turn out very good."

"Sometimes when we were coming out of the tunnel, you could just tell it was going to be a long day for the other team," said McKay. "That was one of those days."

After the Huskies took the opening kickoff and went three and out, Arizona's Terry Vaughan returned a punt sixteen yards to give the

Wildcats the ball on the Washington 48. The huge crowd in Husky Stadium cheered as Arizona quarterback George Malauulu took the first snap of the day and ran an option play to his left. Well, it was *supposed* to be an option play. But in a flash, he was on the turf after Emtman blasted through the line and tackled him.

"On that first play, when Steve got the tackle and threw his hands in the air, there was so much noise and excitement in the stadium," McKay said. "I remember thinking, 'We're just going to crush their soul.' And they knew it too."

On second down, it looked like Arizona wanted to pass, but the play was destroyed so quickly that the world will never know. Emtman roared past Fineanganofo like a commuter going through a turnstile and crushed Malauulu before bouncing to his feet quickly and again throwing both of his index fingers in the air. That pose, that moment of exuberance after the second play, was captured for eternity in an iconic shot snapped by *Seattle Times* photographer Mark Harrison.

Facing third and long, Malauulu approached the line of scrimmage, took one look at Emtman, and promptly called a timeout. In that morning's *Arizona Daily Star* columnist Greg Hansen wrote, "Arizona does not have a chance to win today." Any Arizona fan or player who had disagreed with that pregame conclusion was now in the midst of an agonizing reappraisal. After the timeout, a third-down completion fell short of the necessary yardage to gain, and Arizona punted.

"I felt bad for them," Lincoln Kennedy said. "When Steve had the presence about him, he was going to run you over, and it didn't matter who you were. He was taking you for a ride, and there was nothing you could do about it. He had such a low center of gravity and he was so strong, you couldn't stop him."

"He put their offensive line on roller skates," Shipman said. "He did it to everyone all year, but he really did it to them that day."

"That's the best I've ever seen him play," Hoffmann said. "He just exploded on them."

Arizona's high point of the day was starting its first drive in UW territory. That was as good as it was going to get. In the second quarter, the Wildcats ran sixteen plays. Two resulted in interceptions, two resulted in lost fumbles, and four more resulted in tackles for loss or sacks. Another play went for no gain, and Malauulu threw three incomplete passes. So 75 percent of the plays the Wildcats ran in the quarter gained nothing or lost yards.

Arizona tried running trap plays to neutralize Emtman. Trap blocking is a simple and time-tested technique used against aggressive defensive players. In a trapping scheme, most of the linemen block in one direction, with one lineman pulling toward the play side of the formation. The player they're trying to trap is left unblocked at first before he is hit from the opposite side. In theory, he never sees the block coming. It was a plan. But like Mike Tyson once said, "Everyone has a plan until they get punched in the mouth."

"They intended to trap him and take him out of the play," Hoffmann said. "But they couldn't get over in time to stop him. We started the game in the 'up' formation, where we were all up on the line of scrimmage. They had practiced this all week, and it went smooth. But now, there are all these guys up in your face. Arizona could smell our breath. 'Maybe I'm coming. Maybe I'm not. You don't know, do you?' We ruined their whole plan right away."

By the half, it was 34–0. UW scored three more times but ran the ball the majority of the second half, which kept the score at a respectable 54–0. Six different Washington players scored seven touchdowns on sixteen offensive possessions. Cornerback Walter Bailey accounted for Washington's other TD with an interception return. It was the worst road loss in Arizona football history.

Donald Jones became friends with one of Arizona's assistant coaches from that team, and years later that coach told Jones that the Huskies first-half dominance left Arizona coach Dick Tomey with exactly zero answers at halftime.

"OK, men," Tomey told his offense, "here's what they're doing, and here's what we're going to do." There was a pause as the head coach stood in front of a chalkboard for a moment before turning back to his team. "Guys, I'm not going to lie. I don't know what to do."

The drive chart for the game looked more like an autopsy than a summation of an afternoon of competitive football. Ten of the Wildcats' sixteen drives lasted three plays or less. Seven ended in turnovers. Four lasted less than a minute. Only twice in the game did Arizona string together three consecutive plays for positive yards. Nineteen of the Wildcats' thirty-nine rushing plays resulted in lost yardage. Those nineteen tackles for loss were credited to fifteen different Huskies as everyone got in on the fun. Eight of the rushes were quarterback sacks (the NCAA counts a sack as a rushing attempt), resulting in losses totaling thirty-nine yards.

"Today was the first time we came together as a team and got the job done," Emtman told the TV audience after the game. He had finished the day with ten tackles. Four of them were for lost yards and another was a sack.

"That [game] was shocking," said Bryant, who led the Huskies with ninety-three yards rushing and a touchdown. "I thought we would win, but I didn't think we'd beat them that bad."

After the game, Tomey talked about five lost fumbles and two interceptions and glumly noted, "One thing you have to do on offense is preserve your right to punt, but they even took that away from us with all the turnovers." As for Emtman, Tomey explained what Arizona's plan had been: "In all the film we looked at, teams always double-team him, and that never works. We thought we'd try some schemes that might allow for single blocking. That didn't work either."

In a season in which perfection was the goal, the Huskies came as close to it in a single game as possible. The kicking game continued to be an issue. They missed two extra points and had a field goal blocked. Other than that, it was hard to find anything wrong with their performance. Still . . .

"It's absolutely critical that we keep getting better," Lambright said after the game. "Because we can play better."

The following week, the Dawgs continued their run through the first half of their schedule against the Toledo Rockets from the Mid-American Conference. On paper, it was the easiest game on the schedule. The Rockets were stepping up in class, playing on the road, and facing a superior opponent. On the task of playing the team he had coached for the previous twelve seasons, a team loaded with superstar players (many of whom he had recruited) Toledo head coach Gary Pinkel wryly observed, "It appears I may be shooting myself with a gun I helped load."

Mario Bailey had one of his best days as a Husky with six catches for 170 yards and three touchdowns, and Washington rolled past Toledo, 48–0. Bailey now had seventeen career TDs, making him the all-time UW leader in that stat. At the game's conclusion, Pinkel began looking for James to congratulate him. What happened next nearly overwhelmed him.

"When I got the Toledo job, I had to leave quickly so I didn't get a chance to say goodbye to a lot of guys," Pinkel said. "As I was walking over to talk to Coach James, the entire team was walking toward me to shake hands. It was like a swarm of bees. I got chills, and I was very emotional about it. It was very moving."

Factor in blow-out wins from the previous November against Arizona and Washington State, and now five of the nine most one-sided wins in James's career at UW had happened in less than a calendar year. More impressive than that was a statistical note that served as an exclamation point for UW's dominance of its recent opponents. With 5:26 remaining in the third quarter at Nebraska the Huskies trailed, 21–9. From that point until the end of the Toledo game Washington had outscored its opponents, 185–3, in 200 minutes and 26 seconds of college football.

UW was now ranked third in the national college football polls and was one of five unbeaten teams left in Division I football. One of those other unbeaten was Cal. And the Bears were next on the UW schedule.

Brunell and Billy Joe

AFTER HIS RETURN TO THE FIELD IN A MOP-UP ROLE AGAINST KANSAS State, Brunell played more important minutes seven days later. Hobert suffered two "stinger" injuries (shooting pain from the neck that travels through the arm, making it numb) after collisions in the Arizona game. The first came early in the second quarter; the second, early in the second half. "Nothing I haven't had before," Hobert said with his typical devil-may-care attitude tinged with humor. "It's just a pain in the neck, so to speak." Hobert's numbers weren't bad (5 completions in 15 attempts, 72 yards, zero touchdowns) but Brunell's were better (5 for 7, 93 yards, 2 touchdowns). Given that the Dawgs had won by 54 points, individual stats didn't matter that much—unless, that is, you were a reporter looking for a postgame angle. There were plenty of those, and the angle they were looking for was a quarterback controversy.

For years, one of James's tenets had been that a player shouldn't lose his job due to an injury. Brunell had been the team's number one quarterback when he was injured. Now, he was healthy, and after he looked so sharp against Arizona, it was fair to speculate about whether he should resume his role as the starter. All three of the characters in this melodrama were asked about it after the Arizona game, with James showing little patience for anyone trying to stir up trouble.

"You guys worry about quarterback controversies and all that garbage," he told the media. "Billy Joe is okay physically, and he should be fine."

"No QB controversy at all," Brunell responded. "Billy Joe got hurt, and I stepped in. That's the job of a backup."

Hobert echoed Brunell's thoughts: "I got hurt; Mark's the backup. He came in and filled in for me. That's all."

Still, Brunell had been outstanding in the game. He had been the starter and had gotten hurt. Didn't he deserve a chance to get his job back?

"We had those discussions," Gilbertson said. "But you've gotta be realistic. We were high rolling at the time, and we weren't changing." Gilbertson was right on both counts.

The Huskies were unbeaten, ranked third, and winning by an *average* of seven touchdowns per game. Whatever loyalty James might have felt to Brunell, he was in charge of winning football games, and that's exactly what they were doing with Hobert at quarterback. But there may have been more at work here than simply sticking with the hot hand. James could fall back on two "high-rolling" seasons in his past to give him all the reasons he needed to not upset the Husky apple cart as it rampaged through opponents.

In 1982, the Huskies were the number one team in the country for six weeks in September and October. They were unbeaten, and, like the 1991 team, they were crushing opponents. UW fans had every reason to start dreaming about a run for the national championship.

Then, a very average Texas Tech team came to Seattle, and the Dawgs won a ho-hum 10–3 affair. During the game, James became impatient with his starting quarterback, Steve Pelleur, and replaced him in the third quarter with Tim Cowan. Pelleur remained the starter the next week, although both men played when the Huskies lost at Stanford, 43–31. After that game, Cowan became the starting quarterback. The loss to Stanford ended their hopes of a national title, and a loss to WSU a few weeks later ended their hopes of a third-straight Rose Bowl appearance.

Cowan and Pelleur were friends and discussed how they both needed to react in a positive way to keep the team together. "But there were guys who wanted me to be the quarterback," Cowan said, "and there were guys who wanted Steve."

In 1984, UW was again unbeaten and ranked number one in the polls in late October, when James benched Hugh Millen for Paul Sicuro at halftime of the Arizona game after Millen committed five turnovers. With Sicuro in charge in the second half, they rolled to a 28–12 win. Afterward, the media all wanted to know why James had changed quarterbacks.

"I saw the same thing you did," James said. "Five turnovers. When you're playing poorly but your quarterback isn't making mistakes, he generally feels pretty good about himself. But if he's involved in the turnovers, it's better to make a change."

That part of the story was easy. The next question put James into a corner of uncertainty, a place he seldom visited. Every reporter wanted to know who was going to start at quarterback next week for UW. "I'm not sure," James said. It was a rare public admission of doubt from someone who normally exuded the quiet confidence of a man who always had a plan.

Players and coaches say the right things publicly when there is a change at quarterback. But human nature being what it is, there is always a ripple effect through the locker room. It's only natural that out of over a hundred people affected by a change, some will view it positively, some negatively. It happened in 1982, when Cowan replaced Pelleur, and it happened in 1984, when Sicuro replaced Millen.

In 1982, James made the change after the loss to Stanford, and there was less resulting tension because a quarterback change can be a natural reaction after a loss. But in 1984, the change came after a win. James could have gone right back to Millen; after all, the Huskies were unbeaten and top-ranked. Instead he set up a midseason competition between the two and eventually decided on Sicuro for the next game against Cal.

Both sides in the Millen/Sicuro discussion got a chance to feel good and bad about their opinions in the next two weeks. First, UW routed Cal, 44–16. "See," the Sicuro supporters could say to their teammates. "This was the right move. Look how easy that was." UW then lost the following Saturday at USC, 16–7. "Uh-huh," replied the Millen supporters. "Look what happened. We never should have changed quarterbacks."

The USC game was the Huskies' only loss that season; had they won that afternoon and finished out the year unbeaten, they likely would have been voted national champs over Brigham Young. James didn't spend a lot of time dwelling on the past, but he had to wonder at times if he should have stayed with Millen. It's unfair to pin the USC loss totally on Sicuro, and it's also unfair to say that had Millen started the game, UW would have won. But that didn't mean people wouldn't wonder about it. That's what happens when a coach switches quarterbacks midseason. Twice at Washington James had seen how uncertainty at the quarterback position could derail a team, so there would be no uncertainty in 1991. When Brunell was healthy enough to return to action, the 1990 Rose Bowl MVP was assured he would get playing time, but Hobert remained the top Dawg.

"We made it clear we were going to get everyone involved," said Gilbertson. "But we were not changing quarterbacks. I talked to Mark, and I promised him that we would get him meaningful snaps in every game. We felt we owed him that."

"The team was rolling in such a way," Hobert said, "and as a coach, you don't want to make changes to something that's not broken. I hadn't done anything to lose the job. Whether they believed Mark was better or I was better is almost irrelevant to the fact that things were going well right now, and we didn't want to mess with the vibe of the team or how the offense was flowing. I think that's why Mark wasn't the starter when he came back."

Brunell and Hobert's relationship went a long way toward keeping the situation positive. Teams bring together different personalities, attitudes, and ideas on how to get things done. People who work together don't have to be friends, but they do have to respect each other. Hobert and Brunell shared mutual respect despite the fact it would be impossible to conjure up two more different guys.

"We were opposites," Hobert said. "I was up in the air and flighty and he was way more grounded, but we got along very well. Our meeting room was always fun. Mark has a great personality and a great sense of humor."

Eric Bjornson was Hobert's backup while Brunell was hurt and then moved to third on the depth chart when Brunell returned. He said public images of Hobert as the comedian and Brunell as the studious, silent type were wrong. "Brunell was every bit of a cutup as Billy. He had this image that he was not a smart ass and clean-cut and wholesome. But he would mess with people. They were both funny, and they were both revered by the rest of the team."

Bjornson backed up his assertion about Brunell's being willing and able to clown around with a great story from their days in the NFL. Bjornson was on the Dallas Cowboys kickoff team. He was in line, watching the kicker and waiting to run downfield when he heard Brunell's voice from the Jacksonville sideline. "Hey! Bjornson! Let's get in a fight. You and me. Right now! No one will believe it."

Cunningham kept things simple. In describing the differences between the two quarterbacks, he noted that Hobert was right-handed and Brunell was a southpaw. "To me, the only difference was a different hand under my butt before the snap."

Hart uses a horse racing analogy to describe the duo's differences: "Mark was more the whisper-in-your-ear guy, and Billy Joe was going to go to the whip. He was a rip-snort 'let's go!' guy. Our guys knew how to respond to both approaches."

Orlando McKay is a bit blunter. He lived with Brunell and knew him to be rock solid in his approach to the game. Brunell preferred well-thought-out plans to taking risks. He was always going to be a leader. As for Hobert? "He was a crazy country boy. His attitude was, 'I don't care if I throw a pick. I don't care if I throw six picks. I can't do everything right and I'll make mistakes, but I'm going to keep slinging it around and I'm going to find a way to win, and we're going to have a great time.' And it worked."

Once, during a meeting in 1990 with Gary Pinkel, Hobert cracked a joke that broke the entire room up. As players laughed, an exasperated Pinkel asked Hobert, "Why can't you be more like Mark?" Hobert shrugged his shoulders in a gesture that said, "I am who I am." The staff's willingness to let him be himself was a vital component of Hobert's success.

"You can't contain great players," Gilbertson said. "You've got to let them be who they are and screw things up once in a while. And sometimes, you've got to let them screw up a few times."

Those screwups, and Hobert's desire to occasionally screw around, tried Gilbertson's patience. Everyone involved remembers more than a few times in the middle of practice hearing Gilbertson's voice crackle through the air, "BILLY!," followed by a string of invective. "Hobert would get guys laughing about something before the ball was snapped," said Lambright. "There were more than a few 'What in the hell is going on here?' moments."

The self-confident Hobert knew he was the number one guy. The self-aware Hobert admitted that even he could see the argument that Brunell might be a better fit. "I guaran-damn-tee you I wasn't their favorite guy to have at quarterback. I sucked at practice, I was flighty in meetings, I cussed too much, I partied too much, and my personality was arrogant. Mark was a much more likable guy." This is not to say that Hobert didn't care or didn't want to get better. And while he was often on the receiving end of choicely worded tirades from Gilbertson, he was smart enough to listen and react intelligently.

"I learned a lot from Gilby about the mental aspect of practice," Hobert admitted. "I was such a crappy practice player, and he made me realize how important practice was and how much football is about trust between a coach and player. When the offensive coordinator is calling a pass play, he's saying, 'I'm trusting you to make the right decision here.' There were a lot of plays early in the season that we weren't using because they didn't trust me yet because I sucked so bad in practice. Gilby helped me mature as a quarterback."

Another person helped Hobert develop into a better practice player and thus a better game player: Brunell himself. "Billy was always receptive to Mark's comments and instructions," said McKay. Every player on a championship-caliber team is competitive to a degree most people will never understand. Hobert's and Brunell's competitiveness helped fuel improvements in both players. Conventional wisdom was that Brunell was the better runner before his injury and that Hobert had the stronger arm.

"When Mark got healthy and got back in, he had taken it personally that people said he didn't have as strong an arm as Billy," said Kennedy. "And Billy had taken it personally that people said he wasn't as mobile as

Mark. Before Mark got hurt, he would often audible into the speed option. When he came back, he started to audible into passing plays. Meanwhile, Billy Joe is coming in and checking to run audibles." "Mark became a polished pocket passer," said Bjornson. "The injury forced him to do it."

After his sooner-than-expected return from the knee injury, Brunell's play throughout the season was top shelf. He completed 62 percent of his passes. He helped Washington build on leads and allowed for other players on the second team to show what they could do. His success when he came into games kept reporters nosing around to see if everyone was always okay with the arrangement. Hart said Brunell wanted his job back, but he wanted the team to have success more than he wanted to start, so he kept those thoughts mostly to himself.

"He was the son of a coach," Hart said. "He'd seen his dad lose players to injury, and he knew there were two ways to go. You can take the high road and make it better or become a negative influence. With a negative influence, you can't win. Maybe at the time, he wasn't too fond of Don James. But he couldn't turn on his teammates. More championships are won in the locker room than on the field."

"The most important three things to Brunell were the team, the team, and the team," Gilbertson said. "He was such a good person through it all."

Unlike 1982 and 1984, the way James was using his quarterbacks in 1991 fell more in line with how he had historically handled the position. He had often used two quarterbacks, but their playing time was planned and managed by him and not a surprise to anyone.

"Don always wanted to play backup quarterbacks in meaningful time because you were only as good as your backup, and he wanted that guy to have experience in case you needed him," Baird said. That makes perfect sense, but most coaches didn't play the game that way. Most coaches wouldn't pull their starter in the second quarter of a game to get the backup guy some reps. So reporters pestered James about pulling Hobert to get Brunell time.

"Aw, that's overrated," James would tell the media with more than a trace of irritation. "It's just another position on the field. You want everybody to be competing at the highest level, and the quarterback is no different."

That philosophy came at least partially from how James had been coached and how the game was played when he was in college at Miami. He was the Hurricanes' starting quarterback for most of his time there but shared the job with other teammates. Before his senior year, he found himself in quite the battle in training camp. The student paper, the *Miami Hurricane*, tried to make sense of it all before the season opener against Florida State.

"James has been the number one quarterback for the past two seasons, but Coach Andy Gustafson has experimented with six quarterbacks in practice in an attempt to get good passing and deception into the Hurricane attack. He finally decided on his opening game signal-caller, senior Don James, who will probably start and see most of the action against Florida State."

It turned out that James didn't start but was one of *five* quarterbacks Miami used in the game. Gustafson liked to use multiple quarterbacks anyway, and a rule change in 1953 made that a necessity more than just a coaching philosophy.

The so-called "one platoon" system was instituted by the NCAA for the 1953 season as a way of reducing the cost for colleges competing in football. Players were expected to play both offense and defense, which reduced the number of total players needed and thus reduced costs.

The new system included a series of quirky substitution rules requiring a player who was taken out of the game to stay out until the end of the quarter in which he had been removed. James played in the secondary on defense, but he was only 5'7", so if Gustafson wanted a bigger defender in the game for a certain situation, James came out and by rule couldn't go back in on either offense or defense until the start of the next quarter. So most teams of the era used multiple players at quarterback.

Having been a product of a system in which different guys played quarterback, James saw splitting time as no big deal. But at least one observer thought this was about more than just a reflection of the coach's roots. "It felt like he was trying to prove something," Don Borst said. Borst covered the team for the *Tacoma News Tribune*. "Most coaches didn't do it but to him splitting time at quarterback was no big deal. During games, it would sometimes lead to a loss of momentum, but it just didn't matter."

Part of the joy of coaching is having a little edge that the other guy doesn't have, and James looked at Brunell as exactly that. The other coach had to worry and wonder. When is Brunell coming in? What will they do differently with him in the game? How long will he play? It added an element of confusion for opponents who were already dealing with the fact that they were outmanned when they played UW.

"One of the ways he was better than everyone else was that he looked at things a little differently," Borst said. "Everyone attributed Brunell's playing to DJ being loyal to him. And that's true. But it's also true he wanted to show people. He knew something that not everyone knew, and this was another way for him to prove that he was the best coach in the country."

Close Call at Cal

HOBERT STRODE BRISKLY DOWN A HOTEL HALLWAY, REACHED THE end, opened a door, went down a flight of stairs, and reentered the hotel. He then walked the length of the hallway there until he reached the other side of the hotel. Out the door. Up the stairs, back inside, and down the hallway. It was 2:00 a.m. the night before UW was to meet unbeaten Cal, and like during most nights before games Hobert was too keyed up to sleep.

"I tried watching movies, listening to music, white noise," Hobert said. "I tried everything, and what I eventually did that worked was to power-walk through the hotel and go over scenario after scenario. I'd play the game two or three times so that the next day there was nothing the defense could do that I hadn't already seen in my head." Hobert ran through his checks and talked to himself as he walked; eventually, exhausted, he'd return to his room for a few hours of sleep. On this night he wasn't particularly worried about the opponent, but maybe he should have been.

Cal was not only unbeaten, but also ranked seventh in the country, the highest for a Golden Bear football team since 1951. Berkeley's Memorial Stadium had not hosted a matchup of two teams both in the top ten in the national rankings since October 1947. UW had dominated the series over the years, but the Bears were 11–2–1 in their last fourteen games overall; they were coming into the game after routing Oregon the week before, 45–7; and they were looking to gain some measure of revenge for the 46–7 loss they had suffered the previous year in Seattle.

The stadium was packed for kickoff, a rare accomplishment for Cal home games that did not go unnoticed by ABC's Brent Musberger. "Usually when you come to a game at Memorial Stadium there are more empty seats than folks," Musberger said. "But that is not the case now."

"The whole atmosphere was antithetical to what Cal is all about," Rondeau said. "It was a packed house, and it was noisy. It was an unbelievable crowd for Berkeley. They were into it. It was a hell of an atmosphere."

Days before the game, Cal running back Russell White expressed excitement in the *San Francisco Examiner* about the expected big crowd: "You see those guys at Ann Arbor, at Tennessee, playing in front of 100,000 people, and you think, 'Wow, those cats are living. That's big time.'"

Speaking of big time, the Las Vegas line on the game was a hefty fourteen points, an unusually high number for a matchup of two top ten teams. But that line was likely inflated a bit due to the Huskies' relentless success, not just on the field, but also for gamblers wagering on them. The Dawgs had covered the spread in twelve of their previous thirteen games. "They just keep rolling," Jeff Bauer, assistant manager of Harrah's Reno, told Bud Withers of the *Seattle Post-Intelligencer*. "They can't be stopped by anybody. It's like they can't make the point spread high enough."

The Bears were likely a little hot about being two-touchdown underdogs. They were at home, they were unbeaten, and they'd just drubbed Oregon. Cheers of "ROLLLL ONNNN, YOUUUU BEARRRRRRRRS!" echoed through Strawberry Canyon (the site of Memorial Stadium) from their fans, and when the game began, Cal's defense stopped the Huskies in their tracks on the first three drives. UW's offense helped with some self-inflicted wounds. Hobert fell down on the first play of the game when the Huskies mistakenly left the backfield empty. McKay dropped a pass that would have been good for a first down on the third play of the game.

On their second series, a Hobert pitch bounced wildly on the turf before guard Pete Kaligis recovered it. Their third series ended with a three and out. After that, Cal struck the first blow of the game, a touchdown pass from Mike Pawlawski to Sean Dawkins. The Huskies quickly responded with a touchdown toss from Hobert to Bailey. UW's next drive began with another near disaster when Matt Jones fumbled. The football bounced about ten yards before it was recovered by Rongen. Fifteen minutes into the game the offensive heroes were the guards, Kaligis and Rongen, who had both managed to recover a fumble.

That drive eventually ended up producing points but only after another near miss. Hobert was shaken up by a late hit from Cal's Mick Barsala. Brunell came in to replace him and promptly fumbled on the first play but recovered it himself. An exasperated James wondered how his players were going to win if they kept putting the ball on the ground.

Hobert came back in after two plays and found McKay open on a corner route. For the second time in the game, McKay dropped what should have been a completion, and this time he cost UW six points. A Travis Hanson field goal made it 10–7, but McKay was upset about his mistake. He was sitting on the bench when a coach yelled at him. His day was about to get worse.

"McKay! Gilby wants to talk to you."

"That," McKay said, "is a terrible thing that you never wanted to hear." McKay grabbed the phone. "Yeah, coach?"

"That's TWO!" Gilbertson stressed. "That's TWO, man!" Gilbertson hung up, and McKay exhaled. "He was really upset with me. I assumed I was being replaced, but he just wanted to voice his displeasure. We both understood how big the game was."

The Bears counterpunched with their own field goal to tie the game at 10. The first half was similar to the one at Nebraska in that the Huskies kept stopping themselves: dropped passes; fumbles; interceptions. But on their final drive of the half, the Dawgs took the lead after they got a huge break from the officials. Hobert hit Bryant with a screen pass as Rongen released to move downfield to block. But he didn't have a good angle on defensive back Ray Sanders. So he slid into Sanders with his legs extended. "Tripping!" ABC analyst Dick Vermeil yelled on the broadcast. Somehow, the officials missed it. "I saw it," Kennedy said, "and I was waiting for them to throw a flag."

They didn't, and instead of a penalty that would have pushed the Huskies back to almost midfield, Bryant used Rongen's "block" to advance the ball to the nine-yard line. "I hated going out and blocking defensive backs," Rongen said. "They're shifty and tricky. I'm out there and I've got this kid dead to rights, and he puts a little juke on me and all I had left was that little leg whip. He went flying up in the air, and somehow, they missed it."

Typical of every offensive lineman who ever played the game, Rongen wasn't upset that Vermeil called him out on the broadcast. He was thrilled that his name was mentioned so prominently. Between his recovered fumble and the leg whip, he had gotten more calls on the broadcast than the receivers and running backs. Jay Barry scored on the next play, and UW took a 17–10 lead at the break.

The third quarter featured defense. Cal's four drives finished with two three and outs and two interceptions. The Huskies first three drives ended in punts, and their fourth ended with a missed field goal. Again, similar to the Nebraska game, UW had a huge advantage in yards gained (309–168) but only a slim edge on the scoreboard. And that was about to evaporate on a play that would give the entire UW team a nightmarish flashback. On the final play of the quarter, Pawlawski handed the ball to tailback Lindsey Chapman, who zipped through a hole and was suddenly in the clear and swiftly in the end zone. The sixty-eight-yard sprint was eerily similar to Brian Brown's eighty-eight-yard scamper the previous year in the UCLA game. Like their ursine cousins to the south had done at Husky Stadium in 1990, the Bears took advantage of UW's aggressiveness on defense to score on a simple run up the middle.

With the game tied and the fourth quarter upcoming, Cal fans filled the air with noise. Only twice in their history had the Bears defeated a top-five team: USC in 1975 and Stanford in 1951. Now, they had a chance to do it again. Hobert stood on the field waiting for the fourth quarter to start while his mind raced. "I was devastated," he said. "Cal had a ton of great players, but I had [felt arrogant] about them, and I thought I had screwed the game up."

The Huskies continued their parade of mistakes with a holding penalty on the next drive, which left them in a second and long situation.

Momentum was now completely on Cal's side. From the booth, Gilbertson sent down a handoff to Bryant, who had been sick all week and had suffered nose bleeds in the locker room before the game. Bryant took the ball from Hobert, started to his left but then cut back when he saw a hole open to his right. He shot through the gap, ran between two linebackers, and was suddenly in open field. Sixty-five yards later he was in the end zone. The Huskies had regained the lead and steadied the ship.

After each team punted, Cal got the ball with ten minutes left in the game and strung together a pair of first downs, making one on a third and eleven play, when White ran twenty yards, and making the other on a fourth and one. The Bears were now at the UW twenty-three with a third and short. Lambright had six down linemen in the game for the play. Hoffmann, standing behind them, did a sensational job anticipating the snap and was sliding between D'Marco Farr and Emtman as the play began. Before Pawlawski could even begin to execute whatever the Bears had called, Hoffmann smashed into him and forced a fumble. Cal recovered but faced a fourth and long. Pawlawski overthrew his receiver, and UW took over on downs. James had the lead and the ball with just 5:27 to play. He didn't want to give either back to Cal, and he called upstairs. "Gilby, let's take some air out of this game."

Gilbertson, the offensive line, and the running backs obliged as UW elected to pound Cal into submission. The Huskies ran the ball on seven consecutive plays using halfbacks Bryant and Barry and countering with full back Matt Jones on two plays. After Bryant gained ten yards on his final carry of the day, UW had a third down and four at Cal's thirteen. The Huskies had taken almost four minutes off the clock, and on the next play Barry rolled cleanly into the end zone to put the game away. UW's celebration didn't last long. Officials had called holding on the play. Cunningham turned around, saw the flag, and couldn't believe it when he heard one official say to the ref, "Holding, number 79."

"I had a one-on-one with [Cal defensive tackle] Mack Travis," Cunningham said. He did a stunt where he jumped out of my way and over to another gap. I put my hand down on the ground and dove back and with my shoulder pad and helmet just barely nicked his thigh. My hands were on the ground when I hit him. Any NFL scout would look at that and say it's a really good play. I created an extra foot that gave us a touchdown." But not according to the officials.

"Are you serious?" Cunningham exploded. The video would later back up his claim that he didn't hold on the play. But for now, the call had taken a game-clinching touchdown off the board. Hobert lost two on the next play, and then Hanson missed a field goal attempt. With just under a minute to play, Cal had life. Cunningham was furious as he came off the field. The penalty meant the Dawgs' tired defense had to go back on the field on a hot afternoon and get one more stop. He was so upset that he felt sick to his stomach. Then he got the same dreaded message McKay had received earlier: "Hey, Cunningham. Gilby wants to talk to you."

Cunningham stormed over to the phone. "Yeah?" he half screamed.

Gilbertson unloaded. His offense had spent the entire afternoon taking target practice at themselves. Now, the holding penalty had cost UW a score and might end up costing them the game. Gilbertson left no room for doubt in his monologue about what he thought about that. Finally, he paused to take a breath, and Cunningham, who by now had heard enough, took his opening. "Gilby, I didn't hold him!" Cunningham screamed as he slammed the telephone receiver down.

They would settle things later. For now, they both held their breath as Cal went to work. Pawlawski's first pass found receiver Brian Treggs for seventeen yards, and suddenly the ball was near midfield. Two plays later, Pawlawski found Damien Semien for a big gain, and with just five seconds left on the clock, Cal could take one shot to tie the game from the UW twenty-two. Pawlawski's pass into the end zone hit receiver Mike Caldwell in the hands and probably should have been caught. But it wouldn't have mattered because officials had called Cal for holding on the play. The bad news for the Huskies was that the refs had also called them for being offside. Games can't end on a defensive penalty, so Cal would get one more chance.

Pawlawski looked to Treggs, who was briefly open near the corner of the sideline and the goal line. Walter Bailey quickly cut in front of him and knocked the ball away. No flags. Game over. Huskies win.

"It was so intense out there, you couldn't believe it," defensive end Andy Mason said. "The pressure was building and building, and you could tell it was going to come down to one play. It was going to end with a perfect pass with the ball in the air and the game won by whoever could make that play."

Kennedy lamented the fact that the game had come down to the final play. "There's no reason that game should have been that close. We could have ended it in the first half, but we kept 'em in it by stopping ourselves."

Bailey accepted congratulations and teasing from his teammates—congratulations on knocking away the final pass and teasing because if he had intercepted it, he might have raced untouched the length of the field for a score. "In practice, when he would pick a ball off, he would run and run and run," Dana Hall said. "Now, finally, he had an opportunity in a game, and he just knocked it down."

The truth of the matter was that the pass was high, so an interception and return would have been difficult. By knocking the ball away, Bailey won the game. "God bless him for doing what his coaches told him to do," Hart said.

In the "what if" department, Cal would always wonder if the outcome of the game might have been different if Sean Dawkins hadn't been hurt. He had two catches and a touchdown before suffering a charley horse that knocked him out of the game for most of the second half.

"If Dawkins doesn't get hurt, who knows?" said Rondeau. "He was a real weapon. What if they have him on that last drive? Cal was the real deal, and it was a scary game to me. I was more worried about that game than any other game that season."

"That felt like a game they could lose," said Chuck Nelson. After an All-American career as a kicker at UW, Nelson spent several seasons in the NFL before returning to Seattle, where he worked on Washington's local TV game broadcasts. "It felt like [the Huskies] were lucky to get out of there. [The Bears] were as good as we were."

Cunningham and Gilbertson met in the locker room and hugged. "Dude," Cunningham said. "I don't know what happened. But I didn't hold him."

Some of the Huskies talked among themselves about how the game might cost them in the national championship race. "We felt like we had to have blowouts every game," McKay said, and 24–17 was no blowout.

There were now four unbeaten teams left: top-ranked FSU, number two Miami, and the Dawgs at number three. North Carolina State was also still unbeaten but ranked lower and was not considered a threat to win the title. FSU and Miami were scheduled to play in a few weeks, so one of them would get a loss. Presuming the winner of that game won out and presuming the Dawgs won out, there would be two 11–0 teams left at the end of the year. The problem with that scenario for the Huskies was that they would be obligated as Pac-10 champs to go to the Rose Bowl to face the Big 10 champ.

Hobert thought the whole thing stank. "I hate the polls system," he said. "If it was up to me, I'd have the top three teams in a playoff. Two would play three, and the winner would play one." He then punctuated his thoughts with another one of his unforgettable quotes. "If it was me, I'd dog the Rose Bowl. I'd find some way to kill that obligation, and I'd go find FSU or Miami and play for the national championship."

That notion was popular and also impossible. But that didn't stop people from talking about it. A lot.

You-fense and We-fense

OWING TO GEOGRAPHIC ISOLATION; A CLOUDY, RAINY CLIMATE; and being located in a state that shares its name with the nation's capital (a phenomenon that can lead locals exasperated with the federal government to refer to "the *other* Washington"), people who live in Seattle sometimes possess an inferiority complex about their hometown. But events in the years leading up to 1991 put Seattle at the center of a cultural hurricane.

Starbucks, the little coffee company founded at Pike Place Market in 1971, doubled its store locations between 1989 and 1991 and was gearing up for an IPO that changed the way people thought about coffee and the coffee business.

For those searching for something stronger in their cup, Seattle was one of several cities in the early stages of the microbrewery revolution. A 1982 Washington law allowed for the brewing of draft beer with up to 8 percent alcohol. By 1991 beer drinkers who wanted something different from mass-produced products could wet their whistles at the Redhook Brewery, Pike Brewing, Maritime Pacific Brewing, or Big Time Brewery, which was located a few blocks off campus and was a favorite for UW students and football players.

Nintendo of America had been based in the Seattle area since the early 1980s, and by 1991 it was estimated that one in four American households had a Nintendo console. Yearly sales of Nintendo machines and software approached $3 billion.

In August 1991, Seattle hosted the Microsoft Windows Software Developers Conference. About five hundred people were expected, but over eighteen hundred showed up. Among other things, the overflow crowd required the city to issue a parade permit to Microsoft to get all the developers from one location to another. In November, Microsoft introduced its now iconic Windows logo.

Seattle had also become the center of the musical universe. Pearl Jam's first album, *Ten,* was released in late August 1991. Soundgarden's *Badmotorfinger* and Nirvana's *Nevermind* followed four weeks later. The Alice in Chains song "Man in the Box" was a huge summer hit.

In the spring, Cameron Crowe's movie *Singles,* a romantic comedy set in the increasingly not-so-small world of the local music scene, was filmed at several area locations. Seattle bands with big hits and bands from other cities who wanted to cash in on the excitement regularly played live at venues around town, and UW players who were into music took advantage.

"I grew up in a small town," Hobert said. "I was a big Pearl Jam fan. I loved that part of living there. You wanted to be downtown or in Pioneer Square going to all the clubs and checking out the sound and look of all the different bands. The explosion of art and music coming out of Seattle was insane."

"Oh, yeah, 100 percent," Cunningham agreed. "We were all out all the time. I remember going to the Moore Theatre a lot. Every major rock and alternative band came through Seattle to play concerts because it was the epicenter. The rest of the city was booming; it was cool."

"I liked going to the Fenix Underground in Pioneer Square," Hobert said. "My friends always wanted me to drop my name to get us into places, but I was leery about that. I didn't want Coach James to find out that I was out until three in the morning listening to music."

By the fall of 1991, a person listening to music, working on a computer, playing video games, or having a beer or a coffee was likely using or consuming a product that had a Seattle connection. But it was an innovation from outside Seattle that was of more interest to Washington football fans.

In mid-October 1991 legendary Seattle music station KJR flipped its format to sports talk and rebranded itself as Sportsradio 950 KJR, thus becoming one of the first stations in America to adopt the all-sports format that had originated at WFAN in New York City in 1987. Suddenly, Seattle fans had a place where they could listen to and discuss sports all day long.

And in October 1991 what Seattle sports fans wanted to talk about the most was UW's unbeaten football team—and the brash quarterback who had dared to question the entire college football system and had challenged his school to "dog the Rose Bowl and find FSU or Miami to play for the national championship."

"He sounded like a talk show caller," Nelson laughed. "Billy, from Puyallup. He was saying what the fans all were saying."

Husky fans jammed the phone lines at the radio station. Should the Huskies "dog" the Rose Bowl? Could they? Who was better—Hobert or Brunell? Who was better—UW, FSU, or Miami? Who had played the toughest schedule? Wasn't the fact that UW was ranked behind the two Florida schools the latest indicator of the East Coast bias? Soon, writers and broadcasters who covered the team were on KJR as guests to offer their opinions. Players and coaches made appearances. The arrival of sports talk radio ratcheted up the enthusiasm and hype.

James was like everyone else who heard Hobert's comments about the polls and bowls. A part of him found it funny, and he admired his quarterback's competitive zeal. But he also knew, as did many fans and media members who lined up to "tut-tut" Hobert, that Washington's obligation to the Rose Bowl included contracts that could not be broken. Even if Hobert's idea was a good one, it wasn't realistic.

But Nelson was right. Hobert was only saying what many others were thinking. College football fans were frustrated that the sport they loved refused to develop a playoff system that would allow for a true national champion. Washington fans were acutely aware of the voting system's potential for injustice because of what had happened to UW after the 1984 season. Hobert was right: there *should* be a way to settle things on the field. He wasn't the only one who felt that way.

"When Hobert's comments about the Rose Bowl came out, I had a man in my office [the next] Monday morning who had received a call from a guy in Los Angeles trying to get the names and phone numbers of players at Florida State, Miami, and UW," James told Rick Alvord of the *Bellevue Journal-American*. The man was a former graduate assistant coach who thought James should know this idea was percolating. The plan called for the players to boycott the bowl system and get together on their own to play a game. James was glad to get the scoop but didn't worry about a scenario so far-fetched as to be laughable. He met with Hobert on Monday morning and briefly voiced his thoughts on his quarterback's idea for the postseason. But he was more concerned that Hobert told reporters he thought the UW offense deserved a grade of C-minus for the Cal game.

The game had been frustrating for Hobert. He had thrown two interceptions and pitched the ball wildly on another play. Rhythm was an elusive partner all day, and at no point had he completed three consecutive passes. In the second half, he first underthrew then overthrew McKay in the end zone, potential touchdown plays that instead ended with the ball bouncing in the grass.

"I understood his disappointment because he is a competitor and he didn't play up to his potential," said Gilbertson. "But we still had 441 total yards. There have been times around here where if we'd have had 441, they would have let school out."

James reminded Hobert that the Huskies had won and that the offensive line had done a great job. Barry had run for 143 yards and was named Pac-10 player of the week. Bryant had 99 yards including the game-winning run.

"Be careful when you're talking about the team," he told Hobert. "Don't let frustration over the way *you* played enter into your comments after a win. And if you played well and we lost, you have to think in terms of 'What could *I* have done differently?' because no matter how good you think you played, there's always something *you* could have done better."

"It was a big learning moment," Hobert said. "I needed to learn how to always talk about the team properly. That was a huge thing for me."

James felt so confident that he had gotten through to Hobert that he joked about it with reporters. "What did you think about Billy Joe's comment?" someone asked. "He said your offense's grade versus Cal was a C-minus."

"I disagree with Billy on that, and I explained why to him this morning," James said. "Several of our guys played A or at worst A-minus games."

"What about your quarterback? How was his game?"

"He gets a C-minus," came James's deadpan reply.

Later, Hobert announced he was not going to speak to the media and would decline all interview requests until further notice. He didn't blame the media; he just felt it might be better for everyone involved if he focused on playing football and not talking about football. Seattle reporters could have been excused if they had decided to hold a moment of silence.

But there were other things to focus on, like the improving play of the secondary. Before the season, James had considered it his team's most vulnerable unit. But halfway through the season, they were third in the country in passing efficiency defense, led the Pac-10 in interceptions with fourteen, and had given up just two touchdown passes. Larry Slade was the secondary coach, and given that his job was to put together defensive schemes that make a quarterback's life miserable, it's somewhat ironic that it was a quarterback coach who had led to Slade's getting hired at UW.

Ray Dorr was James's quarterback coach for four seasons at Kent State and nine seasons at UW before he became the head coach at Southern Illinois University (SIU). Two years later, James was looking for a secondary coach and called Dorr, who recommended Slade, a North Carolina native who had coached in the east before joining Dorr at SIU.

Slade embraced the change to an aggressive style at Washington despite the fact it put pressure on him and his players. But he felt they could handle it and pointed out that the key to UW's success wasn't just blitzing all the time. "In 1989 we were a team that showed pressure, but we were predictable, and people knew when we were going to blitz. What we did from an innovation standpoint after the ASU game in 1989 was make our blitzes and our zone coverage all look the same."

Slade said Lambright was constantly asking friends in the business to look at UW's defense and asking if they could tell when a blitz was coming. If they said yes, he would correct whatever the tell was. "By 1990, he had found all of them, and that's when we got really good."

Still, Slade's players had to hold up their end of the deal. The Huskies linemen and linebackers loved playing aggressively, and the only way the head coach would allow them to keep playing that way was if the secondary were taking care of their business.

"We'd always tell the secondary, 'Cover your ass off for three seconds, and we'll either have the quarterback flat on his back or he'll be running for his life,'" Hoffmann said. But sometimes covering a player man-to-man, even for just three seconds, is difficult. When linebackers and linemen noticed receivers getting open, they weren't shy about bringing it up.

"Coach James would not hesitate to shut it down," Clifford said. "When our defensive backs weren't covering, we'd all start yelling at them. 'Man up! Man up! If you don't, James is going to shut it down, and we're going vanilla.'"

Hart said James and Lambright argued all the time about blitzing. Lambo would have done it every play if he could. James saw the benefits of attacking but also worried when he saw receivers get open in single coverage. Their conversations were intense but professional.

"Don, they can't block us," Lambo said.

"But we've got receivers running free," James retorted.

"Yeah, but the quarterback can't find them," Lambright replied, a response that Chris Tormey said was accurate: "We would blitz and bring zero coverage all the time, and it usually didn't matter because we were giving the quarterback less than two seconds to find a guy."

A zero blitz package, which allowed long touchdown runs by UCLA and Cal, leaves no one covering the deep middle, while maximum pressure is put on the quarterback. Lambo loved it, but James thought it was too risky and didn't want to run it. When Lambo would sneak one in, James would ask him about it later.

"I thought I said no zero blitzes."

"Yeah, yeah," Lambright would reply. "One of the players made a mistake. I'll talk to him." James's management style was to let his assistants coach, and that occasionally meant allowing them freedom to do something he might not like.

"He would ask questions and be critical, but when it came to the actual schemes, he let us do it," Tormey said. "He wasn't interested so much in what we did but how we did it." In the case of the '91 team, the "how" involved maximum use of a long list of defensive players who all had devastating talent.

"We walked everyone to the line of scrimmage, and nobody could single block Emtman," Tormey said. "If we walked the two linebackers up, you couldn't double Emtman, and if you couldn't double Emtman, he was going to make the tackle in the backfield. And as soon as you doubled Emtman, Fraley or Clifford came running through. Lambo was great at knowing when to hit it and when not to hit it."

In addition to the vulnerability pressure could create, James worried about his cornerbacks. The Dawgs secondary often began plays at the line of scrimmage instead of staying two or three steps off. In single coverage, this allowed zero margin for error. "We were on an island," Walter Bailey admitted. "It was super dangerous. We were jamming guys and disrupting routes. We were an offensive-minded defense."

"We lined up in your face, we got our hands on you, and you weren't getting a free release," said Dana Hall, "and we didn't worry about getting beat because [safety] Shane Pahukoa was rangy, and we knew that if we missed, he could bail us out."

While James was a constant presence in the defensive meetings, he rarely sat in with the offense. He and Gilbertson talked all the time, but he was more interested and involved in the defense. He had been a defensive coordinator and was always going to lean toward that side of the ball.

"Coach James was always talking during our staff meetings about what the defense was up to," said Gilbertson. "He'd say, 'We are talking about this today. We are looking at this film. We are working on this scheme.'"

Then he'd turn to Gilby. "What are *you* doing today?"

James's love of and interest in the defense led to Gilbertson's hanging a nickname on the two sides of the ball. Gilby started referring to the defense as the "we-fense" and the offense as the "you-fense." Gilbertson's meetings weren't as serious as the ones Lambright and James conducted. He had a great sense of humor, as did his quarterback coach, Jeff Woodruff. Woodruff was a great impersonator, and among his best was one of James, who also happened to be his father-in-law. The defensive staff met in a small room that was separated from the offensive staff meeting room by a sliding curtain–style door. Hart said one day the contrasting styles of the two staffs became an issue.

"We could always hear them. Woody was telling stories and Gilby was making jokes, and they were all just yukking it up over there, laughing their asses off. We've got Don in our room, and there is zero laughter in our meeting."

At one point after some particularly raucous guffaws, James got to his feet. "Enough is enough," he muttered as he walked over and yanked the curtain between the two rooms open. The offensive staff stared at their boss like kids who had just been caught stealing beer from their parents' garage. James stared at them for a moment before speaking.

"Gentlemen, there's a little too much levity in this room."

"Our offensive staff turned into church mice," Hart laughed.

The you-fense began getting serious about what it needed to do; the we-fense returned to its ongoing debate on when, where, and how often to blitz; and they all focused on the second half of the season. It featured five games where UW figured to be the heavy favorite, just like it had been against UCLA in 1990.

15

Beating History

IF THERE WAS A PLACE WHERE THE HUSKIES MIGHT SLIP UP IN THE second half of the season, it was in the venerable Los Angeles Memorial Coliseum. Built to honor the veterans who served America in World War I, it opened in 1923. That fall, USC defeated Pomona College, 23–7, in the first football game played there. The Coliseum had hosted the Olympics in 1932 and 1984; the 1959 World Series; the first Super Bowl in 1967; speeches from John Kennedy, Billy Graham, Nelson Mandela, and Charles Lindbergh; and a Papal Mass for 100,000 by Pope John Paul II in 1987.

Of more importance to James, the Coliseum had always been a vexing spot for Washington. James's only win over USC at the Coliseum had come in 1980. Before that, UW's last win had come in 1964, when Lambright was a senior defensive end for Jim Owens. Many a promising Husky season had faltered at the Coliseum. It was a loss there in 1984 that had prevented UW from being unbeaten and opened the door for BYU.

The Trojans had revenge on their minds, still smarting from the obliteration they had received at the hands of the Huskies in 1990. Todd Marinovich was gone, but several players remained who had suffered through one of the worst losses in USC history.

The Trojans were also ticked off about their 52–20 loss to Cal the previous week. It was the most points USC had ever given up in a game, and it came after a week of pregame trash talk by Cal players. Post-game comments weren't any better as some of the Bears indicated they thought USC had flat-out quit trying during the game. "I didn't see that on tape," said Trojans coach Larry Smith. "But it's human nature to kick a team when they're down."

And make no mistake, the Trojans were down. They were 3–5 and in danger of ending a seven-year bowl streak. A win over UW would go a long way toward lifting USC's sagging spirits, and James wasn't buying into any pregame analysis about USC's being anything other than USC. Kennedy, the native Southern Californian, agreed: "This is a storied program that produced All-Americans every year. Guys won't admit this, but there was always a level of intimidation that came playing at USC."

"The Coliseum is tough," said Cunningham. "You're downtown; it's usually smoggy. It's a sneaky place."

"Just playing in the Coliseum itself, with all that history, that was tough," said Hall, another Dawg with California connections. "We all came out at the same time as a lot of those guys on that team, and we knew they were good, or they wouldn't be at USC."

James also had concerns about his team's intensity after wins over Oregon and Arizona State, although those feelings felt a little contrived. The Huskies had won both games and had done so with ease, but James and Lambright were disappointed with what they felt were late-game letdowns. Against Oregon, the Huskies had scored on four of their first five possessions and had ridden a solid performance from both sides of the ball to build a 29–0 lead in the fourth quarter. But in the final minutes of the game, the Ducks blocked a punt and then scored a touchdown. The final was 29–7, but Lambright was upset that his defense had given up its first fourth-quarter touchdown of the year. It was a meaningless complaint—unless perfection was the goal.

The players agreed and they were ticked off about the late touchdown too. But they also could read a stat sheet, and they knew they had held the Ducks to a miserly 129 yards. They knew they were unbeaten. They had forced twenty-nine turnovers in seven wins, but Lambright wanted more. "If we're getting this much out of you now," he told them, "imagine how good it's going to be by the time we get to the Rose Bowl."

It was more of the same against Arizona State who had a 4–3 record and the second-best defense in the Pac-10. Walter Bailey quickly let them know that none of that mattered. He intercepted Sun Devils quarterback Bret Powers on the first play of the game; then, after Washington scored, he recovered a fumble on the ensuing kickoff. UW scored again and led, 14–0, before ASU ran its second offensive play. It was 41–0 late in the third quarter when ASU scored touchdowns on consecutive drives. UW won, 44–16, and while James was upset about the late scores, he knew what he had seen: "Everybody who went out there went out on the attack—the offense, the defense, and the kicking game. If you were standing on their side, you had to wonder what was going to happen next."

"I go into every game thinking, 'Okay, something is bound to go wrong this week, and we're going to have to get ready to put our nose to the grindstone and come back and overcome some things,'" Cunningham said. "But the way it always happens is something bad happens to the other team. Everyone on this team has such a big play mentality and is looking to make something happen that somebody does something big."

The offense was piling up big numbers each game and making plenty of big plays, but it was the defense that smothered the life out of everyone UW faced. Opponents had started 116 drives versus UW, and only 11 had ended with points. "We would get five or six sacks per game," Hall said. "We'd have all those tackles for loss, and we were constantly forcing turnovers, which shortened the field for our offense."

The Huskies were winning their games by an average of over four touchdowns, and while the coaches continued to harangue the team about playing a full sixty minutes, the players knew they were a part of something special. Kennedy said that self-awareness helped them prepare for USC: "We realized by then that we had the biggest target on our backs. People were getting tired of us. Especially USC. They were used to getting all the attention, and we were taking some of their shine."

The game itself lost some of its shine two days before kickoff. Earvin "Magic" Johnson stunned the world with his announcement that he was retiring from the NBA effective immediately due to an HIV diagnosis. The ripple effect from Magic's news lasted for years, but in the immediate aftermath, most people were simply shocked. Beno Bryant told *Seattle*

Times columnist Steve Kelley that the news impacted the Huskies: "When we found out about it at practice, it messed everyone's practice up. It brought tears to a lot of fellas' eyes in the locker room. It affected us a lot."

It affected USC a lot too, and it was just one more thing added into the Trojans' pregame emotion. They were frustrated about the Cal loss. They were embarrassed about the drubbing UW had given them one year earlier and jealous of the attention the Huskies were receiving. Now, to top it off, the biggest sports superstar in their city might be dying. It wasn't difficult to conjure up a scenario where USC would play with enough emotional fire to knock off UW.

USC did play well. But the game was never in doubt. The final score of 14–3 wasn't as impressive as some of the beatdowns UW had put on opponents, but the Huskies were in control all day. Nothing better illustrated that more than a play that led to their second touchdown. Midway through the second quarter they faced a fourth-down-and-four-to-go situation and sent out the punt team. UW had worked on a fake punt most weeks in practice and gave the play a different name depending on the opponent. This week the play was called "Trojan."

In the huddle, punter John Werdel told his teammates, "Trojan's on!" The fate of the play was now in the hands of fullback Matt Jones, who was the up-back in punt formation and would have the best view of how USC's defense was set up. "If we call it, and you decide to run it," Woodruff regularly told him, "it's got to work."

Asked after the game what the odds were that he would call off the fake once the coaches put it on, Jones replied, "One percent." Jones took the snap, got a nice block from fellow fullback Darius Turner, and ran eight yards for a first down. Six plays later Bryant scored his second touchdown of the game, and UW had a 14–0 lead.

But here's the thing: maybe Jones should have called off the fake because USC had the perfect defensive position to stop it. "We had a pretty good idea they were going to fake it," cornerback Jason Oliver said after the game. "We were in a punt-safe defense. It couldn't have been a better call."

UW was so good that even though the Trojans *knew* the fake was likely, they still couldn't stop it. "We had the best defense out there we could have," Smith lamented. "We were in punt-safe where we don't try to rush, and we don't try to return it. They still ran it right through us."

USC's players wondered what might have become of the game if they had stopped that fake. UW's players never felt any heat. "We were never in trouble," said Hall. "It was just a low-scoring game, and our defense dominated." Not only was that true, but also considering that Bryant fumbled the ball away and Hobert twice threw interceptions (all three miscues deep in USC territory) and Travis Hanson missed a field goal attempt, the Dawgs knew the game should have been even more one-sided.

Bryant was the star of the day. On an emotional day in his hometown, he delivered a career-best performance, rushing for 158 yards and both UW touchdowns on 26 carries. The Huskies gained 237 yards on the ground, which was good because they struggled to move the ball through the air. Hobert had bounced back from his "C-minus" performance against Cal with outstanding games against Oregon and Arizona State. But now, back in the Golden State, he struggled to find consistency.

"He was sailing balls all over the place," Gilbertson said. "Billy's throwing balls up into the seats; balls are landing on the track." Eventually, Gilbertson lost his patience and called down to James. "Don, let's get the other guy in there. Let's give Brunell a chance."

"No," James responded. "We're going to let Billy Joe ride this out." In the games UW controlled, Brunell played as planned in the second and fourth quarters. But in the two games that had been close since he had gotten healthy (Cal and USC), Hobert went the entire way despite subpar performances.

"Don was really good about sticking with guys at quarterback," Gilbertson said. "He had a sense; he knew when to stay the course." And he knew that pulling Hobert in a close game would lead to the inevitable mishmash that came with a quarterback change. He also had an ace in the hole. UW's defense treated USC the way an incoming tide treats a sandcastle. USC ran twenty-eight plays in UW territory. Seven were incomplete passes. Five resulted in tackles for loss. After a third period field goal, USC didn't gain a yard the rest of the day. The defense was buoyed by having Emtman back for the entire game after he had missed much of the Oregon and ASU games with a leg bruise.

"He was everything to us," Walter Bailey said. "You don't always get to make plays, but you can be the disruption. You can cause havoc. That's what Steve always did. Our whole thing was disruption and annihilation. Steve and Tyrone Rodgers and Andy Mason were like a giant tornado. And whatever they spit out, the linebackers would clean up."

UW ended the day with fourteen tackles for loss, totaling minus fifty-eight yards for USC. Hoffmann led the charge with ten tackles, half of them coming for losses of thirty yards. Both numbers were individual season highs for UW. After the game, Hoffmann's family was standing in a common area outside the locker rooms when a gentleman approached them. Dave's younger brother, Matt, was wearing a Husky jersey with Hoffmann on the back.

"Are you Dave Hoffmann's brother?" the man asked.

"Yes."

"Can you give him a message for me?"

"Sure."

"Can you tell your brother that I said he played a helluva game? Can you please tell him that?"

Matt Hoffmann looked into the eyes of the man many consider to be the greatest linebacker in NFL history and told Dick Butkus that yes, he would relay the message to his brother.

"It was one of the best games I ever had," Hoffmann said. "I had a great time that afternoon. Then, to get approval from Dick Butkus? I was so happy I felt like a little kid."

Hoffmann played so well he hoped that maybe, just maybe, people would spell his name correctly. In newspaper stories, on television graphics, and at least one time on his jersey during his career, "Hoffmann" was spelled "Hoffman," with only one "n" at the end.

"It was and still is a pain in the ass. I always tell people that's not my name. I understand it. They've seen Hoffmann spelled with one N all the time. But that's not how I spell it."

The irritation began with his first appearance in a UW uniform during the 1989 spring football game. As he was getting dressed, he noticed that his name on the jersey was spelled incorrectly. "Hey guys," he said to the equipment crew. "I'm sorry, but this isn't how my name is spelled. Can we get this fixed?"

Hoffmann was told that it was too close to game time to do anything. Irritated by the response, he decided it wasn't too close to game time for him to do something.

"Give me that seam ripper."

Hoffmann returned to his locker and cut the Hoffman nameplate off his jersey and played the game with no name on his back. "I'd rather be out there with no name than to have my name spelled wrong."

James could relate to his star linebacker. When he was first hired at Washington in 1975, he drove by Husky Stadium and noticed the reader board, which read, "Welcome Coach Jones." Now, many wins and many years later, he stood in front of the media, happy with his team's win and with history on his mind: "I'm not disappointed at all with our offense. How can I be? It's been since 1980 that I've been able to smile after a game down here. It's a really tough place to play."

Hobert's self-imposed no-interview policy lasted about a week. To the delight of reporters everywhere, he was again delivering outstanding quotes. To the delight of James, he was also proving that even with his youth, a wild streak, and a willingness to say anything anytime, he was coachable.

For Hobert, the game had been similar to the Cal game. But there would be no random assigning of grades to the rest of the team. "I obviously wasn't playing well," Hobert said. "I wasn't throwing strikes. Fortunately, Beno and the rest of the offense did a hell of a job. And the defense saved our butts again. They've proved to me they're the best defense in the country." Hobert being Hobert, he still came up with a bon mot in which he managed to praise the team they had just beaten while criticizing another team that they had beaten. "I was rooting for USC to beat Cal," he told the *Los Angeles Times*. "Because Cal showed little respect for USC and I was hoping the Cal players would have something shoved down their throat because of some of the things they said. USC has a lot of great athletes and nobody has the right to tell them they shouldn't respect themselves."

With his team now unbeaten in nine games, James allowed that the ultimate pinnacle, his goal for years, was coming into view. "When I first came into this league seventeen years ago, my dream was to somehow go into New Year's Day with an 11–0 record. This is the closest we've ever been to that."

Later, the Huskies team plane rolled down the runway at Los Angeles International Airport and took off over the Pacific Ocean. The left side of the plane tilted skyward as the pilot turned to the north to begin the journey home. Those sitting on the right side of the aircraft who had a sense of geography could pick out their next California destination. About twenty-one miles off the plane's right wing, at the foot of the San Gabriel mountains, which glowed red in the setting sun's light, sat the Rose Bowl. The Huskies were now one win away from a return trip to Pasadena. They were two wins away from going there unbeaten, and they were three wins away from a chance to make history.

16

Hungrier Than Ever

CUNNINGHAM WAS IN THE LOCKER ROOM AT PARKER STADIUM IN Corvallis, Oregon, one hour before kickoff when he saw Jim Sprenger and two of the men working on his officiating crew walk in. Officials always have a private pregame visit with coaches to discuss any issues relevant to the day's game. The UW–OSU game was to be officiated by the crew that had worked the Cal game, the same crew that had called the crucial holding penalty against Cunningham that took a game-clinching touchdown off the board.

After seeing the play on tape, the coaches agreed with Cunningham that the call had been atrocious. "They watched the film," he said, "and all hell broke loose. They could see I wasn't holding. Don sent a letter to the league. It was a big kerfuffle."

What disturbed them even more than the call was that it looked as if the official who had made it was reaching for his flag as the ball was snapped. Coaches are a paranoid lot anyway, and it doesn't take much to get them wondering about potential grassy knolls. Was the official in question reaching for his flag at the start of the play? If so, why? Were they making up for the tripping call they had missed on Rongen earlier in the game?

Cunningham figured James's letter was the end of it. He hadn't held his guy, UW had won the game, and the league had been notified of the Huskies' objection. There was nothing more to do. But just the sight of the people who had almost ruined his day in Berkeley was enough to get his blood churning. He knew that now was not the time to say anything, so he sat at his locker doing a slow burn. But someone else felt the time was perfect for a conversation.

"Hey, you guys," James barked at the officials. The volume of his voice cut through the relative quiet in the room. "Come into my office." The men retreated into a small room just off the locker room. "Poor old Oregon State back then," Cunningham said. "Their facility was wood panels, and they had hooks in your locker to hang clothes." The thin walls surrounding James and the officials didn't have a chance of containing James's side of the discussion.

"He shut the door, and he just laid into them," Cunningham said. "He lost his mind on those guys. I'd been around Don five years by now, and I'd seen him mad. But this was different." Everyone else in the locker room heard the entire conversation as James let the referees have it.

"That holding call was terrible," James said. "Do you realize that call could have cost us that game? These kids have a national championship at stake. We've been asking a lot out of them. We are demanding that they work hard and do the very best they can on every play, and I'm telling you right now that I expect the same out of you."

Like a thunderstorm, the tirade was over as precipitously as it had begun. The Huskies already knew their head coach cared about them, but sometimes in the day-to-day interaction that feeling gets lost. But after hearing how vigorously James had defended Cunningham and seeing how much a perfect season meant to their coach, the players felt a mixture of pride, love, and admiration for the man most of them called "the Dawgfather."

"When he came back into the locker room to face us, he didn't say a word about the officials," Cunningham said. "But we heard him, and we knew he had our backs. I'm not sure if he meant for us to hear the conversation, but I'm glad we did."

The Huskies were heavy favorites, and they played the part after a brief misstep. Hobert fumbled on the game's second play, and Oregon State grabbed a quick 3–0 lead. "Overrated! Overrated!" came the serenade from the OSU student section.

Chico Fraley was amused. "Really?" he said. "Are you chanting that we're overrated? You are not ready for what's about to happen."

What happened was an avalanche of domination that the Beavers could not stop. By the end of the first quarter, UW was ahead, 16–3, courtesy of two touchdown passes from Hobert to Bailey and a safety from the defense after Jaime Fields forced a fumble. They had 190 yards and twelve first downs. OSU had minus-one yard and zero first downs. By halftime it was 44–6, and the Huskies had a total yardage advantage of 344–63. Hobert had two TD passes, another to Bailey and one to McKay, and a touchdown run. One of the scores had been set up by a punt block from Hall. It was 58–6 after three quarters, and UW owned a yardage advantage of 433–61. Rules dictate a fourth quarter must be played, and so it was even though it was unnecessary.

"We were just wondering how fast we could get the game over and get out of there," Cunningham said. The final score was 58–6, and with the win, the Huskies had clinched another trip to the Rose Bowl. The accompanying euphoria of that, as well as the smell of roses given to the players as they left the field, evoked strong memories. One year earlier they had clinched the Rose Bowl in a rout of Arizona. Euphoria. Roses. A wild celebration in the locker room when their official invitation was given to them by the president of the Rose Bowl committee.

And then before you knew it, UCLA had chopped them down to size. Each Husky team traditionally chooses a three-word motto to use during a season. The 1990 team chose NBR, which stood for "Nothing but Roses." It was reflective of their desire to return the program to Pasadena, and while words are just words, it was easy to look back and realize that BUT (Beat UCLA Too) should have been added.

The 1991 Huskies, mindful of their late-season flub in 1990, chose HTE, which stood for Hungrier Than Ever, and despite a conference clinching win at OSU, they had one more game to play before the Rose Bowl. Lambright was confident that his players would keep their collective eye on the Apple Cup. "I don't think you can say enough times how much these players learned from the UCLA loss. They all know it takes just one stub of the toe," he said.

There was no official invitation given to the team. There wasn't even a Rose Bowl official. The Rose Bowl committee informed UW that week that its president had another commitment and couldn't attend the OSU game. He was happy to send a lieutenant instead to formally invite the Dawgs. "Thanks, but no thanks," came the reply. Making the Rose Bowl was an accomplishment but not one the 1991 team felt like celebrating.

"We're going to the Rose Bowl," Emtman said. "That means nothing to me right now. The Cougars would like nothing better than to come into our house and knock us off, . . . and I'm focused on them already." All eyes were on the Cougars, but some were willing to reflect on a game that had happened earlier in the day on the other side of the country. Before UW belted the Beavers, FSU and Miami had collided in north Florida. It was only the second time in history that teams from the same state were ranked one-two and met in a regular season game (top-ranked Purdue claimed the Shillelagh Trophy in 1968 with a 37–22 win over number two Notre Dame). The New York Times called the FSU versus Miami game the "most highly anticipated regular season clash" since top-ranked Nebraska's 1971 Thanksgiving Day win over number two Oklahoma. The pregame hype for FSU–Miami reached all the way to Seattle because the Huskies would presumably jump over the game's loser in the national rankings.

Reporter Dan Raley asked sixteen people from the UW team who they thought would win the game. Eight players picked the Hurricanes. Seven took FSU. One person picked a tie—or at least hoped for a tie.

"I think a tie would be the best thing for both of them," James said.

A record crowd in Tallahassee didn't get a tie (FSU fans might have preferred that), but they did get a classic. The Seminoles led most of the day until Miami scored with three minutes left to grab a 17–16 lead. FSU drove into field-goal position, but kicker Gerry Thomas pushed his attempt wide right in the final seconds, and Miami hung on. Mindful of the fact that Miami would now be pitted against Washington in the polls, coach Dennis Erickson politicked for his Hurricanes: "We beat FSU here, and they beat Michigan at Michigan by 25. We deserve to be number one. I don't know about Washington, but I know we'd love to play them. We don't cancel people. They cancel us."

It was a sensational piece of verbiage from the man who, like Lambright and Gilbertson, had grown up in Snohomish County, north of Seattle, and had been a big influence on Gilbertson's offensive philosophy since Gilby had worked for him at Idaho. In one short quote, Erickson pointed out that UW's likely Rose Bowl opponent had been blown out on its home field by the same FSU team his players had just defeated on the road. His line about people canceling Miami was a not-so-thinly-veiled shot at Notre Dame, which had elected to end the series between the Irish and Miami. It wasn't quite "Dog the Rose Bowl," but it was pretty good.

Erickson's squad was free to cut whatever bowl deal it liked, and as the season wound down, there was some thought that the Notre Dame–Miami rivalry might be renewed in the Fiesta Bowl, which hoped to match the Irish against the winner of the Miami-FSU game. But Notre Dame fouled that plan up by losing to Tennessee and Penn State on back-to-back weekends. Miami was 9–0, with two winnable games left against Boston College and San Diego State. It looked like a sure bet to get to eleven wins, and with the Fiesta Bowl plan now kaput, it was open to other options. At least one man, the guy his fans lovingly came to call "the ol' ball coach," had an idea for Erickson to consider.

"We would love to play Miami," Steve Spurrier said of his Florida Gators as they closed in on the school's first-ever SEC championship. The SEC champ received an automatic invitation to the Sugar Bowl, so Spurrier was, in effect, challenging the Hurricanes to come to New Orleans.

The Gators and Hurricanes had played annually from 1944 to 1987, but Florida ended the series when the SEC went from six league games a year to seven. When Spurrier was hired as Florida's coach the day after UW demolished the Gators in the 1989 Freedom Bowl, he said he wanted to play Miami. That off-season, the SEC added another game to the schedule, so each school had to play eight league games. For budgetary reasons, the Gators wanted to play six home games a year, and due to other commitments, the only way they could schedule Miami and still get six home games was if the 'Canes agreed to play the game at Florida every year. That wasn't going to happen. So as quickly as the agreement was reached, Florida broke it and made the Gators another target for Erickson's "We don't cancel people" comment.

"We've been called chicken and everything else," Spurrier said, "and now here's an opportunity for Miami. We're going to get a chance to go to the Sugar Bowl. All they have to do is say, 'Hey, let's go play the Gators.'"

But there was another bowl in the equation. The Orange Bowl wanted its hometown club to play Big 8 champion Nebraska. Miami had defeated the Cornhuskers in the 1984 and 1989 Orange Bowls. Attendance and TV ratings for both games had been good, so why not do it a third time? In addition, from the Hurricanes' point of view, staying at home for a bowl game made sense for all the obvious reasons. That logic didn't sit well with the Huskies, who felt that Miami should have to play the toughest available team in a bowl game. Given that Florida was ranked fifth and Nebraska eleventh, the choice was clear to Cunningham, who was asked after the game about comments from various Miami players that UW wouldn't fare well against them.

"What do they know? They've never seen us play. I'll tell you one thing. We'd hit them harder than they've ever been hit, and I don't know if they could stand up to it. So if Miami wants to talk a little trash, fine, but I still think we're a better team. I know we could run the ball all day on them. They play hard and they've got a lot of speed, but I don't think they could hang with us physically." Cunningham was just getting warmed up and continued his soliloquy in quite personal terms as tape recorders whirred and writers scribbled frantically.

"If Miami does not go and play the highest-ranked opponent in another bowl, I don't respect them right off the bat. If they don't go play Florida, they're wimping out. I can't use bad words in the newspaper, but I don't think they have the testosterone level they need right now, and I think we all know where testosterone comes from. They're running and hiding in the Orange Bowl, and I think that's a joke."

Cunningham's anger was fueled partially by the vagaries involved with the polls system that had been on display in recent weeks. Florida

State and Miami had been ranked first and second all season. UW had moved into third place after the win over Kansas State. In both polls the Huskies gained ground on Miami throughout October. Voters in both polls ranked the top twenty-five teams. There were sixty voters in the AP poll and fifty-nine in the coaches' poll. The team they ranked first got twenty-five points. The second got twenty-four, and so on. By the end of the month, UW was only three points behind Miami in the AP poll and fifteen behind in the coaches' poll. Miami fans and players could be excused for wondering how the 'Canes could keep losing ground when all they were doing was winning games.

Then, in the first week of November, Washington defeated Arizona State while Miami enjoyed a week off. Imagine how Miami's players felt when after that weekend they found themselves tied with UW for second place in the AP poll. The coaches' poll still had UW nine points behind Miami and in third place.

On the same day Washington defeated USC, Miami knocked off West Virginia, 27–3. Those two results caused one voter in the AP poll to drop UW one spot in the voting, and the next week's poll showed FSU at number one, Miami at number two, and UW back at number three, now one point behind the Hurricanes.

The result of the vote allowed for the easier promotion of the FSU-Miami game as a "one versus two" matchup, and cynical Husky fans suggested that was the reason behind the changed vote. It probably wasn't, but the entire situation illustrated how voting to determine a champion made it possible that the entire process could turn into a beauty contest. UW had been named Miss Congeniality in 1984, and the 1991 Huskies were nervous after they watched their ranking bob from third to a second-place tie back to third in just over a week for no discernible reason.

When the next polls were released, the 'Canes and Dawgs were at the top, with Miami enjoying a wide lead in both. UW went from one point behind Miami to forty points behind in the AP poll and from nine points to thirty-three behind in the coaches' poll. Both teams had won, but one had lost ground. UW fans wanted to know how they could be one point behind Miami and then, after both teams had won, suddenly be forty points behind. As the Huskies rolled out of Corvallis for the five-hour bus ride home, players stewed about their collective fate. It seemed increasingly possible that they might finish the year unbeaten but ranked second.

"I hated it," Hobert said. "I hated that anyone voting in the polls thought that Miami was better than us." But many did, and at least one of those was close to home and about to put himself and his team right in the Husky crosshairs.

17

The Apple Cup

HOBERT AND OTHER PEOPLE WHO FAVORED A PURPLE AND GOLD hue didn't feel any better when they read a story by Dan Raley in the *Post-Intelligencer*. Raley had spoken to some of the voters in the AP poll, and their comments not only irked Husky fans, but they also confirmed a belief that the poll was biased against UW.

"I have Washington third," said *Knoxville News-Sentinel* columnist John Adams. Adams said he moved Miami to number one after they beat FSU. He dropped FSU to number two and kept UW third. Why? "From everything I've read about Washington, it seems like they're a good team. I just have a hard time believing they're as good as Miami or Florida State." "Read"? "Seems"? "Hard time believing"?

Bob Gillespie was a columnist for the *The State* in Columbia, South Carolina. "I couldn't tell you about a player on that [UW] team. I've heard of Emtman, but I couldn't tell you what he's done this season. I see three paragraphs and a box score on Sunday. That's about it."

The truth is that with a little effort, Adams, Gillespie, or any voter could have seen at least some video on the Huskies. But in 1991 there wasn't as much college football on TV as there is today, and West Coast games were often just shown on the West Coast. The UW game against Nebraska was the only one televised coast to coast. Miami, owing to an agreement it had with ESPN, had five national telecasts.

Some felt the coaches' poll had more credibility, but the fallacy in that thinking was that coaches spend Saturdays coaching and not watching other teams play. Furthermore, it had long been an open secret that many coaches didn't bother filling out their ballots, leaving that task to a graduate assistant or someone in the school's sports information department. That the system used to settle rankings in college football was ridiculous and riddled with problems was inarguable. But it was better than it used to be.

For many years, the final polls were taken *before* the bowl games. The AP decision to take the final vote after the bowls came in 1968. The coaches didn't make this change until 1974. Before that, it was possible for a team to be named national champion and then lose in a bowl game. That happened in 1964, when Alabama was named national champion, then lost to Texas in the Orange Bowl. Arkansas finished 11–0 and defeated Nebraska in the Cotton Bowl. But the Razorbacks finished second.

The Crimson Tide felt Arkansas's pain two years later when they were unbeaten and routed Nebraska, 34–7, in the Sugar Bowl but finished third in both polls behind Notre Dame and Michigan State (both of whom had finished 9–0–1, with the tie against each other). Neither played in a bowl because Michigan State had played in the Rose Bowl the year before, and Big 10 rules at the time forbid a team from going to Pasadena in consecutive years. Notre Dame refused to play in bowl games between 1925 and 1970 because the school considered them meaningless exhibition games since they happened after the final polls.

A similar fate befell UW's 1960 team. The Huskies were ranked sixth in the final polls but then defeated top-ranked Minnesota in the Rose Bowl. Nevertheless, Minnesota is listed as the AP and UPI national champ for 1960. Making matters even more chaotic was that in 1960 at least seventeen different athletic clubs, foundations, and media outlets chose national college football champions every season, and that is how the 1960 Washington team won a piece of the national title. The Helms Athletic Foundation was a Los Angeles–based organization founded by Paul Helms, who used proceeds from his bread bakery to finance the "foundation." His organization picked a national college football champion yearly from 1947 to 1982 and named UW the 1960 champs after the Rose Bowl win over Minnesota.

Even after the writers and coaches started waiting until after the bowls for their final votes, there were still five teams that finished unbeaten but did not get a share of the national title. It happened to Penn State three times and Arizona State twice.

Now, in 1991, UW fans watched helplessly as their unbeaten team was seemingly locked into second place in the polls (and with at least one voter who had them ranked third) and wondered if they could end up as the first team since the 1975 Sun Devils to go unbeaten and still finish second. James pointed out that since the Huskies had no say in how people voted in polls, he wanted them to focus instead on their final two opponents. But he was close enough to the prize that he allowed that he'd like to "give 12 and 0 a try" and that he'd like to be number one in "one poll or the other, just to make that claim."

The players had an eye on the polls too, but they also kept a firm eye on Washington State and the Apple Cup. It was the one game still left to win on the regular-season slate, and it had picked up extra heat when one particular coach revealed who he liked in the Washington/Miami debate. Mike Price was in his third year as the Cougars' head coach and was a media favorite because he was open, honest, and funny. On the Monday of Apple Cup week, he offered up a nugget that got everyone in the state talking. "I don't really care to share my thoughts," Price began on a conference call with Seattle reporters before doing just that. "But I voted for Miami for number one. Am I supposed to say that or not? I don't know." Price said the main reason he picked Miami was that he had gone to high school with Dennis Erickson, and the two remained close friends. "Any success he gets is great for him."

That Price had stuck with his friend was admirable, but announcing it was questionable and not well received at Husky Stadium. The top Cougar may as well have walked into a kennel wearing pants made of raw meat.

"People say we don't have East Coast respect, but we don't have West Coast respect, either, even in this state," Cunningham said. "I think you have to be objective when you vote, and I'm pretty sure he [Price] knows more about Washington than he does about Miami."

"I guess it's our job to go out and impress him this weekend," Hoffmann added.

"He'll get his opportunity to see what the Huskies are all about," said linebacker Brett Collins.

"I've never been around a team that takes comments like that as personally as we do," Cunningham said. "Our coaches know that. They're not dumb. They put 'em up in the locker room and let everyone know what's been said."

Gilbertson was bewildered by Price's comments. "I've known Mike since we were in high school. We were going to play hard anyway, because we knew we were close to the prize. As soon as he said it . . . now everyone is upset, and now we're really going to show them." Gilbertson was on his way to the field for warm-ups when he ran into Price. "Why would you say that?" he asked while shaking his head. Price just shrugged his shoulders.

The truth was that Price could have said he was voting for Miami, the University of Florida, or the Daytona College of Cosmetology. The Huskies knew that while they had moved from third to second in the polls, they had still lost ground to Miami, and they knew there was one way to regain that ground.

"Our feeling was that we had to score a lot of points to impress everyone," said Kennedy. "Washington State became a huge emphasis for us. We were talking about earning respect, and the only way to do that was to beat the snot out of somebody."

The Cougars did more good things than most teams against the Huskies. Running back Shaumbe Wright-Fair and receiver Phillip Bobo both had big days as did Drew Bledsoe, who threw for 295 yards, more than any other quarterback the Huskies had faced. "I remember you could hear his passes whistle," Cunningham said. "It was easy to see he was going to be great." The Cougars also had 430 total yards, more than any other team had all year against UW. They still lost by five touchdowns.

The Huskies were behind, 7–6, after one quarter (the first time they'd trailed after the first since the Nebraska game), and they responded with five consecutive scores. First, Hobert hit fullback Darius Turner for a touchdown. Three plays later Walter Bailey returned a Bledsoe interception for a touchdown. It was Bailey's sixth interception of the season and his second touchdown return.

After a three and out, Brunell entered the game and connected with Mario Bailey for another touchdown. The teams exchanged punts with John Werdel's boot pinning the Cougars inside their own five. The defensive coaches had again spent the week manufacturing tales of predicted doom for their players when it came to stopping Bledsoe. "Drew's a big boy," Lambright repeatedly told them. "I'm not sure we're going to blitz this week because I'm not sure you guys are big enough and strong enough to get him down."

After several days of that kind of talk, and with WSU in a vulnerable position on the field, the UW defense went into full Cougar hunting mode. "Hoffmann and I were both on the line," Fraley said, "and then at the snap, we backed off. We called that 'cat and mousing.' Bledsoe thought we were going to blitz, so he rolled to his right. But the blitz was actually coming from the outside, and he rolled right into Jaime Fields, who just unloaded on him." The resulting safety gave UW a 28–7 lead, and early in the third quarter, Beno Bryant rolled twenty-one yards for a score to cap the scoring blizzard and put the Cougars in a hopeless 35–7 hole. UW added three more scores and prevailed, 56–21.

During this game, Gilbertson's offense was a football version of a Swiss army knife. McKay caught a TD pass from Hobert, and Bailey caught two, one from Hobert and one from Brunell. Hobert also had the short TD pass to Turner. Beno Bryant and Jay Barry both scored on touchdown runs. The Apple Cup was the best example yet of how Gilbertson wanted his offense to function.

"We could go one back, one tight end, three wide receivers, or we could go one back, two tight ends, two wide receivers, or we could go two backs, one tight end, two wide receivers, or we could go one back, three tight ends, one receiver," Gilbertson said, rattling off formations like an auctioneer. "The message was always, 'If your personnel group is in the game, it better hum, buddy. You better make yards and be productive, or we'll go with another group.'"

The Apple Cup win concluded UW's first unbeaten regular season since 1915, when Gil Dobie's team went 7–0 in the middle of his remarkable 58–0–3 run over nine seasons as head coach. It featured another afternoon of devastation wrought by the defense. Bledsoe rolled up impressive yardage, but he was sacked seven times, part of UW's twelve tackles for loss. The Huskies also forced three turnovers and six three and outs.

"We were competing against Miami, and we knew they were unbeaten so we couldn't have a letdown," said Donald Jones. "We planned to physically beat WSU, and that is what we did."

"We want to play at a level so we can look back as alumni and say, 'Hey, that 1991 squad was the greatest team in Washington history,'" Kennedy told *Tacoma News-Tribune* columnist John McGrath. "That's what I want to be a part of. To be able to come back here and know that people would always respect what we have done."

Players celebrated the win later by watching Miami play at Boston College on ESPN. It happened to be the seventh anniversary of BC's miracle win in Miami in 1984 in the "Hail Flutie" game, when BC quarterback Doug Flutie threw a touchdown pass on the final play of the game to Gerard Phalen to lift the Eagles to a 47–45 win.

On this night, while Flutie watched from the press box, quarterback Glenn Foley's pass on the final play of the game bounced into the end zone, and Miami escaped with a 19–14 win. It was the coldest kickoff temperature of the season for Miami, and the Huskies snickered at how cold the Hurricanes looked in 50-degree weather. But the result left UW's players frustrated and unimpressed. Voters in both polls were also unimpressed with Miami's close call with a four-win team. Miami's lead in the AP poll was slashed in half, from forty to twenty points. The Hurricanes' lead in the coaches' poll shrank even more dramatically, dropping from thirty-three points to just three.

UW's season was over, but Miami still had one game left to play, and the Huskies spent their Thanksgiving weekend watching them defeat San Diego State, 39–12. The Hurricanes seemed intent on making a statement. *Orlando Sun-Sentinel* reporter George Diaz wrote the following about the game: "Using its first-string quarterback the entire game, going for a two-point conversion with a 25-point lead in the fourth quarter, and continuing to throw long and often, top-ranked Miami lashed back at its critics who whined about its lousy schedule and unimpressive victories."

On a night when his quarterback, Gino Torretta, set a school record for passing yards (485), Erickson said after the game that he kept calling pass plays because San Diego State kept blitzing. "If we wanted to run it up, we would have run it up," he remarked. Erickson and the rest of the Miami camp were a bit puzzled by what happened next. The Hurricanes had won a game by twenty-seven points and had lost more ground in both polls. Their lead over UW in the AP poll fell to fourteen points. Their lead in the coaches' poll dropped as well—to zero.

The coaches' poll had both Miami and UW with 1,443 points. But Miami still had three more first-place votes than UW (31–28), and the way the math of the poll worked, that meant some coaches were ranking Miami third or lower. In a season in which only two teams ended up 11–0, it seemed natural that they would be ranked one-two on most ballots. This was not the case here, and Miami's head coach knew why. Some of Erickson's colleagues didn't like his team's brash, in-your-face style of play (like going for two when you're up 25). But that some of them were showing their displeasure in their vote irritated him. "When you're on that panel, you can do anything you want. If there are coaches who don't like us, they can leave us out of the top twenty-five."

Erickson's center, Kelvin Harris, went further. In remarks that showed that UW wasn't the only team frustrated by a system that wouldn't allow the best two teams to play, Harris took a full roundhouse verbal blast at the Dawgs when he announced that his top five national rankings would leave UW fifth, behind Miami, Florida State, Florida, and Florida A&M. The Florida A&M Rattlers were a Division I-AA school, and while they had had some successful teams over the years, their 1991 team was 5–5.

"They'd have a hard time beating Florida A&M," Harris said about UW before going full Hobert. "If I had my druthers, instead of playing in the Orange Bowl, we'd line up with Washington and settle this once and for all. We'd play them in Seattle. It wouldn't make any difference." Hobert wanted to dog the Rose Bowl. Harris wanted to do the same thing to the Orange Bowl. If only there was a way.

Roy Speer thought there was, and he didn't think it was necessary for either team to back out of their bowl commitments. Speer was the chairman of the Home Shopping Network, the first-ever TV network dedicated to pitching products. With the explosive growth of cable and satellite delivery systems, combined with low overhead, Speer's idea was a money maker. Now, he had another one.

Working with a UCLA booster and former Bruins equipment manager named Angelo Mazzone and a pay-per-view-TV expert named Rich Kulis, Speer formed a company called the National College Football Champion Game Group and proposed that should Miami and Washington both win their bowl games, they would meet in a championship game to be played at a neutral site the weekend before the Super Bowl. The game would be available to fans via PPV-TV at somewhere between $35 and $40 per home.

Speer said that from the revenue he thought the game would generate, he could guarantee the NCAA $30 million. Miami and UW would get $4 million each, every Division I team would get $150,000, and the NCAA could keep the remaining $6 million.

The idea was intriguing, but the NCAA wasn't exactly ready to jump into a proposal that involved so much speculation; moreover, it couldn't. Its by-laws required a vote on a proposal of this nature, and the earliest that could happen would be at the annual meeting in 1992. Speer's proposal didn't stand a chance, but that didn't mean people weren't excited about it. Everyone wanted to see Miami and Washington play, and the fact that college football's clunky postseason system was preventing it made for compelling discussions. The Miami-UW debate was one of the first major national topics that benefitted twenty-four-hour sports talk radio stations.

A good talk radio topic has two good sides. It spurs debate, and it allows people to choose which side they're on. When the topic has no answer, it can have a good, long shelf life. The Miami-UW debate was all of those things. Sports radio stations in both Seattle and Miami ran computer simulation games, complete with announcers describing the action. In stunning news, Seattle station KJR had the Huskies winning,

19–17, while Miami station WQAM's simulation ended with Miami on top, 17–10.

Undoable proposals and computer simulations: that's what fans were left with as it became obvious to all that there was no way Miami and UW would ever meet on the field to settle things. Miami enjoyed a slim lead in the AP poll, the coaches' poll was tied, and each team had one more game left to impress the voters.

18

The Weak Link

ROSE BOWL PRACTICES DIDN'T BEGIN UNTIL MID-DECEMBER, SO the Huskies enjoyed a couple of weeks away from football while receiving daily affirmation that what they had just done was worth celebrating.

Steve Emtman and Mario Bailey were both named to the AP All-American team. It was the second time in school history that two players had received that honor. Kicker Chuck Nelson and linebacker Mark Stewart had been named to the 1982 team. Emtman also won the Outland Award, given to the best interior lineman in America; the Lombardi Award, given to the best overall lineman; and the Morris Trophy, given to the top defensive lineman in the Pac-10. He was also named to five other All-American teams and finished fourth in the Heisman Trophy voting, the best finish at the time for a defensive player in Heisman history. The Huskies had what many considered the best defense in America in 1991, and it all started with a farm kid from a dot in the road in eastern Washington.

"A lot of people recruiting him [Emtman] questioned whether he could play defense," Gary Pinkel said. "He was being looked at as an offensive lineman. He was a dominating player, and as I got to know him, I knew we had something really special." Pinkel was driving Emtman to the Seattle airport after his recruiting visit when the Cheney High School senior asked him a question: "How does this commitment thing work? What do I do?" Pinkel's heart rate quickened as he realized he was close to landing a very big fish.

"Steve, you just pick up the phone and call me. I don't care if it's three in the morning. When you're ready to commit to UW, you just call."

Emtman assured him he would. Several hours later, at exactly three in the morning, Pinkel was startled out of a deep sleep by the telephone ringing. "I thought for sure someone was in trouble," he said. He picked up the phone and mumbled a groggy "hello."

"Hi, Coach; it's Steve."

Pinkel's mind was awash in middle-of-the-night fog. Finally, the voice said, "Steve! Steve Emtman. You said I could call you at 3:00, and that's what I decided to do." Pinkel had forgotten he had told Emtman that he could call anytime, and now he smiled as it all came back to him. "Steve, I think you've made the right choice, and we can't wait to get you in here."

Pinkel and Emtman made a little small talk before the coach and his new recruit agreed on what should happen next. "Coach James is asleep," Pinkel said. "I think we should wait until the morning to give him the news." Pinkel hung up and sat in bed, now wide awake. He'd likely never get a better piece of news at 3:00 a.m.

"You've got to have a bell cow if you're going to be good on defense," said Baird. "Steve was dominant. He refused to be blocked by one guy. His attitude was that if you're using one guy on me, you're insulting me. He was the force and that's who we built the defense around."

Emtman had sixty tackles on the year, 19.5 for losses (including 6.5 sacks). The totals would have been higher if it weren't for the fact that he had sat out the entire second half of five of the team's games. Playing time was a season-long issue for the defense for three reasons. First, the Huskies had tremendous depth, and the coaches wanted to reward second-team players good enough to start for other teams with time on the field. Second, Lambright's intense and aggressive style demanded fresh players, so the coach insisted on a liberal substitution philosophy.

"We understood that the twos needed to get their reps," Hoffmann said, "but playing was our pay. Most of the time we were forcing three and outs, so how many plays were we getting in a game? I needed more. I wanted more."

"Our attitude was, 'Let us get our candy.'" Fraley said. "At times, there was anger involved. But you never knew when your number was going to be called, and that helped keep the sense of competition [among teammates] healthy."

James Clifford saw the discussion from both sides. He had been a starter and led the conference in tackles in 1989. After his knee injury in 1990, he found himself backing up Hoffmann. He knew how the starters felt when they came out but also saw that the rotation of players on defense allowed the Huskies to play their high-energy style with no worries about fatigue.

The third reason so many guys played (on both sides of the ball) was that James steadfastly refused to run up the score. Of all the things James accomplished during his career, near the top of the list of what made him proud was the fact that he never scored 60 points against an opponent. He had a sense of what was fair, what was right, and when his point had been proven. "As a young player, I remember being frustrated by it," Hobert said, "but I understand it better now." The 58 points the 1991 team scored at OSU was the high-water mark for James's teams in games he coached.

There's little doubt the Huskies could have named their score and impressed voters in the polls with more touchdowns in at least half their games. But during the third quarter or sometimes even at halftime Gilbertson and Lambright would get the message from the sidelines: "That's enough," James would say. He expected everyone to keep playing and coaching hard, but he wanted the offense's flair and the defense's attack dialed down.

Similar to Emtman, UW's other All-American took a good season in 1990 and found a way to build on that success in a remarkable, record-breaking 1991. Bailey's seventeen touchdown catches were not only the most in UW history, but they were also the most ever in the Pac-10. He set career records for UW for yards receiving and TDs. His emergence as a star receiver dramatically impacted Hobert, who began the year as the only quarterback on a top-fifteen team who had never started a game. For the season, Bailey was on the receiving end for 32 percent of Hobert's completions, 40 percent of his yards, and 64 percent of his touchdowns.

"He became a nice security blanket for Billy Joe," said McKay. "[Hobert] knew he could throw to Mario even if he was double covered. He [Bailey] was good in his junior year, but the improvement to his senior year was a big reason we did what we did." McKay said Bailey had something in common with his fellow All-American: "He was never shy about letting you know when you weren't playing up to his standards. He was a leader."

Bailey, Cunningham, and Kennedy were named to the All-Pac-10 team on offense. Kennedy also gave the Huskies a clean sweep in the Morris Trophy award by claiming the offensive player trophy. Emtman, Hoffmann, Fraley, Jones, and Hall were all named to the defensive All-Pac-10 team. Larry Slade was happy for all the players who were honored but thought the selection committee had missed one obvious choice: "Our philosophy was we would blitz you anytime, anywhere. That's who we were, and because of the nature of our defense, on that team our MVP was Shane Pahukoa."

Pahukoa was the team's free safety. Due to the number of blitzes UW used and the number of players who were involved in those blitzes, he was often their last line of defense. "He stopped a lot of big plays," Slade said. Pahukoa was also one of the hardest hitting players on a team that craved physical contact.

"That's how we were wired," said Hoffmann. "Our guys were starving to get to the ball, and when we got there, we were going to unload. Guys did not want to be hit by us." Slade agreed that he could sense that feeling from opponents. "There were people who were fearful of us. They knew our guys could hit, and they didn't want to get hurt."

"We had some crazy people on that team," Walter Bailey said. "When we went onto the field, it was a straight party out there. We were going to hit someone in the mouth and have a great time."

Hobert didn't receive any postseason honors but did set the school record for touchdown passes with twenty-two. He had started 1991 in the spring as an unproven talent whose teammates loved him but at the same time wondered about his youth and inconsistencies. After the Brunell injury, he emerged as a leader who always found a way to win. "We didn't realize how good Billy Joe was," said Donald Jones. "He was one of those cats who, when the lights come on, he becomes something special."

"Billy had so much confidence," said McKay. "He liked to spread the ball around, and I was a big beneficiary of it. It was easy to rally behind him. A guy who is confident like that . . . it's easy to follow his lead."

Kennedy thought Hobert's stepping into the number one role also added layers to the Huskies' already versatile offense. "We were a one-back team, but we could run power football with two backs, and with Billy, we could also spread you out, and that added more diversity to our play calling; it opened up a whole world of possibilities."

Yet Hobert faced critics and critiques all season long. In a game broadcast in November, ABC's Bob Griese said that he thought Hobert was the "weak link" of the Huskies' team. Cunningham took that as an insult. "The media's been giving Billy a lot of flak," he said, "and I'm pleased Coach James has been sticking up for him. First of all, he's a sophomore. And second of all, he had barely any game experience coming into this year. Bob Griese can stick his comments as far as I'm concerned. We're the best team in America."

Hobert, for his part, was not offended. He put a positive spin on it: "Griese is a quarterback. He understands. It's no big deal. If I'm our worst link, then I think UW is gonna be all right."

One of Hobert's friends thought the comment was so funny that he had "Weak Link" bumper stickers made. Soon, many of Hobert's teammates, as well as the man who had inspired the comment, had the sticker on their cars, lockers, notebooks, and any other place a sticker could be stuck.

Sports radio stations weren't the only ones cashing in on the "Who is better, Miami or Washington?" debate. The *Tacoma News Tribune* and the *Miami Herald* worked together to poll the sixty voters in the AP poll. Thirty of the thirty-seven voters who had Miami ranked first said they would consider changing their vote if UW won the Rose Bowl—no matter what Miami did in the Orange Bowl. Fourteen of the twenty-three voters who picked UW as number one said they were firm as long as the Huskies sealed the deal in Pasadena. The story also reiterated a geographic fact of life and an ongoing concern to UW fans. Of the sixty voters, only fifteen worked west of the Rocky Mountains.

James went to Pasadena in early December for a press conference about the game. He told reporters he wasn't obsessed with winning a national title but he did crack open the curtain about what it would mean to him. "I don't judge myself or my success on whether or not I win a national championship," he stated. "But I go to meetings and see Johnny Majors with his championship ring. [Majors coached Pittsburgh to the title in 1976.] It would be fun to have one."

Lambright was asked about his boss's statement and was more forthcoming: "He wants this bad. He's very quiet about long-term goals. But there's no question that as our success mounted this season and his intensity's grown, he's made number one the primary goal." James wasn't alone. The players and coaches who joined him on the team plane bound for Pasadena all had the same thought.

"We all knew what was out there," said Gilbertson. "When you're getting the amount of attention we were getting, you know you're doing something special. Coach used to say anytime you win, there are more chips on the table. And the next game is bigger. And then the next game gets even bigger. When you've gone undefeated, you know where you're at."

Where the Huskies were at now was one win from history.

19

We Fear No Man

A FEW DAYS BEFORE THE ROSE BOWL, WOODRUFF WALKED INTO A meeting room with Washington's punt team to explain how they were going to defend against Michigan star Desmond Howard. Howard had set or equaled five NCAA records and owned another twelve Michigan school records. His senior season he had sixty-one catches for 950 yards and twelve touchdowns, scored two more touchdowns on reverses and another on a kick return.

Howard ended his career in Ann Arbor with a spectacular ninety-three-yard punt return for a touchdown against Ohio State. As well over 100,000 Michigan fans roared their approval, Howard became the first player ever to strike what became known as the "Heisman pose," lifting his left leg up and thrusting his left arm out to mimic the bronzed football player atop college football's top individual trophy as he stood in the end zone.

Three weeks later Howard won the Heisman Trophy, and Michigan fans still hadn't stopped cheering. Howard had a big smile, and the Heisman pose showed he had a propensity to attract the spotlight. Seven of Michigan's games had been on ABC, and two more had been televised on ESPN, so naturally ESPN focused much of its attention on him leading up to the Rose Bowl. To UW players it felt like every time they turned on the TV, there was another feature on Howard. "I was jealous, envious, and pissed about all the credit the media was giving to Michigan talking about all their great players and what they had done," Hobert said.

Howard also had the full attention of the UW coaches. After much consideration they had decided that the prudent thing to do with Howard on punts was to avoid him. If that meant kicking out of bounds, so be it; better to sacrifice a little field position on a punt than to watch Howard burn them like he had burned the Buckeyes. Woodruff's explanation of the proposed strategy was rejected by the punt coverage team.

"Bullshit!" came a voice from one of the players. It was immediately echoed by others. "We want to kick to him! Kick to him!" Before long, the entire room was buzzing with voices of young men who defied the notion of avoiding Howard. The coaches exchanged wide-eyed looks and realized that not kicking to Howard went against the grain of the team's personality. "We had a lot of those guys," Gilbertson said. "Cocky, championship guys. They weren't afraid of a challenge. That's who we were."

But the coaches wanted the defense to understand how dangerous Howard was, so they put together a video of his season highlights. Lambright told them, "All of you need to see this so you'll know what we're facing and in particular what our defensive backs are facing."

Lambright pushed "play," and here was Howard scoring on a touchdown run and catching a touchdown pass against Notre Dame. Players watched as he scored three times against Boston College and three more times against Indiana. He caught a touchdown pass in every Michigan game in 1991, and the tape ended with his romp through Ohio State's punt coverage team, which everyone in purple had seen several times by now.

"Everyone in the room is going 'ooh' and 'ahh,' and they're all talking about Desmond and all these plays," Slade said. The lights in the room came back on, and the players then all heard the voice of Dana Hall, who spoke directly to Lambright. "Coach," Hall said. "We fear no man."

Slade almost burst with pride. Hall and his fellow defensive backs had adopted that phrase after the Huskies had gone to the aggressive style in 1989. Their style—"We will blitz you anytime from anywhere on the field"—meant that anyone playing in Slade's secondary was going to be occasionally left on an island in one-on-one coverage. In those instances, the receiver has the distinct advantage of knowing where he is going. The defender must be quick, talented, and perhaps most of all, fearless.

"We. Fear. No. Man," Hall repeated.

It was more than just a slogan to Hall. By now, it had become the way he and the defense did business. And business was very much on his mind when he sat down to speak with Keith Jackson. TV broadcasters meet with players and coaches before game broadcasts for informal interviews that aren't recorded. Broadcasters use them to get a feel for what a player or a coach is thinking. Jackson sat at a table with Hall, Walter Bailey, Shane Pahukoa, and Tommie Smith, the starters in the UW secondary and the men tasked with keeping an eye on Howard. "How are you guys going to cover him?" Jackson asked in his pleasant Georgia drawl.

Hall looked at his teammates and then looked back at Jackson. "Desmond Howard should be worried about how he's going to get open," he replied. "It's not our concern about whether we can cover him because we've got the skills to get that done. And we don't have to cover him very long because our front guys are going to get after their quarterback. Nothing against the competition he's faced all year, but we think we're pretty good, and we think we can handle him."

Hall and the rest of his teammates respected Howard's talent, which was real and obvious. But, like Hobert, they had grown weary of all the media attention he received. Given that Bailey had more catches for more yards and more touchdowns than Howard, they thought their own teammate was his equal in terms of talent and was being overlooked.

Howard fueled those feelings when he was asked about Bailey in an interview. His answer caused UW ears to prick up, as though someone had offered a pack of hungry Huskies a crate of Milk Bones. "I'm not familiar with Bailey," Howard said. "Does he return punts and kickoffs?" Told that he didn't, Howard replied, "Oh. I'm not familiar with him."

Howard also said that he thought Miami should be ranked number one ahead of UW because the Hurricanes had beaten FSU, and "playing a formidable opponent like that deserves a higher ranking." The Huskies were amazed at Howard's attitude, and Donald Jones thought it was going to backfire on the Wolverines. "Desmond was arrogant,"

Jones remarked. "He was the Heisman Trophy winner and he was the darling of the country, but I knew he was in trouble. All our guys wanted a piece of him. They were after him, and I don't think he knew who he was messing with."

Among the things Howard was messing with was a defense that was getting a daily dose of intensity from Lambright. "We are not going to let you guys fail," he told his players in a rising voice. "We did not come all this way undefeated to let this game stop us. You're not going to screw this up, fellas. Does anyone want to challenge me on that point?" That question was always answered with silence.

But Hobert had an answer for Howard's line about Bailey's not being a return man: "The only reason he didn't return punts and kicks is that we had so much depth and talent, we didn't need him to. If Mario had been a return guy, Howard would have finished second in the Heisman voting."

It's an interesting point to ponder. Among those who thought about it, years after the fact, was the man who had decided Bailey's role in the first place: Don James. "Don said the one mistake he made coaching that team was that he should have used Mario on kick and punt returns," Carol James said. "He rarely second-guessed himself, but he did about that. He felt Mario probably could have won the Heisman Trophy if he had let him return kicks."

Fearful of injury, James kept Bailey off special teams, so it was a moot point to everyone, including Bailey, who had no quarrel with Heisman voters. "In my honest opinion, Howard deserved the Heisman. He was on special teams, returning punts and kickoffs. He deserved it." But Howard's comments about not being familiar with Bailey bugged the Seattle native. "I had watched him all season. and I loved him," Bailey said. "I was looking forward to meeting him. But we were at several events together, and he was over-the-top arrogant and cocky, and he blew me off. I took it personally. You've got to respect your opponent, and it felt like he didn't have respect for any of us."

A lot of the events Bailey spoke of were open to the media. Reporters surrounded Howard, but Bailey usually sat by himself. "That's okay," he said to *Tacoma News Tribune* reporter Don Borst. "I'm used to it. It's just another perfect page in the story. I promise you it will change January 1."

Hobert's personality was on full display at every Rose Bowl event. At Disneyland he said Goofy was his favorite Disney character. "I'm more like him than anyone else." He admitted that too often he played the game with his mouth. "Ever since I was a little kid, I've had too big a mouth for my actions and said some asinine things. I just keep talking and eventually something comes out that I know I should take back." Told that some of his comments about being tired of all the media attention given to Howard and Michigan had made it onto the Wolverines' locker room bulletin board, he said, "That doesn't bother me. They can't hit me in the locker room."

Hobert said he wanted to atone for a subpar performance as a backup in the 1991 Rose Bowl, where his only pass attempt was intercepted. "Playing in the Rose Bowl and throwing an interception showed the world what a slouch Hobert was, so I've got to prove otherwise." Asked if he got along with center Ed Cunningham, he said, "I've got to touch his butt every day. So we better get along." He started one session with reporters by saying, "I should probably just apologize now for whatever it is I'm going to say."

Three days before the game, at the urging of James, Hobert announced he was done talking. "This is my last interview. It's more of a safety factor. I don't want to be assassinated before the game." Reporters from Washington smiled knowingly, and reporters from around the country ate it up. His media obligations over, Hobert had one more person he wanted to talk to. On his own, he sought out the president of the Rose Bowl committee and apologized for the "dog the Rose Bowl" comment.

The Huskies may have grown weary of all the attention the Wolverines were getting, but they were everything a Big 10 champion should be. They were big and strong, talented, and smart. They had blown through their conference with eight wins in eight games by an average of 28 points per game. Only Indiana (who inexplicably through history has almost always played Michigan tough) came within a touchdown of the Wolverines.

"They were a marquee opponent," Gilbertson said. "Howard was only one of their great players. They had that great Michigan defense that people thought was almost as good as ours. [In their final five games the

Wolverines' defense had given up just 23 total points.] Every kid in our program knew who Michigan was."

Gilbertson's assertion was correct, due at least partially to a quirky fact that benefitted the Huskies. Michigan football had become a regular part of UW's Saturday pregame routine thanks to the fact that the teams played in different time zones. The Wolverines' victory over Notre Dame came during a bye week for UW, and on five other occasions while Washington was preparing for an afternoon kickoff on the West Coast, Michigan was kicking off on ABC or ESPN at noon EST.

"We'd finish breakfast and then watch them on TV before we went to the stadium," Bailey said. Every week they listened to announcers fawn over the Wolverines, and the memory of those games served to gin up the team even more. Oddsmakers established UW as a touchdown favorite, and most of the Huskies' players, given the chance, would have gleefully laid the points. Publicly, they only wondered why everyone ignored them to talk about Michigan. Privately, it was a different story.

"It was not a matter of whether we were going to win; it was a matter of by how much," said Hobert.

"The way we practiced, and particularly the way our defense practiced, it was going to be a long day for Michigan and a long day for Howard," said Bailey, who spent two weeks in practice pretending he was Howard to help the defense prepare. When Bailey wasn't impersonating Howard, he was just being himself. And according to McKay, that was more than enough to frustrate his teammates in the UW secondary. "Mario was trash-talking all the guys. He just started calling people out. He'd yell out the name of the guy he wanted to go against. He was over the top, and it was awesome to watch. I knew I could never be like that, but I enjoyed watching it happen."

"I'm so good, I'll tell you the damn route I'm running, and you still won't be able to cover me," Bailey said. "I'm going to run a fade."

"I think that [comment] was against Dana," McKay said. "And he [Bailey] ran the fade and caught it for a touchdown. He was telling them what he was going to do. The supreme confidence of Mario Bailey. He calls out the route he's going to run, and you still can't stop him."

The confidence about UW's chances permeated pregame media coverage. Much of the coverage ignored Michigan as writers, broadcasters, and analysts debated the Miami versus Washington question. Who would win between college football's best two teams?

All that Miami talk was being used by Michigan the same way the Huskies were using all the Howard hype. Michigan quarterback Elvis Grbac wondered aloud if it might be better for UW to just go play Miami. "They don't seem to have as much interest in playing us," he said. "We'll see."

Besides Howard, the UW coaches, coming into the game, were concerned about two potential problems. First, Emtman had a severe case of the flu. Southern California health officials said the flu outbreak in their region was the worst they had seen in a decade, and they used the word "epidemic" to describe it. Emtman made two trips to the hospital for IVs and antibiotics.

"I was his roommate that week," Cunningham said. "He was sick. He couldn't get out of bed." Emtman's sickness was exacerbated by dehydration because he didn't like the way the water tasted at the team hotel. When UW team doctor Steve Bramwell heard that, he went to a convenience store and bought as much water as the store had. Flu be damned; everyone thought Emtman would play in the game.

"He could not practice all week, get out of bed, and play," James said. "I'm not worried about him." But James was worried about another problem: the inconsistencies of kicker Travis Hanson, which had been a pebble in his shoe all season. Hanson had missed four extra points and seven of his fifteen field goal attempts during the year. The Huskies hadn't needed him to win any of their games. Yet. Now, in California, things went from bad to worse as Hanson forgot how to kick.

Dick Baird, the assistant in charge of kicking, was feeling the pressure as the game drew near. "All kicking is about keeping the mental side of the equation clean," Baird said. "Kickers can do it in their sleep. It's all about getting the kinesthetic feel. But that week, Travis went into a deep, mental funk. He couldn't make an extra point in practice, let alone a field goal."

Finally, Baird and the rest of the coaches gathered to discuss the situation. "Don was very concerned," Baird said. "Here we've got the biggest game of our lives, and we've got a kicker who can't make a kick."

"What are we going to do with this kid?" James asked in a flat, matter-of-fact tone. Everyone in the room looked at Baird, who was searching for the right answer. After a period of silence, he responded with the best he had: "I have an idea. Let's try to get him to relax a little bit." James looked at Baird in cool exasperation while everyone else in the room did their best to stifle a laugh.

"Well, gee," James replied sarcastically. "He needs to relax? Thanks, Dick. That's a really good idea." The coaches all thought Baird should work on visualization techniques with the kicker, and that's what he did. "Just put yourself into a trance," Baird suggested. He had no idea if his advice was going to work, and his biggest hope was that the Huskies would play so well that they wouldn't need Hanson to make any clutch kicks.

Baird wasn't the only coach who attracted unwanted attention before the game. Gilbertson found himself in hot water when the boss became suspicious about the size of his offensive line. "Don was adamant about guys weighing in each day," Gilbertson said. "He wanted to know that kids were staying in shape. We'd been there a week, and our kids were going out to nice dinners. They had gone to the Beef Bowl at Lawry's [the Los Angeles steak house hosted a yearly steak-eating contest between the Rose Bowl teams]; they had gone to Disneyland and Knott's Berry Farm. They were having huge breakfasts every morning. As college kids will do when there's food around, they were eating."

James was looking at the list of player weights one day when something struck him as odd. "Wait a second; something is wrong here," he said to Gilbertson. "How come every one of our offensive linemen weighs 320 pounds?" Gilbertson, who, like his linemen, was not shy about food consumption, told James that the scale being used to weigh the players only went to 320 pounds.

"I knew as soon as I said it; I knew they were in trouble, and I knew I was in trouble too," Gilbertson said with a laugh. James told Gilbertson they were going to do something else so they could get accurate weights. "Don arranged to take all the linemen to a meatpacking place down the street from where we were practicing, and each guy gets on this huge industrial scale and they're all overweight."

After the weigh-in, James informed Gilby that he would be leading his hefty crew on daily jogs to trim some weight off the players before the game. "I wasn't crazy about doing it," Gilbertson said. "But we did it, and we got some weight off them."

Gilbertson might have needed an extra lap one day after he decided to buy his offensive staff a treat. The players had been excused for the day, and James was locked in a room with the defensive coaches where, according to Hart, no mirth was present. In another room, Gilbertson ordered up a pitcher of margaritas. The men in charge of the Huskies offense enjoyed a quick drink before getting back to figuring out ways to beat the Wolverines.

"We were watching how they defended short-yardage, and their defensive backs were just smoking," Gilbertson said. "They were so quick to the line." Gilbertson then noticed that when teams ran pitch plays against Michigan in those situations, the Wolverines had a habit of ignoring the tight end while they attacked the pitch. He had a simple idea. "Guys, if we fake the pitch and [tight end] Aaron Pierce goes for the reach block, he's going to be in a seam, and there's going to be nobody there." A reach block is used by offensive linemen on runs to the outside. Defenders who see a lineman executing it would assume that the play call is an outside run.

"I'm telling you; fake pitch, Pierce releases, and he'll be wide open," Gilby enthused. They drew a few ideas out on paper and came up with a plan to burn Michigan's speed if they had the Wolverines in a short-yardage situation. That the play wasn't named "the margarita special" must be chalked up as one of life's missed opportunities.

Finally, New Year's Eve arrived, and the Huskies had their final practice. For the seniors, it was their last practice as UW players. The group had arrived at UW, some in 1987 and some in 1988, when James and the program were at a low point. They didn't go to a bowl in 1988, and some in the media said James was overrated and washed up. That was the year all the coaches received "No Bowl" watches as Christmas gifts from James. They had grown together with their coach through the tough times of 1988 and 1989. They had learned a crazy and fun new offense and an intense and fun new defense. They had authored one of the greatest wins in Husky history over USC in 1990 before suffering a crushing defeat weeks later to UCLA that cost them a shot at a national title. They had then redoubled their effort to reach perfection and had delivered one of the greatest seasons in Husky history with but one game to win to give them at least a piece of the national championship.

They were a free-spirited bunch, and James had given them more leeway than he had previous teams. They responded by not taking advantage of their coach and by policing themselves and taking care of any problems that came up in the locker room. At the end of their final practice, which fell on James's fifty-ninth birthday, he wanted to do something special for the group of seniors who had lifted his program back to where it had once been and were potentially taking it to a height never before reached.

"All the underclassmen lined up in two parallel lines to form a tunnel," Rondeau said. "Each senior player then ran through the line. Guys were slapping on their shoulder pads, pushing them a bit, hitting them on their helmets. Don was standing at the end of it." They came through the line at intervals long enough to give James a minute with every player. "He was greeting each guy, shaking hands with them," Rondeau continued. "He was so relaxed and loose and happy, and he looked like the proudest dad you could imagine. He was loving up on these guys and enjoying the moment. I think his attitude reflected his feelings about the game and the team. It was as animated as I ever saw him in a practice situation. . . . I knew then they were in pretty good shape."

20

The Purple-Shirt Hurt

NEW YEAR'S DAY 1992 DAWNED SUNNY AND COOL IN SOUTHERN California. Bleary-eyed Huskies fans awoke and began clearing the detritus of New Year's Eve revelry from their brains with coffee and maybe something stronger. And they smiled at the familiarity of it all.

This was the fifth time since 1978 the Dawgs and their fans were going to spend the first day of the new year playing in the Rose Bowl, the aptly nicknamed "granddaddy of them all." The moniker (given to the game by ABC's Jackson) served as a reminder that no matter how many bowl games there were, the Rose Bowl had been the first, it paid teams more than any other bowl, and it was considered the most prestigious.

Ed Cunningham boarded one of the two buses that would ferry the Huskies to the stadium and took a seat next to Beno Bryant, directly behind Don and Carol James. They rolled up the highway toward the stadium, where they were all going to play the biggest game of their lives and talked about various things.

"We talked about school and our plans for the break after the game and what we had done with our free time the past two weeks," Cunningham said. "It felt like Don and Carol and Beno and I were a family going to Pasadena for the day. It was a fun, relaxing ride." That mood belied a team that after almost two weeks in Anaheim was past ready to play a football game according to Carol James. "You could see, as the game drew closer, how focused they were," she said. "They had had their fun. They were ready to start hitting. They weren't going to lose. I'd never quite seen a team so intense."

When the Huskies arrived in Pasadena, thousands of Washington fans lined the narrow street used to get to the stadium. They cheered, woofed, and slapped the sides of the buses as the drivers carefully steered through the crowd. The players had experienced the same thing the previous year when they had defeated Iowa, but McKay echoed the thoughts of everyone: "The national title was on the line. The Heisman Trophy winner was in the game. The Michigan game felt a lot bigger than the Iowa game did."

Hobert was anxious to get into the stadium. Like many great competitors, he used anger as his primary emotion to get ready to play, and he had manufactured plenty of it during the past few days. "I believe the game should be played mad, with a big chip on your shoulder. Going back to middle school, and high school, I always played pissed off. Before a game, I was always hard to get along with and hard to please."

Hobert was angry at Howard for his dis of Bailey, at the media for showering too much attention on Michigan, and at the poll voters for even debating who was better between Miami and Washington. By game day he might have found a reason to be mad at the hotel ice machine.

"A little sprinkling of frost over the San Gabriels, which loom behind the ol' Rose Bowl," Jackson said as he welcomed the TV audience to the game while viewers saw a gorgeous shot of the mountains behind the grand stadium.

One area where the Huskies were expected to have an advantage over the Wolverines was in overall team speed. The Huskies were fast, and they showed off that speed right away when freshman Napoleon Kaufman raced through Michigan defenders on the opening kickoff return before being tackled at midfield. The Huskies exploded on the sideline, pogoing up and down, screaming, and high-fiving each other.

"Napoleon's return set the tone," Mario Bailey said. "We were coming for Michigan. We were going to kill them."

But the Huskies looked nervous on their first possession and after three plays were forced to punt. The snap bounced on the ground at punter John Werdel's feet, and Husky fans' hearts paused before he expertly fielded the ball and got the kick away. The Wolverines quickly ran the ball twice for six yards a pop and a first down.

Maybe they were mad, like Hobert. Maybe they were tired of hearing that UW was a touchdown favorite. Maybe they were tired of hearing all this talk about the Huskies playing for a share of the national title. Maybe they were mad that everyone seemed to focus on what would happen if unbeaten UW and Miami played. Mighty Michigan was the Big 10 champion after all, and the maize and blue weren't about to be anyone's pushover. Then they tried their first pass play.

Elvis Grbac was big, smart, and accurate. He'd led America in passing efficiency and had completed 65 percent of his passes for almost 2,000 yards and 24 touchdowns. With him at quarterback and the speedy Howard on the wing, the Wolverines were confident they could move the ball through the air against UW. Before the play, while introducing the UW defense, Jackson referred on the broadcast to Emtman as the "big wrecker inside." Emtman lived up to that billing as Grbac took the snap and quickly retreated five steps to set up to pass.

At almost the same rate of speed, Emtman pushed Michigan guard Joe Cocozzo straight backward. Cocozzo would become an All-American in 1992 and then play five years in the NFL. But against "the big wrecker" he shuffled his feet like a cartoon character trying to keep his balance.

Fullback Burnie Legette's arrival to set up a double team was akin to throwing a tissue into the wind as he found himself instantly back-pedaling alongside his guard under the behemoth's relentless advance. Promptly, all three players crashed into Grbac. Emtman reached over the two men trying to block him and smacked the ball out of the quarterback's hand. Michigan recovered the fumble, but Emtman's arrival as a dominant factor in the game had been announced and noticed, just like the start of the Arizona game. He seemed personally offended that the Wolverines had bothered to show up.

"I don't know what film they watched, but that move Steve made, he'd made it all season," said Fraley. "He would get underneath the guard and drive him back. Then, the poor little fullback; once all that weight was moving, you weren't stopping Steve."

"It was funny watching Michigan after that play," Bailey laughed. "Looking in their eyes it was like, 'Oh, my God! This is worse than I thought.' Watching Steve on tape was bad enough. Seeing him in real life . . . he was a monster. You should have seen the look in their eyes."

"That play was a signal to Michigan," Rondeau said. "This is the kind of day you're going to have. It's not going to get better."

The Wolverines ran the ball for no gain on second down, and then Grbac retreated to the shotgun formation in an attempt to buy some time for a third down pass. But shortly after the ball arrived, so did Jones, who had zoomed around the right tackle and quickly deposited Grbac to the turf. "Watching them try to deal with Jones," Hoffmann said with a laugh and a shake of his head, "was funny."

"That was our most focused game," Jones said. "I played my best two games in the Rose Bowls against Iowa and Michigan. It was the only time my family came to watch me play, and I had to make sure they were proud." The rattled Wolverines went to the sidelines and found themselves thinking the same thing every Washington opponent had thought that year: "They're bigger, faster, and stronger than we thought. How are we going to stop them?"

The Dawgs moved the ball deep into Michigan territory, but Hobert's second pass of the game was thrown directly to Michigan safety Otis Williams, who returned the interception to midfield. "I was so pissed," Hobert said. "And I remember thinking as I came off the field, 'The little guy is going to kill me.'" "Little guy" was Hobert's nickname for Gilbertson and his assessment was correct. "He lit me up, but I had so much respect for him, it didn't matter because I agreed with him. I was the only guy in the stadium madder than he was. It was a dumb pass to throw."

The Wolverines had tricked Hobert. They had shown a formation that left the middle of the field wide open. But they had jammed Aaron Pierce at the line of scrimmage and forced him to run his route into an area where Williams suddenly appeared. Hobert has seen the play a few times over the years, and it always ends the same way: he watches himself throw the interception, and then he throws his remote at the TV.

"Their defense was a lot like ours," Gilbertson said. "There was nothing easy." Gilbertson knew Michigan would overplay Bailey, and he had designed a lot of plays to the tight ends to take advantage of it. But the first one hadn't worked. It was the twenty-first turnover of the year for UW. But in yet another example of their defensive dominance opponents managed only two scores and ten points on those miscues. That total wasn't going to grow today. The defense continued to relentlessly pressure Grbac, and the Wolverines ran three plays and punted.

The first quarter continued in this fashion; similar to the Nebraska and Cal games, UW's offense kept stopping itself with dropped passes, penalties, and poor decisions. But the defense rose to the challenge of stopping whatever Michigan threw at them. In practice and meetings, Lambright had emphasized Michigan's history of not making changes to terminology or formations for bowl games.

"Michigan doesn't respect you," he bellowed at his team. "They think they're going to be able to line up and run over you like they've done everyone else. They won't change anything they're doing." The players wondered how that could possibly be true. Teams almost always do a few new things in bowl games. But Lambright was correct about Michigan.

"They weren't changing anything," Fraley said. "We watched so much film, and we knew their playbook and tendencies. We were calling out plays they were going to run, we'd yell at each other, and they wouldn't check out of it. We knew what was coming, and we attacked."

"These guys don't have a chance," Clifford told his teammates. "You can tell by the look in Grbac's eyes. He has no idea what's happening. They don't have an answer for Emtman; they don't have an answer for anything we're doing. It's not going to get better, and I think Grbac knows it."

Michigan was overmatched, undermanned, and confused. Finally, on its fourth possession of the game, Michigan tried to get Howard involved, Grbac targeting him with a deep pass on first down. "Howard ran a post corner post and lost me," Walter Bailey said. "Fortunately, I had help over the top, and Shane came over. He really should have had the interception."

Instead, Pahukoa got himself between the football and Howard and deflected the former into the air where it was caught by Bailey, who was immediately tackled. Bailey popped back up, and as he was running toward the UW sideline, he paused, raised his knee toward his stomach, and stuck his arm out to briefly mimic the Heisman pose.

"Bailey kind of gave us the Heisman step there just as Desmond had done in the Ohio State game," Griese said to viewers. It had happened quickly, but it was a brazen act from a confident player, and it foreshadowed a similar move by a different Husky later.

As the first quarter wound down, Mario Bailey hauled in a strike from Hobert that put the Huskies in a first and goal situation. Then, on the first play of the second quarter, Hobert scooted around the left side of the line to score the first touchdown of the game. Baird and the rest of the coaches held their breath as Hanson came on to attempt the extra point. "Visualization, Travis," Baird said to himself. "Lock everything else out and put yourself in a trance."

Whatever trance Hanson may have been in, he quickly emerged when the snap to holder Eric Bjornson bounced on the turf. Bjornson fielded the ball, which arrived on its side and quickly flipped it upright and into proper position. Baird felt his heart sink. His kicker had had a terrible week of practice, and now, for his first kick of the Rose Bowl, the snap was bad, and the timing was way off.

Hanson's approach was tentative. He swung his leg forward and didn't get much on the kick, but the ball somehow, some way, miraculously got off the ground and barely cleared the crossbar of the goal post. The Huskies led, 7–0, and the Husky coaches resumed breathing.

Michigan tied the game on its next possession. Grbac completed his first pass of the day to Howard to set Michigan up inside the UW ten-yard line. Howard caught the ball in front of a leaping Hall, who bounced to his feet after the play and slapped both hands on his helmet in frustration. "I should have intercepted it," Hall said. "I mistimed my jump." Michigan scored three plays later.

Running back Beno Bryant's best day in 1991 was in his hometown against USC when he ran for 158 yards and two touchdowns in the Huskies' win.
(PHOTO COURTESY UW ATHLETICS)

"He did more things as a freshman than any other tight end we ever had."

Don James on tight end Mark Bruener: "He did more things as a freshman than any other tight end we ever had." (PHOTO COURTESY UW ATHLETICS)

Husky Stadium on game day. 70,000 fans—some who tail-gated and others who sail-gated. (PHOTO BY MARY LEVIN, COURTESY UW ATHLETICS)

Sundodger Denali keeps an eye on things at Husky Stadium. At the airport before the trip to the Rose Bowl, Sundodger accidentally was almost loaded into an unpressurized cargo hold. Band staff member Ken Noreen spotted the mistake and made sure Washington's canine cheerleader was moved to a pressurized hold for a safe flight to Pasadena. The 1992 Rose Bowl was Sundodger's last game before his retirement. (PHOTO COURTESY UW ATHLETICS)

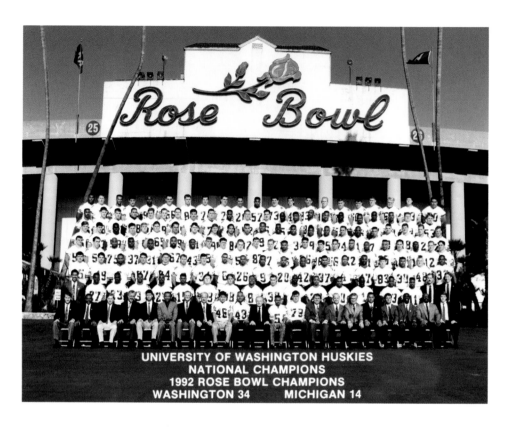

UNIVERSITY OF WASHINGTON HUSKIES
NATIONAL CHAMPIONS
1992 ROSE BOWL CHAMPIONS
WASHINGTON 34   MICHIGAN 14

The players and coaching staff of the 1991 Washington Huskies pose for a team photo before the Rose Bowl game with Michigan. (PHOTO COURTESY UW ATHLETICS)

Don and Carol James outside the Rose Bowl the day before the Michigan game. (PHOTO BY DOUG GLANT, COURTESY CAROL JAMES)

James watches a Rose Bowl practice from his tower. He became a "tower coach" because Bear Bryant did it that way. "I can see everything that's going on, and I can help make good decisions because I've seen everything." (PHOTO BY DOUG GLANT)

James addresses the team after a Rose Bowl practice. Gary Pinkel said James had success because he "saw the big picture, listened to his assistants, and did the right things." (PHOTO BY DOUG GLANT)

Lincoln Kennedy interviewed after a Rose Bowl practice. He switched from defense to offense in 1989, and by 1991 he was considered the best offensive lineman in the conference. (PHOTO BY DOUG GLANT)

At a team dinner, Mario Bailey looks 100 percent comfortable with the mic. Behind him are (*left to right*) Donald Jones, Chico Fraley, Kris Rongen, and Orlando McKay. (PHOTO BY DOUG GLANT)

Keith Gilbertson with his wife, Barbara. Gilby might be fired up about a play he just thought of to run against Michigan. Or he might just be excited about the deal on Italian sausage and meatballs side orders. (PHOTO BY AND COURTESY OF CHRIS TORMEY)

Lincoln Kennedy prepares to dine like a King at Los Angeles restaurant Medieval Times. (PHOTO BY DOUG GLANT)

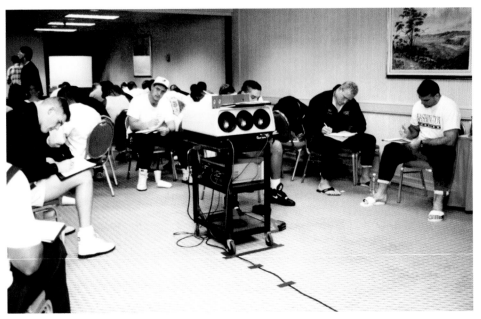

The night before games, players would gather in hotel meeting rooms and take written tests devised by James and his staff as one final check to make sure every player knew the game plan. The night before the Rose Bowl was no exception. (PHOTO COURTESY DOUG GLANT)

Lambo and Gilby, architects of the "we-fense" and the "you-fense," on the field before the Rose Bowl. (PHOTO BY DOUG GLANT)

"Seeing him in real life? You should have seen the look in their eyes."

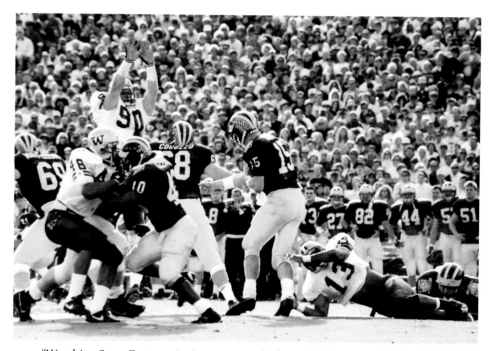

"Watching Steve Emtman (90) on tape was bad enough," Mario Bailey said. "Seeing him in real life? You should have seen the look in their eyes." (PHOTO BY DOUG GLANT)

Some of his teammates thought tight end Aaron Pierce (84) should have been the Rose Bowl MVP given his day in Pasadena: seven catches, 86 yards, a touchdown, and a two-point conversion. (PHOTO BY DOUG GLANT)

"We fear no man."

Don James and Dana Hall on the sideline during the Rose Bowl. Hall and his secondary teammates had a simple motto: "We fear no man." (PHOTO BY ROD MAR, COURTESY OF *SEATTLE TIMES*)

Quarterback Billy Joe Hobert (12) at the Rose Bowl. The stage was never too big for him. (PHOTO BY DOUG GLANT)

Backup quarterback Mark Brunell (11) was on target with seven of his eight passes for 89 yards and a big touchdown to Mario Bailey. (PHOTO BY DOUG GLANt)

Kicker Travis Hanson (7). After a tough week of practice, he came through for the Huskies on game day with a successful extra point off a bad snap and two tough-angle field goals. (PHOTO BY DOUG GLANT)

Wide receiver Mario Bailey (5) and tight ends Aaron Pierce (84) and Mark Bruener (85) each caught a touchdown pass in the Rose Bowl. (PHOTO BY DOUG GLANT)

"Any guy from Washington."

Dave Hoffmann (54), Donald Jones (48), Chico Fraley (39), and Tommie Smith (15). Asked before the season who the best linebacker in the country was, one coach replied, "Any guy from Washington." (PHOTO BY DOUG GLANT)

"I could stand on that field and look at that scoreboard until they turn it off."

James with the Rose Bowl trophy signals the crowd as to where he thinks UW should finish in the national rankings. (PHOTO BY MARK HARRISON, COURTESY OF *SEATTLE TIMES*)

"I could stand on that field and look at that scoreboard until they turn it off." Jim Lambright. (PHOTO COURTESY UW ATHLETICS)

At the 1999 ceremony where James was honored as a Husky Legend. "You couldn't talk about Don without talking about Carol," Baird said. "They were a team." (PHOTO BY BRUCE TERAMI, COURTESY UW ATHLETICS)

UW's next two drives ended in successful field goals by Hanson. Both were short kicks from difficult angles, one from the left hash mark and one from the right. UW's struggling kicker had successfully delivered despite a bad snap on an extra point and had then banged home two tricky field goals. The Huskies had a 13–7 lead, but there was frustration among the offense because the team was squandering opportunities. Hobert's interception stopped one drive, a Jay Barry touchdown run was called back because of a holding penalty, and Beno Bryant dropped a pass for a touchdown that hit him in his hands.

"We were ahead 13–7," Hobert remembered. "But it felt as if we had left at least 14 and probably 21 points off the board. We should have been ahead 21–7 or even 28–7."

Michigan's players were thinking the same thing. The Wolverines had been almost completely shut down on offense, but they were just one big play from having the lead. And for a moment, it looked like they might get that chance.

Late in the half, the Huskies had the ball near midfield and were driving. But the frustrating misfires continued. Hobert slipped and fell for a big loss. On the next play, he hit Pierce with a pass, but the ball ricocheted off his tight end's hands and into those of Michigan sophomore linebacker Steve Morrison. The interception deep in UW territory gave Michigan a golden opportunity to take the lead before halftime or at least cut UW's margin in half with a field goal. But in a response that sapped whatever hope Michigan might still have had, the Huskies defense quickly reminded everyone who, exactly, was in charge.

On first down, Emtman blew past the offensive line like an express train roaring through a local station and smashed Grbac to the turf for a loss of twelve yards. On second down, Andy Mason chased Grbac into Emtman for a two-yard loss. TV cameras found Michigan coach Gary Moeller, who looked like a man who had just found out his taxes were going to be audited. On third down, Fraley tackled running back Tyrone Wheatley for a one-yard loss. In what could be described as their biggest defensive series of the year, Lambright's relentless crew delivered three stunning body blows to Michigan's offense.

"The Rose Bowl was a big-time shining moment for Lambright," said Cunningham. "Michigan saw a bunch of stuff they hadn't seen, and they couldn't solve it. That was all Lambright's brilliance in that game."

The Wolverines weren't going to take the lead with a touchdown or cut into the deficit with a field goal. On fourth and long they punted the football away, and the first half ended. Outside of his one long completion to Howard, Grbac had completed just one other pass for eight yards. UW's defense had played a flawless first half.

In the second half, the offense began to move. Bryant carried the ball for six and two yards to set up a third down and short situation. It was the perfect scenario for the pass to Pierce that had been concocted over margaritas.

"Billy fakes the pitch to Beno," Gilbertson said, "and all their guys are coming in screaming. They're going to kill Beno. Kill him. Aaron goes for the reach block and then sneaks into the seam."

As Gilbertson had predicted, Pierce was wide open. He hauled in the pass from Hobert, and twenty-one yards later the Huskies had the ball at mid-field. "Pretty good-looking play," Jackson said to viewers. "It was well designed," agreed Griese. Gilbertson laughed like a man whose plan was working out. That drive, UW's best of the day, featured six passes and six rushes, covered eighty yards, and ended in a short touchdown pass off a broken play. Hobert was scrambling when he found freshman tight end Mark Bruener, who hauled in a pass thrown through traffic while tight-roping the backline of the end zone. "It was a play-action to the left, but something took my vision off of it, so I immediately reversed field," said Hobert. "The entire play was designed to go the other way."

Bruener was originally the first option. When Hobert pivoted to his right, Bruener adjusted his route but now didn't expect to get the ball since Hobert would have to throw to his left while running to his right. But when they locked eyes, he knew that was exactly what was going to happen. "He was going to do something he shouldn't do, something bad, and I was involved," Bruener laughed. "That pass took forever to get to me."

Bruener began the year by pancaking and eliciting a "Who the hell are you?" from Stanford linebacker Dave Garnett. He was ending it with a touchdown catch in the Rose Bowl. Not bad for a freshman. "The second he put his foot on the practice field, he jumped out at us," Gilbertson said. "He was smart, powerful, and mature beyond his years."

A Michigan penalty on the play meant UW kicked off from midfield, and Wheatley was swarmed at his own five after just a couple of steps. "Watching that team run to the football, every guy, it was like they couldn't wait to get there," Rondeau said. "The speed with which they played was unbelievable to watch."

Michigan ran for two yards, then on second down Emtman again shredded Michigan's line, pushing past a double team from center Matt Elliott and Cocozzo and spinning into the feet of running back Ricky Powers, who was subsequently brought down by Mason and Clifford for a four-yard loss. After an incomplete pass, Michigan punted. The Huskies then went forty-eight yards in eleven plays, with Hobert hitting Pierce for a two-yard touchdown pass on the second play of the fourth quarter that gave UW a 27–7 lead. It was the first score of the year for the Seattle native.

"I almost started crying," Hobert said. "All season long I'd been telling him, 'I'll get you in the end zone.' Then to have it happen in the Rose Bowl. That was great." That Hanson then missed the extra point became a footnote to the game but nothing more. The Dawgs were having their day, and nothing could spoil the party.

ABC had invited former Michigan head coach Bo Schembechler to sit in on the broadcast and used him throughout the day to provide analysis. With the Huskies rolling he was asked by Keith Jackson for his assessment of the game. "I think we've run into the number one team in the country," Schembechler said. "I've never seen a defense quite this good." Jackson agreed and pointed out that the Wolverines' longest sustained drive of the day had gone for just five plays. The dominance by UW's defense was inarguable, and after Michigan turned the ball over on downs, the Huskies sent out Brunell to put an exclamation point on the day.

On first down, he threw a pass down the right sideline that nestled into the hands of Bailey as he tumbled into the endzone. Bailey's momentum caused him to roll over twice. When he came to a stop, he popped up, tucked the ball against his body, stuck his arm out, and did his best Heisman pose toward the Michigan bench. Unlike Walter Bailey's pose from earlier in the game, which came and went like a shooting star, Mario Bailey held his long enough to make sure everyone saw it. McKay was crossing the end zone from the other side of the field. "Did he just do the Heisman pose?" McKay asked himself. "Well, okay! It was a crazy moment."

"Our sideline just exploded," Hall said. "We all started screaming and high-fiving each other. We couldn't believe he did it."

"I had no plan at all," Bailey said. "It was just a spur of the moment thing. It all had to do with how he [Howard] had acted around us that week. If he hadn't been so arrogant, I wouldn't have done it."

On the broadcast, Griese said that he didn't think Bailey had caught the ball. In the (glorious?) days before replay, the analyst's opinion didn't matter. The refs had called the play a touchdown, so it was a touchdown. ABC had only two angles to replay, and neither one showed conclusive evidence. Bailey may have trapped the ball against the ground, but it's also possible he got his hands under it and made the catch. He offers two solid arguments in favor of the latter situation: "First of all, I wouldn't have popped right up to do the Heisman pose if I hadn't caught it," he said. "Second, after all these years, I'd admit it if I hadn't caught it. I caught the ball."

Bailey laughs when he thinks about the Heisman pose now. "I call it a blessing and a curse." The blessing part is obvious. It's an iconic moment, and Bailey seldom meets a fan who doesn't ask him about it. Therein lies the curse part. "I couldn't escape it," he said. "During my pro career, everyone kept bringing it up. Even today, people meet me, and they want a picture with me striking the pose. I won't do it. I did it one time. I've never done it again."

It was one of the most in-your-face moments in college football history, and it was behavior that Bailey's coach wouldn't have tolerated in a different situation. But timing is everything. By that point the game was no longer in question.

"Don let that team have a good time," said Chuck Nelson. "He wasn't always happy about some of it. The Heisman pose . . . 90 percent of him hated that. But 10 percent thought it was the greatest thing ever. I think he appreciated why Mario did it."

"He didn't like it," Carol James said, "but afterward he thought it was kind of cute. Mario was such a great player."

"The timing was perfect," Bailey said. "It was like, nail in the coffin and game over. The best thing was that when I got to the sideline, I was hamming it up for the camera, saying 'I love you' to all my people. Then I looked up, and it was like the Red Sea had parted. Everyone moved out of the way, and I thought, 'Uh-oh. What happened?'"

James was striding to where Bailey sat, and everyone else scrambled out of his way. Bailey and his teammates wondered how the coach would react. Would he understand the spirit of the moment? Or was he angry? Bailey nervously stood up and James gave him a huge hug. "Good job, Mario," James said.

"That was the only time in my career he ever did that," Bailey said. "And the funny thing was, he never pronounced my name right. My name is pronounced Mah-rio, and he always called me Mare-e-oh. He was the only guy I allowed to say it like that. Mrs. James used to tell him all the time, but it just didn't matter. I was always Mare-e-oh to him, and by then, I didn't care anymore." Bailey received praise from James.

Hobert was more critical. "I didn't see the Heisman pose until I watched the game a few days later," he said. "I was amazed he had the guts to do it. It was so classic, but I always have given him crap because it was the wrong pose. His arm needed to be extended farther out. He should have practiced it more."

Truth be told, Bailey nailed the pose more accurately than Howard, who had stuck his left arm out and tucked the ball with his right arm. The bronze figure atop the Heisman Trophy uses his right arm as a stiff arm while cradling the ball in his left arm. That's how Bailey did it after his touchdown.

Michigan added a late touchdown to make the final score 34–14. The game ended with UW on the five-yard line with James refusing to add a touchdown late in a one-sided game. By then, Bjornson was in the game. It was his seventh appearance of the year, and he was the third-string quarterback. "Given what was on the line, it's pretty remarkable that we didn't try to score at the end," Bjornson said. "41 sounds better than 34."

Players, coaches, family members, fans, and media all milled around on the field after the game. Hugs were the currency of the moment and were exchanged between people who knew each other and people who didn't. There were no purple-clad strangers at that point. The architect of the perfect season walked around the field giving and accepting congratulations. After being presented the Rose Bowl trophy, James smiled and briefly stuck his arm in the air with his index finger extended. UW fans roared, "We're number one! We're number one!"

James's playful side was on display during a live interview with Jack Arute of ABC. Asked about the Orange Bowl, James said, "I'm a Miami man, but I'm going to have to say, 'Go Nebraska!'"

After the game, Carol stood outside the UW locker room. She planned to give each player a high-five, but that was quickly abandoned due to the over-exuberant nature of the players giving those hand slaps. "My hands got sore," she said, "so I started giving them hugs instead." The hugs weren't quick or casual. The players loved Carol and realized she was as much a part of the success they now enjoyed as anyone.

Gilbertson happily summed up the game with one of his favorite lines. "We put the purple-shirt hurt on those guys." Lambright had spent all season in high intensity mode, but now, with the Rose Bowl and a perfect season in hand, he was satisfied. "I could stand outside and look at that scoreboard until they turn it off."

Emtman and Hobert were named co-MVPs. Cunningham said the game should have included Aaron Pierce as a third MVP. Pierce had been a problem for Michigan all day, hauling in seven catches for eighty-six yards, a touchdown, and a two-point conversion. The defense ended the game with an astonishing thirteen tackles for loss against the number four ranked team in the country. During the entire season, Grbac had been sacked just six times. The Huskies sacked him five more in one afternoon and got his backup, Todd Collins, for a sixth sack. Three of those were courtesy of Donald Jones, who remains today the career leader in Rose Bowl sacks (five), tackles for loss (five), and yards (minus forty).

Legendary *Los Angeles Times* columnist Jim Murray showered praise on Emtman and his merry band of defensive wrecking balls: "The UW showed up with a defense resembling nothing so much as a school of piranhas." About Emtman Murray wrote, "The Rams had the fearsome foursome. Washington has the fearsome onesome. He was all seven blocks of granite on Wednesday. On wheels."

Bailey's Heisman pose allowed Howard to deliver at least one memorable moment on the day. He missed it when it happened, and when he found out, he smiled thinly and delivered a gem: "Tell him if he wants to see the real one, it's at my house." Howard had just one catch on the day and was a non-factor in Pasadena.

"Walter and Dana just took it upon themselves to shut Howard out," Baird said. "Their ability to play man to man against a guy like that allowed us to bring the house up front. Lambo was not bashful in bringing five, six, or seven guys on passing plays. That was all based on having such good cornerbacks. Their ability to lock guys down allowed us to bring the heat."

That had been the plan. The coaches had noticed that Big 10 teams played off Howard at the line of scrimmage. That strategy allowed him to catch short passes and turn them into long gains. Howard was fast, and James was nervous when Lambright and Slade talked about having the corners play right on him. But he let them start the game that way, and Slade said they never had to change: "We planned to point at him before every play, so we'd all know where he was, and we had a little combo coverage package on him to mix things up. But the big thing was they had no fear of him. They got right up in his face, and that was different for Desmond. He had not faced that before."

The players were happy, but there was still a bit of mystery as to exactly what they were celebrating. Since Miami was just starting the Orange Bowl against Nebraska, they wouldn't know for sure until the next morning if they were national champs, co-national champs, or runners-up. Hoffmann said that it didn't matter: "I remember celebrating on the field, and we knew we were the national champs. We knew, and we stayed out there for a while."

"We were ecstatic," Hall added. "We were unbeaten, we were back-to-back Rose Bowl champions, and we all thought we should be national champions."

Gary Moeller was a believer. "I've not prepared or played against Miami," he said. "But I can't envision a football team any better than that one. We lost to as good a football team as I've ever seen."

Grbac agreed. "UW is the best team we've played by far. Notre Dame and Florida State aren't even close. They're ten times better than anyone else."

The UW radio broadcast wound down, and Rondeau, who was terrific during his career at producing prose that rose to the occasion at hand, delivered the goods in describing the Huskies: "Everything they could do, they have done. Every goal they have set, they have achieved. There is no way this team is not a national championship football team, and if they take it away from them, it will be one of the great crimes of all time."

That didn't mean it couldn't happen. Everyone in Washington was rooting for Nebraska. Emtman even wore a Nebraska hat in his postgame interviews. Nebraska had support. What they didn't have that night in Miami was a chance. Miami prevailed, 22–0, to finish up 12–0. It was anyone's guess how the polls would end up.

"Don was afraid they were going to go with Miami," Hart said. "We were in his room, and he was concerned about it. Because of what happened in 1984, he knew it could happen. That was in his mind after the Rose Bowl."

21

Champions

AT THE AP OFFICE IN NEW YORK, THE OVERNIGHT SHIFT WAITED anxiously for one more voter to cast his ballot in the final poll of the season, the one that would determine the 1991 national champion. Fifty-nine of the sixty votes were in, and as the clock nudged past 3:00 a.m., the conversation again returned to a conspiracy theory the staff had concocted.

"I've done the math again," one man said. "If he wants Washington to win the national title, he'll have to vote Miami seventh."

"If he votes Miami that low, we're going to have to challenge him," another person replied. "He's going to have to justify that, and he's not going to be able to do it."

A phone on one of their desks rang and was answered.

"Hi, this is Don Borst of the *Tacoma* . . ."

"Hey!" the man interrupted and screamed at his coworkers as he held the phone triumphantly in the air. "I've got him! I've got Don Borst!"

Borst had no idea he was the last to call in his vote and was also unaware that while they were waiting for him to call, the AP staff wondered if he would purposely rank Miami low enough to help UW win the national title. He couldn't believe they would think he would do that, and he *really* couldn't believe they *told* him they were thinking that. Nothing irritates a reporter quite like having their integrity questioned.

"I was pissed," Borst said. "I thought UW was clearly the best team in the country. I thought they'd most likely beat Miami if they played. But I wasn't going to take anything away from Miami's season just because college football hadn't figured out a way to get these two to play." He informed the AP staff that he had Washington at number one and Miami at number two. The AP poll was now complete, and Miami was its national champ. Borst realized he had some news and decided, even though it was after midnight in California, that he should call James. Carol answered the phone and handed it to her husband.

"Don," Borst began. "I was just on the phone with the AP in New York, and . . ."

Borst was cut off for the second consecutive phone call. "They went with Miami, didn't they?" James asked.

"Yeah. Miami by four points," Borst said. The four points eclipsed the previous closest finish in the AP poll's history, which was the twenty-point margin in 1984. James had now been on the wrong end of the two closest championships in college football history. UW's performance had changed eleven voters' minds. Three of them had abandoned the Hurricanes and selected UW as the number one team. The remaining eight split their votes among the two unbeaten teams. In the final math, the Huskies had needed to pick up fifteen total points. They had picked up eleven.

"Well, maybe we'll get the nod from the coaches in the morning," James said before hanging up. Borst was certain that was the case. "There was no chance [the Huskies] weren't going to be named national champs by the coaches. Don had more respect than anyone in the business. That's the one he wanted anyway. That's the one that meant more to him."

After a fitful night's sleep, James woke up at 6:30 a.m. No news at this point was not good news. He and Carol both feared that the coaches' vote had gone against them, and no one wanted to call to give them the bad news. "We were nervous," Carol James said. "As it got later, we started thinking that we didn't get it. Again."

Eleven long minutes of silence passed before the tension was broken by the jangling of the hotel phone. James nodded at his wife. "Might as well answer it."

Carol picked up the phone, and a huge smile creased her face. "Yes!" she shouted gleefully before handing the phone to her husband. The voice on the other end informed James that the *USA Today*/CNN coaches' poll had selected UW as the 1991 national champions. Like the AP poll, the vote was close. In the poll at the end of the regular season (where they were tied) Miami got thirty first-place votes, and UW, twenty-nine. Now, thirty-one coaches had picked UW as number one, and twenty-three had taken Miami. Five split their votes, making the final first-place votes tally 33.5 to 25.5. That gain in first-place votes lifted UW to a nine-point win in the final poll.

James was thrilled. He started calling his coaches to spread the news. Many of them had been up late celebrating and were in various levels of mental acuity. One of James's first calls went to Baird, who he figured might be a bit groggy.

"Hello," Baird muttered.

"Good morning, Coach Baird," James said in a very businesslike manner. It took Baird a moment to realize who was speaking to him, and when he figured it out, he briefly panicked.

"Oh, my God! Did I forget about a meeting?"

James laughed and gave him the good news. Before long, the word filtered through the hotel. As soon as one person found out, he or she would call someone else. Unlike the coaches, most of whom had gotten a little sleep, many of the players had kept the party raging until morning and were still awake when they heard. "I remember partying like we were rock stars," Mario Bailey said. "We celebrated with family and fans."

"There was an annex, a separate building from the main hotel, and that's where we all were," Kennedy said. "It was like a large dorm, and nobody was sleeping. Everyone was hanging out, partying, and having fun. Everyone's door was open, and people were just going from floor to floor. Everyone had the TV on ESPN, waiting for the news to drop."

When it did, Kennedy felt the urge to inform anyone in the neighborhood and did so shortly before 7:00 a.m. by taking all 6'6" and 320 pounds of himself out onto the balcony to deliver the word in a huge, booming voice: "WE'RE NUMBER ONE! WE WON THE NATIONAL CHAMPIONSHIP!"

Kennedy reflected about the meeting in 1988, when they had had to reckon with the uncomfortable truth that they were not going to a bowl game. Three years later, he and his teammates were atop college football's mountain. "We realized that it was special," Kennedy said. "We had not lost a game all year, and no other UW team had achieved that since 1915."

About thirty minutes later, Cunningham was walking around the hotel looking for something to eat. He turned a corner, looked in a banquet room, and saw his coach at a podium surrounded by several media members. He slipped into the room and listened to James tell everyone what it felt like to win a national championship. That's how he found out. Bailey eventually came into the room. "I had been around coach for four years. When I saw him, the joy and the happiness on his face . . . that's something I'll never forget. I get teared up thinking about it."

At the press conference, Don and Carol both began to cry as they recounted the eleven long minutes between the time they woke up and when they got the news, convinced as the clock marched on that they had fallen short.

"For these guys not to get a part of it would have been a tragedy," James said in a voice shaking with emotion as tears spilled out of his eyes.

"How about when the call came?" a reporter asked. "How was that?"

James laughed. "Talk about from the outhouse to the penthouse."

In interviews leading up to the game, James had insisted he was not consumed by the thought of winning a national title. Maybe it didn't *consume* him, but the emotion he showed now that he had one was proof that it was something he very much wanted to achieve. "Winning the national title was complete validation for him," Chuck Nelson said. "He had come so close, and now, finally, he had finished it off."

James had also maintained for most of the past month that he'd be fine sharing the national title with Miami if both teams finished unbeaten. He (only half kiddingly) said the coaches knew more than the media, so he was happy to be their choice. But he was delighted for his alma mater and Erickson, and the 'Canes' head coach echoed that thought from Florida. "Believe me, I'm not complaining," Erickson said.

"We don't want to take anything away from Washington. We both had great seasons." Miami quarterback Gino Torretta agreed: "We'd like to settle the debate on the field, but I think the split is fair."

Even Hobert sounded a conciliatory tone: "I don't like sharing. We all feel like we could beat them, but I'm not going to dog Miami. They deserve it just as much as we do."

Some players had received permission to begin vacations with their families and weren't at the hotel when the news arrived. Chico Fraley spent several hours with teammates after the game, but about midnight he and his family departed in an RV for Mexico. He was on a beach, near Rosarita, Mexico, on the Baja Peninsula the next day when he heard that UW had won the national title.

"The pride in saying you were going to do something and then doing it, I had never done anything like that before," Fraley said. He and his father, Charles, and two friends spent the day sitting on the beach and celebrating. "We bought four cases of beer for the week. I think we went through all four that afternoon. It was great."

A year earlier, Fraley had given his dad his Rose Bowl ring with the promise that he "would get another one next year." Mission accomplished. Now they sat and laughed and quaffed cervezas while the sun marched lazily across a blue sky.

So who would have won if Washington had played Miami? There's plenty of evidence to pore over, some of it statistical, some of it anecdotal, and most of it bendable to fit anyone's argument.

The teams had two common opponents, Arizona and Nebraska, and in that comparison, UW comes out ahead. The Huskies had annihilated Arizona in their most dominant performance of the year. Miami beat Arizona (in Tucson), 36–9, but didn't impress Dick Tomey as much as UW did. "We hung in with Miami for a while," he said. "Washington? We were never in it; they could have named their score. That team was incredible. Their defense was suffocating, and their offensive versatility was extraordinary. I thought that team was better than Miami."

As for Nebraska, the Hurricanes' shutout win in the Orange Bowl was impressive, but UW beat the Big Red in Lincoln and posted statistical anomalies that hadn't been achieved against Nebraska since the mid-1950s.

"Comparatively speaking, Miami catching Nebraska in Miami was laughable," Rondeau said. "It's understandable why they did that instead of going to the Sugar Bowl to face Florida. But if UW had played Nebraska in Seattle, it would have been a mismatch."

Maybe the best question isn't necessarily who would have won but instead whether either team would have even scored? Miami and UW finished first and second in scoring defense during the regular season, with UW surrendering 101 points while Miami gave up 100.

But the Huskies were slightly better than Miami defending the pass and much better than Miami in rushing defense and total defense. Washington was second in the country against the run (sixty-seven yards per game) and posted that impressive number despite facing Nebraska, Michigan, Cal, and Arizona, all of whom finished among the leaders in rushing offense.

Washington gave up over 100 yards rushing in a game only to Nebraska and Cal. Eight teams rushed for triple digits versus Miami, including San Diego State, who, behind 154 yards from Marshall Faulk, put up 214 yards. Arizona had 188 against Miami (compared to 30 on the Wildcats' miserable afternoon at Montlake). Arkansas also slashed Miami for 188 yards on the ground. Tulsa got 181; West Virginia, 150.

Washington rolled up 232 yards per game, so given that several teams easily ran for big yards against Miami, it's reasonable to posit that UW could have moved the ball on the ground. Miami finished seventieth in the country in rushing (146 per game), and given UW's rush defense, it's hard to see the Hurricanes having a lot of success on the ground.

Miami featured two spectacular receivers in Kevin Williams and Lamar Thomas. Plus, in Gino Torretta, they had a future Heisman winner at quarterback. The Hurricanes averaged nearly 300 yards a game passing, and it's fun to wonder how they would have stacked up against UW's defense. UW's passing numbers were good (240 yards per game) but not as gaudy as Miami's. They would have been significantly higher if James had been willing to step on the gas longer in routs.

"If Coach didn't have the integrity he had, the passing stats would have been even more impressive," Gary Pinkel said. "The Huskies' stats were great, but they didn't accurately reflect how dominant they were."

"Our offense could have easily been number one [statistically] in the nation," Bailey said. "I saw Coach James's point, but in at least four games I was done at halftime. I played in the fourth quarter only three times all year."

Both teams were difficult to pass against, finishing third (UW) and fourth (Miami) in the country in pass efficiency defense. Washington's pass defense was built around the team's ability to pressure opposing quarterbacks and thus disrupt offensive game plans. Evidence indicates they were successful.

In twelve games, UW's opponents ran 791 plays. Of those, 417 resulted in a tackle for loss, no gain, a turnover, or an incomplete pass. So 52 percent of the plays opponents ran went nowhere or backward. UW's defense regularly put the other team in down and distance situations that were nearly impossible to overcome. In the Rose Bowl, Michigan ran sixty-one plays, and thirty-two ended with one of the four outcomes above.

"They [Miami] just wouldn't have been able to handle our defense," Walter Bailey said. "There wasn't a team that was equipped to handle what our defense was doing. We were able to run it in a way no one could do, and that's why we go down in history as one of the greatest defenses ever."

The truth of that statement owes no small debt to the presence of one of the greatest defensive players in college football history: Emtman. He was an unsolvable problem, and if Miami had come up with a way to neutralize him, it would have been the first team to do so. Miami was pretty good at protecting Torretta (who was not known for his mobility), but Florida State sacked him six times and Oklahoma State got to him four times. It's not a stretch to think UW's defense would have done the same.

"One of the first things we did was analyze how opponents protected the QB and how we could beat it," Dick Baird said. "Lambo loved to pressure from all over the field, so everyone was involved. We had fifteen guys who had tackles for loss and sacks because of the pressure package he developed."

UW finished second in the country in turnover margin with a whopping plus-nineteen margin (thirty-nine turnovers created versus twenty given). Miami's margin was plus five (twenty-nine versus twenty-four). Twenty of Miami's turnovers were interceptions thrown by Torretta. "We would have had so many opportunities to make plays," Bailey said.

Another intangible that favored UW was penalties. Washington averaged seven for sixty-six yards a game. The Hurricanes, who had infamously set records with fifteen violations for 202 yards in the 1991 Cotton Bowl against Texas, made it a point of emphasis to reduce transgressions in the 1991 season. Yet they still racked up an average of eleven flags for ninety-five yards a game. They had forty-one penalties in their final three games.

UW had only one close call all year in the game at Cal. Miami had three games decided in the final seconds. Boston College threw an incomplete pass in the end zone on the last play of a five-point loss. Penn State's Tony Sacca was intercepted at the one-yard line in the final minute of a six-point loss, and the 'Canes needed a missed field goal on the last play of the game to prevail by one at Florida State.

Miami played more bowl teams (five) than UW (two). Three of Miami's opponents were postseason winners. Penn State won the Fiesta Bowl; Florida State, the Cotton Bowl; and Tulsa, the Freedom Bowl. UW's only opponent to win a bowl game was Cal, who dismantled Clemson in the Gator Bowl, 37–13. Stanford lost by a point to Georgia Tech in the Aloha Bowl.

So what does it all mean? Ultimately, it was two perfect teams playing a game within the confines of an imperfect system that wouldn't allow them to meet. It's maddening. The statistics seem to favor Washington. The Huskies were better at running the football, they were better at defending the run, they were better at defending the pass, they scored more points, they created more turnovers, and they committed fewer penalties. Tomey maintained that UW would have won in a low-scoring close game.

"Right now," Hobert said, "[If] I've got one series left in my lifetime, I would take it against Miami. Let's go. Let's see what happens."

22

Team Perfection

"HOW DID UW FINALLY GET A NATIONAL CHAMPIONSHIP?" GARY PINKEL asks. "They had a head football coach who saw the big picture, listened to his assistants, and did the right things."

In a perfect world, Pinkel would have stayed at UW for one more year before beginning his head coaching career. But when the right chance came, he took it. So except for the long day he spent on Toledo's sideline against his former team, he witnessed what UW did in 1991 from afar. "Don was so disappointed after 1984, and that's what led him to make the decisions he did. He wanted a national championship on his resume. He didn't talk about it much, but deep down in his heart, he wanted to win one really bad."

Change is never easy, and it can be particularly challenging for a man in his late fifties. But the brightest and best leaders in any situation realize that for themselves and for the people they're leading, evolutionary change and adjusting to what's happening around them is necessary to achieve success.

"There was a willingness to understand and embrace the new stuff," Rondeau said. "Don is perceived as this starched, stoic, my-way-or-the-highway guy, and that's not true. He committed to doing things differently, analyzing data differently, and having a team with a different personality."

"It's hard to admit 'The direction I've been taking is wrong, so we're going to turn the ship and go this way,'" McKay said. "That's hard to do when you have a lot of pride. He did it."

James's decision after the 1986 Sun Bowl to emphasize speed in recruiting took a few years to take hold, but by the time Gilbertson arrived in 1988, Baird was an experienced recruiting coordinator and was helping coaches find players who could play the game the way James now wanted UW to do it.

"Baird had a massive impact," Rondeau said. "He brought in a personality, a free-spiritedness that hadn't been there, and that played well with the kids. He was a great example of Don's willingness to change. He understood that Baird had some abilities and relationship talents that he didn't have and was never going to have."

While Baird formed a fun counterbalance to James's serious side, Gilbertson and Lambright did the same thing to each other. Gilbertson wasn't quite as free-spirited as Baird, but he leaned more that way. "We're going to be around each other so much," he told his players; "let's make sure we have a few laughs. Let's make sure we all enjoy this."

Ed Cunningham loved pushing Gilbertson's buttons, offering up different ideas on how to do things. Gilbertson found many of his center's suggestions overly thought out and needlessly complex and would often remind him in an exasperated tone, "Football was developed by PE majors for PE majors. It's not that hard."

Lambright possessed a sneaky sense of humor, but his overall personality was much more like James's. "His intensity was beyond the limit," Tormey said. "His focus and what he demanded of the players and the coaches around him defined our defensive group. You could see the evidence in how we played." Lambright used his intensity as a means to an end in 1991, when he was coaching a team that was so talented, experienced, and deep that it presented the coaches with a bit of a conundrum.

"Don always made you think about ways a player could improve," Lambright said. "In 1991 we had to convince a group of players who were already great to believe they could be better. That's why I was always screaming at them about giving up a touchdown or a field goal. I knew we had the potential to be even better."

Lambright was a chess player and loved the complexities of a game that forced players to always think several moves ahead. It was the same thing with football. He enjoyed the challenge of finding an opponent's weakness, something new each game that the other guy just couldn't handle.

"I played for Bill Belichick [in Cleveland in 1995], and he is the most brilliant defensive guy who ever coached a game," said Dana Hall. "Most offenses are going to run a certain play out of a certain formation. Belichick was able to see in his mind that team running that play out of various formations, and he could predict what formations they were going to use so you were always ahead of them. That's the kind of mind Lambo had. His ability to prepare us for an opponent is what set him apart."

"You couldn't be dumb and play on our defense," Fraley said. "We had the belief in Lambright. There were certain situations where he'd tell us, 'If you see this, make this check.' We were just as smart as we were athletic."

Hoffmann developed a friendship with Lambright. "He was my coach, but we had a great relationship. I could articulate things to him, and he'd understand me. I wanted to be in the quarterback's head, and I wanted to be in the offensive coordinator's head. And on some days, when it was really going well, I'd be thinking, 'OK, Lambo, scoot over. I'm getting inside your head too.'"

Most of the time, when Hoffmann ended up there, it was to urge Lambright to be more aggressive. "C'mon, c'mon! Let's blitz more," he would say on the sideline phone. "Settle down," was the usual reply. "We'll get to it, Dave. We'll get to it."

"They never took a day off," said Bjornson, who grew weary of facing them in practice. "As a quarterback, you're trying to read the defense. But they were so smart. They all would read you and figure out what you were doing. It was so hard to do anything against those guys."

Working against Gilbertson's offense was no picnic either. "By reputation, people point to that team's defense as among the best of all time, and I think it was," Rondeau said, "but look at the offense and note how many guys went on to play at the next level and how many guys were the best at their position Washington has ever seen."

That offense also had to find a way around the one injury problem UW faced in 1991. Brunell's going down in spring led to two questions.

First, would Hobert be able to handle the number one job? Some thought so in April. Some were converted by the fall. Everyone believed after the Nebraska game. "His ability lived up to his swagger," Chuck Nelson said. "In the Don era, it was refreshing to see a guy who was free-wheeling it a little bit. Don let him have a good time, and he worked well with that group of guys."

Second, would Brunell complain about being the number two quarterback when he returned to the team? No, he would not.

"Mark Brunell's not playing did as much to help us, and Billy, as anybody," Baird said. "Brunell's presence and the kind of leader he was . . . people don't understand the value of the backup quarterback."

Once Hobert proved that he could handle the number one quarterback job, his and Gilbertson's biggest problem became what to do with their embarrassment of riches. "We got to the point where we were unstoppable," Kennedy said. "With all the different weapons we had, we were going to run all over you and put a lot of points on the board."

Kennedy said the offense was so good that he remembers that both Hobert and Brunell, during games, occasionally told the defense at the line what they were going to run. They'd run the play, gain yardage, and Hobert would say, "I *told* you we were going to run there. What else do you want me to do?"

"It was unique that they were all so good," Gilbertson said. "They could all catch, they could all block, they could all run, and we had a lot of big playmakers. It was unique to have that many great athletes there at the same time."

When Gilbertson arrived at UW in 1988, he found a group of players who admitted they were not always on the same page. That changed immediately. "He fit us perfectly," said Rongen. "He had flair and swagger, and that was what we needed. He instantly transformed our program."

"When our offense changed, it helped the defense," Bailey said. "They got better by practicing against us. Our 11-on-11 at the end of practice was more Gilbertson versus Lambright than anything. That competition, their competition, made us better." To keep a fire burning under his players during those drills, Gilbertson reminded them that James was a bigger fan of the defense.

While Lambright might win an intensity contest against him, Gilbertson was not exactly undemanding in his pursuit of perfection. "I remember at halftime of the Freedom Bowl in 1989," Rondeau laughed. "We're kicking Florida's ass and I ran into Gilby in the press box. He was fuming. He told me he thought we should have at least 50 points by now. This from a guy who was ahead 27–7."

Cunningham calls Gilbertson, Lambright, and Baird the "three-headed beast." "[These were] two really good coaches who knew how to play the modern game and a guy who knew how to set up a great recruiting system."

Baird prefers the "who guy," the "what guys," and the "how guy." "I was involved heavily in the 'who' part of things," he notes. "Who are we going to get? Gilby and Lambo were involved in the 'what' part. What are we going to do? But it was Don who was the master of the 'how' part. Here's how we're going to do things."

Washington's players also had a unique collective trait: a willingness to accept coaching not just from their coaches, but also from each other. "Sometimes we'd have good talks about what was happening on the field," Fraley said. "But sometimes it was more like, 'What the f— are you doing? You're supposed to be here.' You said it, you defended it, and then you were done."

"Getting peers to criticize peers doesn't happen at a lot of places," Hart said. "Our guys weren't afraid to say to each other, 'That's wrong; we're not playing that way.' Coaches can say that, but when a player says it, that's when it gets better. Our locker room won a lot of games. They liked each other, listened to each other, and corrected each other."

The players also had an obsession with the game. When they weren't playing or practicing, they were talking football or watching tape. They studied other teams and found strengths, weaknesses, and ideas they could use.

"The best place I coached as far as having guys who were students of the game was the last couple seasons at Washington," Slade said. "They were football nerds. Certain formations tipped certain plays, and through film study they'd find things I didn't see. It was as good a situation like that as anywhere I've ever been."

"You've got to be totally in," Gilbertson said. "You've got to love it. You've got to be dying to win, dying to learn; it's got to be important to you. [With] some other teams I was around, it wasn't as important. Winning and being good and competing were all real important to that group of people."

"They were able to take the individual 'it's about me' thing out of the equation," Pinkel said. "They had a determination to play their very best every game. That came from the coaches, but it also came from the leadership on both sides of the ball. And they were all loyal to one another. That's how that national championship was born." As for loyalty and national championships, a box arrived at Pinkel's office in Toledo in the spring of 1992. It was a gift from James: a national championship ring.

James ever so slightly loosened the reins on his talented 1991 group too. It wasn't exactly like Miami, where on-field celebrations seemed to follow every play. But as evidenced by his reaction to Bailey's Heisman pose in the Rose Bowl, James realized he had a rare group of passionate guys who played with unrestrained enthusiasm that was sometimes joyfully expressed on the field. He allowed his approach on some things in that area to evolve.

"They had more swagger than Miami in my opinion," said Keith Shipman, "but they channeled it better. It didn't come off as arrogance or cockiness. They were going to test the boundaries like a bunch of teenage kids and young adults will, to help them excel. Don was smart enough to allow that to a certain degree. If it spilled out into the public eye, he'd reign it in." Usually.

"Earlier in the year," Hall said, "we got him to wave a towel, which was way out of character for him. What DJ morphed into over my five years at UW was totally different. He was still the Dawgfather. That mystique was still there. He was still a disciplinarian and he was still very stern, but where he was when I was a true freshman to where he ended up in terms of relationships with his players was a 180-degree turn."

Another change that benefitted Hall (and others) was James's philosophy about young players. "The best time to play a freshman is when he's a senior," James had famously said. But by the time the 1980s ended, he began to see value in using the best players for what he was trying to accomplish, regardless of experience. He also didn't worry as much about how his players looked.

"When I came to Washington," Bailey said, "we were the team that wore the pro socks. You couldn't have a beard. You couldn't have earrings. Suddenly, we're wearing black socks, black shoes. Guys had their jerseys pinched up to show off their ab muscles. Coach James adapted to some of the changes we wanted to make, and that made a difference."

Rondeau watched most of James's career at Washington and agrees with the notion that he was able to view the 1991 team with a slightly different eye than earlier teams. "Don was a very observant coach, and he understood what he had. Great teams have great attitudes and characters. It wasn't going to be a team that you could try to suppress. He allowed them to have some fun. The joy with which that team played is unlike any Husky team I saw before or since, and I think Don felt that joy himself."

What didn't change was James's devotion to punctuality. Meetings and practices always started on time, which meant early. And while the practices were hard, they were efficient, with no wasted time. "If it said on our sheet that a drill was to run for exactly six minutes and seven seconds," Baird said, "at 6:07 on the dot the whistle would blow, and we were on to whatever was next."

James always arrived for meetings exactly one minute before they were scheduled to start. The players lived in a perpetual state of concern about being late, but they appreciated that James had a reason for preaching punctuality. "When you're on time," he told them, "you honor other people. You're showing them that they're important and that you value their time. If you're on time, we can start the meeting or the practice on time. Then, we'll finish on time and you can get to where you need to be next."

When James spoke at area banquets, Rondeau often accompanied him to introduce the coach. Banquets often drag a few minutes behind. That didn't matter, according to Rondeau. "Whenever I was emceeing a banquet and [Don] was ready, he'd catch my eye and tap his watch three times. He never said a word. He just looked at you, tapped his watch, and you knew it was time to go."

James never had to tap his watch three times to get his 1991 players ready. They answered the bell each week during the greatest season in UW football history.

"We knew we were good," McKay said. "But I don't think any of us realized we were going to be the only national championship team for Washington for thirty years, or maybe forty or fifty. Who knows? We didn't understand that part."

USA Today computer expert Jeff Sagarin rated UW number twenty-one on his 2019 list of the best teams in college football history. The 1991 Miami squad finished eighty-second. One thing is certain: the 1991 team would enjoy playing against any of the teams ahead of them on that list.

"Typically, when you go back and look at old football video, things look slower and more ponderous," Rondeau said. "But even now, the 1991 team looks so perfect in how they played. Explosive with everyone running to the ball. They should show footage of that team to every team every year and tell them, 'Watch these guys and be like these guys.' They were a fabulous team. They were timeless. They could compete with teams today. They were that good. They were what a championship football team looks like."

23

History

COACHING TREES ARE THE BEST EXAMPLE OF HOW HISTORY IS CARRIED through college football. A great coaching tree contains strong roots and flowering branches. James worked for and was influenced by several legendary and innovative men, and his influence is felt today in dozens of football programs throughout America.

Fielding Yost is considered one of the pioneers of college football. After playing at West Virginia University, he began a legendary coaching career in 1897 at Ohio Wesleyan University. At Michigan, between 1901 and 1926, Yost won six national championships, and in 1902 his Wolverines defeated Stanford, 49–0, in the first Rose Bowl.

Yost was born in 1871 in Fairview, West Virginia. Eighty years later, just six miles down Paw Paw Creek Road and another fifteen miles down Monumental Road, Nick Saban was born in Fairmont, West Virginia. Saban's coaching career has entered its fourth decade, and he is considered by many to be the greatest coach in college football history. In addition to their West Virginia heritage and their success, another connection ties Yost and Saban together, and that's Don James.

When James was an assistant coach at Michigan in 1966, his friend and colleague Bennie Oosterbaan gave him a copy of Yost's book, *Football for Player and Spectator*. The book was written in 1905. James loved to point out that it didn't give tips on how to defend the forward pass, which hadn't yet been invented. Instead, Yost wrote about organization, practice habits, daily schedules, proper nutrition, and player and coach conduct. "It's amazing how little the basic fundamentals of football and life have changed over the years," James said.

Oosterbaan played for Yost in the 1920s and then coached at Michigan for several years while Yost was athletic director. He shared many stories about his mentor, and Yost became one of several coaching legends who influenced James's career.

Prior to his time at Michigan, James spent seven seasons at Florida State, coaching for Bill Peterson. Peterson was an assistant for Paul Dietzel at LSU in 1958, when the Tigers won the national title, and he brought Dietzel's organization structure to Tallahassee. The system leaned heavily on ideas Yost had written about in 1905, and Peterson expanded them from the season to the off-season. "We had a detailed plan for everything," James said. "It was a year-round concept of developing a program. The way to a good program, how to organize and administer it, I got that from Bill Peterson."

When James changed both his defense and his offense in the late 1980s, he had his year-round organizational plan in place. He realized that updating a strategy about how to play the game was simply good leadership. How he ran that program on a daily basis would stay the same.

After Michigan, James's final stop as an assistant was at Colorado, where he was the defensive coordinator for Eddie Crowder. Crowder had worked for Bud Wilkinson at Oklahoma and Red Blaik at Army. Wilkinson's teams won forty-seven consecutive games and went unbeaten in conference play for twelve straight seasons. Both of those records still stand.

Blaik is credited with being one of the first coaches to use players exclusively on offense or defense. Twenty of his assistant coaches became head coaches, including Andy Gustafson, who coached James at Miami.

James was also influenced by legendary Alabama coach Bear Bryant. James played against Bryant's Kentucky teams in 1951 and 1952. While at FSU, James made regular off-season pilgrimages to Tuscaloosa to listen to the man he called "the guy" in college football. Among the ideas James scribbled into his notebook included Bear's belief that a coach needed a high perch to best view practice. James thus became, in his words, a "tower coach," observing his players and assistant coaches from a platform high above the field: "I can see everything that's going on, I can settle any debates on personnel at the next morning's staff meeting, and I can help make good decisions because I've seen everything." When Bryant greeted him warmly in an airport in the 1980s, James told Carol that the fact that Bear knew who he was meant he had arrived in coaching.

The 1991 Huskies were the crowning achievement of James's career, and that season serves as a milepost of sorts on the college football highway. James left coaching less than two years later, and it's easy in retrospect to view his championship and retirement as a passing of the torch to two men who had played on his first team at Kent State and who had cut their teeth in the coaching business under the wise and watchful eye of Don James: Nick Saban and Gary Pinkel.

Seventeen years after James talked him into taking a graduate assistant coaching job at Kent State, Saban got his first head coaching job in 1990 at Toledo. He left after just one year to become the defensive coordinator for the Cleveland Browns and was replaced by his former college teammate Gary Pinkel, who thus received the dubious honor of playing UW in 1991. Saban jokes that avoiding a trip to Seattle to face the mighty Huskies was one reason he took the Cleveland job.

Pinkel spent ten seasons at Toledo before moving on to a fifteen-year career at Missouri. He is the all-time winningest coach at both schools, one of only three coaches to pull that off, joining Bryant (Alabama and Kentucky) and Steve Spurrier (Florida and South Carolina) in that exclusive club. Ask Pinkel the key to his success as a head coach and he credits James: "I took what worked in Kent and what worked at Washington and dropped it in to Toledo, and it worked. Then I took it to Missouri, and I told everyone that it had worked everywhere it's been."

After Toledo and his stint with the Browns, Saban coached at Michigan State, LSU, and Alabama. By at least one measure, Saban stands alone among all college football coaches. When Alabama defeated Ohio State in January of 2021, the Crimson Tide won the national championship. It was the seventh time a team coached by Saban has been so honored. Yost and Bryant each won six titles. And Saban's coaching tree is arguably the most impressive in college football history. Over two dozen men have jumped from being a Saban assistant to head coach. Several of them are still active, and they all owe a debt to James. Pinkel sees James's influence when he thinks about Alabama's success: "Nick is as good as Coach James at the daily operations of a football team in all levels: spring camp, fall camp, regular season, off-season conditioning, nutrition, academics. Every day he gets the most done, and then they cross it off and go to the next day. They're not worrying about next week or next month. Today. Then tomorrow."

James's place in college football history is at least partially as a link between two of the most successful modern day coaches and the ideas of pioneers like Yost. Saban regularly credits James for many of the organizational ideas he adheres to at Alabama, and when he does, he is in effect giving credit to some of the things Yost started doing in 1897 at Ohio Wesleyan University.

David Gilbertson is an offensive analyst for the University of Oregon football team, where he works for Mario Cristobal. He was talking to his father, Keith, one night about the organization within the program and began to describe something Oregon was using called the "Thursday checklist." Keith Gilbertson began to tell his son the various items that were on the list: details on travel plans, hotels, flight times, meals, meetings, and bus times. "I'll bet you've got a Friday checklist, too," the senior Gilbertson continued. "That one has more football stuff. 'What's our best short yardage play? What's our first third and long play going to be?' Stuff like that, right?"

The son was surprised his dad knew so much, and the dad just laughed. "I know where those checklists came from, and I know where Mario got it," he told his son. The checklists had been part of UW's ritual during the James years. They had been borrowed and used by Saban at Alabama, where Cristobal had been an assistant for five years before he became the head coach at Oregon.

In his book, Yost's colorful description of an afternoon of football ends with his team winning, and that's appropriate to this discussion.

Yost, James, Pinkel, and Saban have coached in more than eleven hundred games, and their teams have been victorious nearly 75 percent of the time. And winning is as sweet today and is celebrated in much the same style as Yost described in 1905:

"Let us start homeward. It is time for us to prepare for the festivities of the evening. There will be lively times around the old campus tonight."

Epilogue

ED CUNNINGHAM TOOK A MOMENT TO MARVEL AT HIS OWN GENIUS. He had concocted a foolproof plan, and now, as the leader of the free world prepared to exit the room, Cunningham was perfectly positioned to introduce himself to President George H. W. Bush.

The plan had been hatched in Cunningham's mind just a few minutes earlier. "How often am I going to get the chance to shake hands with a US president?" he asked himself. "Today is going to be it."

He and the rest of the 1991 Washington football team (along with the 1991 Miami football team) were guests of President Bush for a White House ceremony to honor both of the national champions and their coaches. Jerseys from both schools were presented to the president, who congratulated them for their championship seasons. Parents of players beamed as they watched from risers set up in the ballroom.

Dennis Erickson and Don James made their way around the room, with James shaking hands with several Miami players and Erickson doing the same with the Huskies. James was a Miami alum, and Erickson had grown up outside Seattle. Their praise for one another and their players was genuine and heartfelt.

There had been some (mostly) good-natured banter between the Huskies and Hurricanes about which team was better, and someone joked about going to the South Lawn outside the White House and settling things once and for all. Pity that decorum and common sense prevailed.

Cunningham got the feeling that the brief ceremony was winding down. He guessed that President Bush would exit where he had entered earlier, so he stood near that door. His plan was to step into the aisle, extend his hand, and thank the president for hosting the party. Simple. And for the rest of his life he could brag about shaking hands with a president.

Cunningham watched as aides approached Bush. He nodded to them, smiled, thanked everyone for being there, and began to make his way toward the door where Cunningham stood. "Here he comes," Cunningham thought to himself as he rehearsed his line in his mind. "Hello, Mr. President; I'm Ed Cunningham. I wanted to thank y. . . ."

"Hey! Ed!"

Cunningham was startled to hear his name called and turned toward the voice. It was his father, Emmett, who was standing on a riser behind him holding a camera. "Hey! Smile!" His dad snapped a photo. By the time Cunningham turned back around, the president had left the room. Sadly, Cunningham lost track of the photo. But he said it was a classic. "It's me, with a dumb look on my face, and in the background, you can see President Bush hurrying past."

So much for a handshake. And while that plan was an unmitigated failure, Cunningham's other plan had gone off beautifully. Cunningham grew up in northern Virginia and knew the area well, so he had become the de facto host of a party for his teammates the night before. His sister Shirell and many of her friends worked at bars, and Cunningham thought it would be fun to rent a bus and do a pub crawl. A week before the trip he floated the idea to his teammates. "Every guy was like, 'In, in, in, in.'" he laughed.

Shortly after they landed, the players wasted no time lighting the fuse on their bus tour of DC-area watering holes. That they all had a relatively early wake-up call and an appointment the next morning at the White House was forgotten. Throughout the night they rolled from one hot spot to the next, players clambering off the bus and into the bars, drinking, eating, and laughing as the party gained steam. Nachos, pizza, and burgers were devoured and washed down with beers and shots.

At one of the bars they met a bouncer named Dave Bautista, who would go on to a successful career in acting and professional wrestling. Bautista stood 6'6" and weighed 320 pounds. Bautista and other wide-eyed bouncers at each bar slowly relaxed once they realized that this group of giant young men was out for a fun night and no trouble. A few of the security guards asked Steve Emtman and Lincoln Kennedy for photos. "It's pretty rare that we get this many guys in here who are bigger than us," they told the players.

Many of the players had first met in 1987, when the season had ended with a trip to the Independence Bowl. They had all promised themselves then that things were going to get better, but after the 1988 season they had missed out on the bowls entirely. There were divides within the team, such that some players (including Cunningham) considered transferring out of the UW program. From that low point it would have been difficult to imagine they would end up here, partying in the nation's capital the night before a White House soiree.

It was one of life's wonderful nights, where stories kept beginning with, "Remember that time?" and ended with uproarious laughter. They laughed about it all now: the close calls at Nebraska and Cal, the blowouts, and the Rose Bowl. They talked of the endless meetings and practices and the laps they had had to run when they irritated one of their coaches.

The defensive players could all imitate Randy Hart yelling at them. The offensive players could all imitate Keith Gilbertson doing what Orlando McKay called his "cool walk." Most had funny stories about being terrified the first time they had gone in to talk to Don James. The word had been passed down from earlier generations that a player had better write down on a card what he wanted to say because once it was just him and the Dawgfather in the office, he was bound to get flummoxed.

James would watch a player squirm in his chair before finally taking the pressure off. "I see you have a note card," he'd tell him. "What did you want to talk about?"

Every story, every mimicked gesture, every hardship and triumph relived was met with laughter. It was one of those nights that you hope never ends.

But it did, and it also became the last time they were all together. There would be other times down the road that they gathered: weddings, funerals, reunions. But on this night, for one more time, they gathered as the 1991 Washington Huskies. The best team in UW history. And for that matter, the best college football team in Washington, DC, on that night.

ACKNOWLEDGMENTS

Any story involving history tends to lean heavily on the memories of those who lived it and the prior work of those who wrote and talked about it. This story is no different.

A large portion of the details, quotes, and stories in this book was obtained through interviews with a number of people in 2018, 2019, and 2020.

Thanks to Carol James, who was generous with her time and enthusiastic about the book. Her encouragement in the early days of this project was a big help, and her love for the players who played at UW during all of Don's years there is deep, true, and unending. It's also reciprocated from each player.

Thanks to Keith Gilbertson and Jim Lambright. I've been fortunate to know both men for many years, and the chance to relive so many fun stories with them made for enjoyable conversations. I'm particularly grateful that I was able to spend time visiting with Jim before he died in 2020. If the reader gains any insight from this story, my hope is it will be to fully appreciate the groundbreaking innovations that Gilbertson and Lambright brought to the UW football program that led to the 1991 title.

Thanks to Dick Baird, a masterful storyteller, a fellow broadcaster, and a friend.

Thanks to Randy Hart, Another great spinner of yarns who dedicated his entire professional life to helping young men get better at football and life.

Thanks to my Whidbey Island neighbor Chris Tormey, who was part of the entire story from the 1985 Orange Bowl to the 1992 Rose Bowl.

Thanks to Larry Slade for filling in some important details and for giving me a great title for the book.

Thanks to Gary Pinkel, a sharp offensive mind who saw where the game was going and was willing to accept help to get UW there. He's also the winningest head coach in Toledo and Missouri history. He knows what he is doing.

Thanks to Nick Saban for providing the foreword for this book.

Thanks to Bob Rondeau, who is a friend, a mentor, and—as much as it hurts this native Hoosier to admit—a better euchre player than I am.

Thanks to Don Borst, who has been a constant source of encouragement and honesty during my second act. He's a good man and a great friend.

Thanks to Chuck Nelson and Keith Shipman, who had interesting views of the 1991 team and all that they accomplished.

Thanks to Kris Lambright for her help and friendship.

Hugh Millen and Tim Cowan were both great Husky quarterbacks who helped color in some details during the early timeline of this story.

Thanks to all the players who spent time visiting with me about this team. They trusted a guy who came parachuting into their world with details and stories that only they could know, and I am most grateful.

Thanks to Mario Bailey, Walter Bailey, Eric Bjornson, Mark Bruener, James Clifford, Ed Cunningham, Chico Fraley, Dana Hall, Billy Joe Hobert, Dave Hoffmann, Donald Jones, Lincoln Kennedy, Orlando McKay, and Kris Rongen.

Thanks to Jeff Bechtold and Brian Tom from the University of Washington for providing access to and help with the UW archives.

Thanks to the photographers whose work appears in this book: David Gaddis, Doug Glant, Mark Harrison, Joanie Komura, Bruce Terami, and Corky Trewin,

Thanks to Andrew Berzanskis for editing help and unwavering enthusiasm and encouragement during this project.

Thanks to Bojana Ristich for an eye like an eagle when it came to copyediting.

Thanks to Margaret Sullivan and everyone else at UW Press who helped make this project a reality.

Thanks to Renee for an unending stream of support and great suggestions.

Finally, thanks to every player, coach, and staff member who was a part of the 1991 UW football team. What they did will live on forever, putting together not only the greatest team in UW history, but also one of the greatest teams in college football history. For what it's worth, I think they would have drilled Miami.

1991 UNIVERSITY OF WASHINGTON TEAM ROSTER

NUMBER	NAME	POSITION	YEAR	HOMETOWN
38	Ricardo Aguirre	LB	Fr	Seattle, WA
9	Eric Alozie	SE	Sr	San Bernardino, CA
53	Jeff Aselin	OT	Fr	Huntington Beach, CA
88	Bruce Bailey	TE	Jr	Seattle, WA
5	Mario Bailey	WR	Sr	Seattle, WA
23	Walter Bailey	CB	Jr	Portland, OR
99	Angelo Banchero	TE	Fr	Seattle, WA
83	Doug Barnes	LB	Fr	Carson, CA
21	Damon Barry	SE	Fr	Northglenn, CO
42	Jay Barry	TB	Jr	Northglenn, CO
67	Charles Battle	OL	Fr	Carson, CA
51	Bruce Beyers	LB	So	Burien, WA
14	Eric Bjornson	QB	Fr	Oakland, CA
56	Jeff Bockert	LB	Fr	Vancouver, WA
62	Todd Bridge	OT	Jr	Montesano, WA

81	Mark Bruener	TE	Fr	Aberdeen, WA
93	Shermonte Brooks	SE	So	Tacoma, WA
11	Mark Brunell	QB	Jr	Santa Maria, CA
29	Beno Bryant	TB	Jr	Los Angeles, CA
27	Brandon Bunch	WR	Fr	Federal Way, WA
13	Eric Butler	FL	Fr	Osceola, FL
45	Hillary Butler	LB	So	Tacoma, WA
32	Richie Chambers	LB	Fr	Lake Stevens, WA
53	James Clifford	LB	Jr	Seattle, WA
12	Ricky Cobb	FS	Jr	Reno, NV
46	Brett Collins	LB	Sr	Portland, OR
73	Brian Conlan	OT	Fr	Delta, British Columbia
82	Ernie Conwell	TE	Fr	Kent, WA
24	Shawn Cox	CB	Jr	Bellevue, WA
97	Jason Crabbe	K	Jr	Laguna Beach, CA
79	Ed Cunningham	C	Sr	Alexandria, VA
41	Shandon Cyrus	MG	Jr	Kaneohe, HI
37	Mike Derrow	LB	Fr	Federal Way, WA
36	Demetrius Devers	LB	Fr	Seattle, WA
68	Robb Dibble	DE	Fr	Bellingham, WA
76	John Disante	OT	Fr	North Hollywood, CA
10	William Doctor	CB	Sr	El Paso, TX
87	Rodney Ellison	TE	Jr	Sacramento, CA
92	P. A. Emerson	TE	So	Irvine, CA

90	Steve Emtman	DT	Jr	Cheney, WA
88	Mike Ewaliko	DT	Fr	Seattle, WA
75	D'Marco Farr	MG	So	San Pablo, CA
3	Jaime Fields	LB	Jr	Lynwood, CA
47	Jamal Fountaine	LB	So	San Francisco, CA
39	Chico Fraley	LB	Sr	Rowland Heights, CA
36	J. J. Frank	FB	Jr	Everett, WA
66	Tom Gallagher	OT	So	Puyallup, WA
65	Frank Garcia	C	Fr	Phoenix, AZ
17	Curtis Gaspard	SE	Sr	New Orleans, LA
9	Lawrence Goncalves	CB	So	Spokane, WA
20	Darrell Green	CB	Fr	San Francisco, CA
32	Charleston Grimes	FB	Fr	New Orleans, LA
26	Russell Hairston	CB	Fr	Bellevue, WA
5	Dana Hall	CB	Sr	Diamond Bar, CA
7	Travis Hanson	K	So	Spokane, WA
11	Darren Harrell	CB	Jr	Tacoma, WA
41	Eugene Harris	TB	Jr	Bellevue, WA
79	Trevor Highfield	MG	Fr	West Linn, OR
50	Mike Hill	LB	So	Bellevue, WA
12	Billy Joe Hobert	QB	So	Puyallup, WA
54	Dave Hoffmann	LB	Jr	San Jose, CA
91	Steve Hoffmann	DE	Fr	San Jose, CA
18	Damon Huard	QB	Fr	Puyallup, WA

24	Eteka Huckaby	TB	Fr	Sunnyvale, CA
54	Jeff Hudson	OT	Fr	Tacoma, WA
49	Larry Humble	FL	So	Vancouver, WA
77	David Ilsley	OG	Jr	Napa, CA
85	Jeff Jackson	TE	Fr	Newport Beach, CA
1	Denton Johnson	SE	So	Missouri City, TX
34	Leif Johnson	FB	So	Seattle, WA
48	Donald Jones	LB	Sr	Gladys, VA
29	Louis Jones	FS	Fr	Los Angeles, CA
22	Matt Jones	FB	So	Portland, OR
95	Virgil Jones	LB	Sr	Tacoma, WA
56	Pete Kaligis	OG	So	Bellingham, WA
8	Napoleon Kaufman	RB	Fr	Lompoc, WA
75	Lincoln Kennedy	OT	Jr	San Diego, CA
69	Patrick Kesi	OT	Fr	Honolulu, HI
35	David Killpatrick	ROV	Fr	Anchorage, AK
3	Joe Kralik	SE	So	Puyallup, WA
90	Clayton Kuhrau	C	Fr	Seattle, WA
25	Sanjay Lal	SE	Jr	Los Angeles, CA
64	Scott Leick	OT	Fr	Renton, WA
74	Mike Lustyk	DT	Jr	Bellevue, WA
25	Lamar Lyons	S	Fr	Los Angeles, CA
6	Damon Mack	SE	Jr	Gardena, CA
18	Marshall Magee	LB	Sr	Kent, WA

70	Siupeli Malamala	OT	Sr	Kailua, HI
13	Andy Mason	DE	So	Longview, WA
86	Shell Mays	DE	Sr	Tacoma, WA
83	Jim McCoy	TE	Sr	Redmond, WA
4	Orlando McKay	FL	Sr	Mesa, AZ
86	LaMar Mitchell	FL	Sr	Stockton, CA
7	Josh Moore	CB	Fr	Torrance, CA
80	Shaun Moore	TE	So	Spanaway, WA
16	Tom Nakane	QB	Jr	Spokane, WA
99	Keith Navidi	DT	Fr	Yorba Linda, CA
20	Leon Neal	RB	Fr	Long Beach, CA
52	Jim Nevelle	OG	So	Palmdale, CA
61	John Norman	OG	Jr	Battle Ground, WA
21	Shane Pahukoa	FS	Jr	Marysville, WA
60	Andrew Peterson	OG	Fr	Port Orchard, WA
84	Aaron Pierce	TE	Sr	Seattle, WA
71	Pete Pierson	OT	So	Portland, OR
66	Tyson Pollman	LB	Fr	Randle, WA
19	Dana Posey	CB	Jr	Arlington, WA
71	Terrance Powe	MG	Sr	Carson, CA
23	Terry Redmond	FL	So	Novato, CA
63	David Reiner	C	So	North Hollywood, CA
4	Reggie Reser	DB	Fr	Pasadena, CA
27	Dante Robinson	ROV	Jr	Santa Barbara, CA

57	Tyrone Rodgers	MG	Sr	Carson, CA
72	Kris Rongen	OG	Sr	Federal Way, WA
19	Joel Rosborough	WR	Fr	Long Beach, CA
89	James Sawyer	SE	Sr	San Jose, CA
52	Donovan Schmidt	LB	Fr	Palm Springs, CA
10	Kaala Shea	QB	Fr	Honolulu, HI
22	Eric Simpson	CB	Fr	Portland, OR
55	Danianke Smith	DE	Jr	Long Beach, CA
15	Tommie Smith	ROV	Jr	Lancaster, CA
37	Matt Spillinger	FL	Fr	Port Orchard, WA
15	Travis Spring	WR	Fr	Seattle, WA
49	Steve Springstead	LB	So	Lacey, WA
6	Michael Steward	DB	Fr	Long Beach, CA
8	Paxton Tailele	ROV	Sr	Laie, HI
93	Justin Thomas	LB	Fr	Spokane, WA
30	Richard Thomas	FB	Fr	Kent, WA
17	Andy Trimakas	FS	Fr	Seattle, WA
31	Darius Turner	FB	Jr	Gardena, CA
30	Jayson Turner	ROV	Jr	Redmond, WA
28	Richard Washington	DB	Fr	Long Beach, CA
48	Jay Wells	FB	Fr	Arroyo Grande, CA
58	Paul Wight	LB	So	Seattle, WA
78	Donald Willis	OT	Fr	Lompoc, CA
16	Zario Ziegler	ROV	So	Lewiston, ID

COACHES

Don James	Head coach
Jim Lambright	Defensive coordinator
Keith Gilbertson	Offensive coordinator
Dick Baird	Recruiting coordinator
Myles Corrigan	Tight ends coach
Matt Simon	Running backs coach
Bill Wentworth	Wide receivers coach
Jeff Woodruff	Quarterbacks coach
Randy Hart	Defensive line coach
Chris Tormey	Linebackers coach
Larry Slade	Secondary coach